# THE DIGITAL INNOVATION PLAYBOOK

## CREATING A TRANSFORMATIVE CUSTOMER EXPERIENCE

### Nicholas J. Webb

WILEY

John Wiley & Sons, Inc.

Published by John Wiley & Sons, Inc., Hoboken, New Jersey.
Published simultaneously in Canada.

For general information on our other products and services or for technical support, please contact our Customer Care Department within the United States at (800) 762-2974, outside the United States at (317) 572-3993 or fax (317) 572-4002.

Wiley also publishes its books in a variety of electronic formats. Some content that appears in print may not be available in electronic books. For more information about Wiley products, visit our web site at www.wiley.com.

*Library of Congress Cataloging-in-Publication Data:*

Webb, Nicholas J., 1958–
   The digital innovation playbook : creating a transformative customer experience / Nicholas J. Webb.
       p.   cm.
Includes index.
   ISBN 978-0-470-94470-7 (hardback); ISBN 978-1-118-11301-1 (ebk);
ISBN 978-1-118-11302-8 (ebk); ISBN 978-1-118-11303-5 (ebk)
   1. Business enterprises – Technological innovations.   2. Technological innovations – Economic aspects.   3. Business enterprises – Computer networks.
4. Digital media – Economic aspects.   I. Title.
HD45.W396 2011
658.4'063–dc22

                                                                2011014261

Printed in the United States of America

10   9   8   7   6   5   4   3   2   1

*I would like to dedicate this book to my family:
my amazing wife and lifetime cheerleader, Michelle;
my daughter and creative genius, Taylor;
my daughter and daily inspiration, Madison;
my son and the pride of my life, Chase Parker;
and my youngest daughter, Paige, who taught me
that the real genius of innovation resides in kindergarten.*

# Contents

# Foreword

It's a little embarrassing to admit, but I spend far more time in the digital world than I do in the real one. When I'm not creating digital documents, e-mailing, reading RSS feeds, tweeting, using Facebook, texting, blogging, or listening to podcasts, I'm thinking about the future of all those things. Since my job is all about developing new growth opportunities for a Fortune 500 company, being obscenely connected doesn't seem that strange. Sad? Maybe. But not strange. I am happy to report I am not alone. I take no small comfort in knowing that as I cradle my CrackBerry, thumbing bite-sized musings into the digital ether, Justin Bieber, Kim Kardashian, and Barack Obama are doing the same. This is an unusual turn of events for humanity and a bit of an omen.

Much like my friend Nicholas J. Webb, I am both an innovator and author. At heart, I'm a pragmatic futurist. In fact, my forthcoming book is an unconventional look at the U.S. economy over the next 10 years and the innovation opportunities it will create. Not surprisingly, many of these will be digital. Why? Evolution. From the moment our furry ancestors discovered that it's way easier to smash open a coconut with a rock than a claw, we haven't looked back. Each invention—shoes, the wheel, clocks, electricity, assembly lines, cars, and computers made life on earth a little more bearable. These advances made it possible to sustain larger populations, trade globally, and communicate in ways that make the deck of the Starship Enterprise look like a finished basement from the 70s.

In economic terms, we are part of a massive shift from labor to capital. Wealthy countries build machines that run factories, seed crops, and transport energy. Some, like the United States, can't be bothered with making things. They leave industrial work to developing nations. Our days of slaving over hot assembly lines are long gone. We are hyper-connected cubicle dwellers now. Every tweet, every Like on Facebook, every Angry Bird is the shout of a plump nation reveling in victory.

A funny thing happens when your world turns digital—it starts to move and evolve faster than ever. In the analog world, trucking companies upgrade their fleets every five to seven years. Furniture stores change models every three to five years. Electronics companies release new devices once or twice a year. Software companies send patches monthly (weekly if it's Windows XP). Web services change daily, while digital media flow in an endless tsunami that in Biblical times would have required an ark. The less friction, the faster the flow.

As life digitizes our expectations for all things—digital or not—accelerate. We begin to expect food, FedEx packages, and relationships delivered as quickly and successfully as text messages. Enterprising individuals and corporations are swimming in possibilities. Some will leapfrog each other in the digital realm—gaming, search, social networking, and so on. Others will dare to apply digital tools to the analog world. From faster food to personalized retail to workforce productivity—if people do leave the house, innovators can strive to make that intrepid journey at least as good as Second Life on Xbox.

For every brilliant go-getter, there will be hundreds, if not thousands, that recede into their safe digital cocoons. If you haven't yet seen *The Matrix*, I highly recommend it. The film presents two distinct worlds. The virtual one offers pleasure, beauty, and Keanu Reeves. By contrast, the real world is a gray, metallic wasteland where humans struggle to survive in poorly-tailored outfits. Why would anyone choose the real world? In the movie, there was no choice. Most were unaware that everything they believed to be real was completely synthetic, like Baked Lays.

Already, most interactions we have are either completely digital or getting there. Consider these five pieces of evidence.

1. The web is more omnipotent than Oprah. Almost everything we own, from cars to appliances is now connected to it.
2. Social networks

   Facebook and Twitter are just embryonic examples of things to come, although they are technically opt-in networks that are becoming mandatory through peer pressure. As Heidi

Klum says, in her warm Germanic way, "You're either in, or you're out."

The viral outbreak of social networking tools across every web is unprecedented. There are thousands of ways to tweet, share, or social bookmark anything.

Entire businesses, like Groupon, were built on the power of social media.

Digital is the default medium for dating and net-working (LinkedIn, Facebook, Monster, Match.com, Adult-friendfinder).

Often, online relationships take precedence over real ones. You can spend hours on Facebook writing to people you'll never see in person, while ignoring calls from your own parents.

Twitter and Facebook helped spark revolution in Egypt and other parts of the world. By helping people connect and organize in ways never before imagined, social media proved that it's not just a one trick pony. Its powerful tentacles extend well into the physical world.

PR power. When director Kevin Smith tweeted about being thrown off a Southwest flight for being too fat, he didn't quite stir an Egyptian-style revolution. He did, however, give the airline a black eye and showed that those with followership also wield economic power.

3. Digital entertainment

Video games are more realistic than ever. It's just a matter of time before you can plug them right into your head—or worse.

Most media—books, music, and video—are moving to Web distribution, legal or otherwise.

Cheap consumer electronics have moved every imagin-able kind of entertainment into the home, even if that home is on wheels.

3D is one of many features that make media more real and addictive.

4. Mobile connectivity

Do you have any friends who cradle their cell phones or BlackBerries like limbs? Are *you* that friend? The phone is both a guide and your master.

Text messaging is how kids communicate. The phone is always with them, always on. And Verizon never sleeps. If it did, they'd charge you a fee for it.

New devices like tablets and netbooks allow you to connect almost anywhere.

Broadband and wifi are cheaper and more abundant than Starbucks.

5. Obesity is rampant, and it's technology's best friend. The more virtual your life, the less you move. The heavier you get, the less likely you are to disconnect. The Wii is not a Stairmaster.

6. The military recruits gamers as it shifts from a human army to one of remote drones right out of a movie.

So why should companies care if we're hurtling toward life in *The Matrix*? The best explanation I can offer is it gives purpose to what looks like chaos. Customer expectations now move at a digital pace, while most companies are still painfully analog. Power shifted toward Droids, Twitterers, and doughy MIT brainiacs faster than anyone could imagine. The race to meet those expectations and to wield that power will range from slow to impossible. In the meantime, the most important step any business can take is changing how it communicates, both internally and externally. By embracing the spirit and tone of social networking, countless doors to innovation will open. Just maybe that simple act of honest dialogue is all that is really missing.

Before I suffocate under the melodrama of those last three sentences, I'd like to briefly mention Nicholas J. Webb. Writing this introduction to his book is the easy part. *The Digital Innovation Playbook* is the product of Nicholas's inventive mind, countless hours of research, and keen perspective on all things digital. Not only do I value Nick's advice, but I enjoy the passion with which he delivers it. That said, I couldn't imagine leaving you in more capable hands.

Steve Faktor
American Express
New York
March 2011

■ ■ ■

*Steve Faktor leads Growth and Innovation for the Vice Chairman of American Express. He is also a futurist, author, and frequent keynote speaker on the future of business. His forthcoming book is about innovation opportunities after the recent great recession. To learn more, visit ideafaktory.com, where Steve explores, predicts, and provokes new thinking on innovation.*

# Acknowledgments

This book would not have been possible without the support of some amazing people. My development editor, Jennifer Dean; my Wiley editor, Susan McDermott; Paul Pluschkell and Jim Heilig at Spigit; Rick Calvert, CEO and co-founder of Blog World and New Media Expo; Marcel Lebrun, CEO of Radian6; Philip Nelson, senior vice president for strategic development of NewTek; Christi McNeill of Southwest Airlines; Thomas Hoehn, director of Interactive Marketing and Convergence Media at Kodak; Bruce Jasurda, chief marketing officer with the U.S. Army; Ken Robbins, CEO of Response Mine; Robert (Bob) Siminski, Intellectual Property Counsel at Harness, Dickey & Pierce, PLC; Art Beckman, director of the innovation program office for Hewlett-Packard's Software and Solutions operations; and IndyCar's Daniel Incandela and Julie Dolak. I would also like to thank my good friend Matti Palo, M.D. for all his support; Patrick Tickle, executive vice president of products at Planview; and last but not least, my twin brother, Charles A. Webb.

# Introducing the Next Step

## NAVIGATING NEW MEDIA

Social media and other new digital media have been on the tip of many a tongue for the last several years. Some companies are embracing it while others . . . well, not so much. The fact is that very few are getting it right. Why is this? For most organizations the major problem is that they don't understand the relevancy of what digital, social, and new media mean to their organizational goals and objectives.

The truth of the matter is, it couldn't be simpler. It's not about your company or the significance of your products and technologies. It's about the customer. It starts and ends with the customer. Digital media—Facebook, Twitter, blogs, YouTube, and all the others—they're simply another tool to connect with the person who gives your company purpose: your customer.

You may be asking yourself why an innovation strategist is writing a book about social, digital, and new media. The best way for me to answer that question is to briefly define innovation. As you know, there are literally thousands of definitions of innovation. In my humble opinion, there is but one correct definition.

*Innovation is the process of delivering exceptional customer value through active listening.*

It's interesting to me to read the protracted and frankly convoluted definitions of innovation by many so-called innovation experts. In fact, it's their sheer complexity that makes these definitions so flawed. The lack of a customer-centric definition is why so many innovation initiatives fail. For the sake of this book's message, I would like to categorize all forms of digital communication as *digital media*. Remember that social media, new media, digital media, and Web 2.0 are all forms of digital communication. Throughout this digital

1

innovation playbook I will be using these terms as specific facets of the overarching definition of digital media. So here's the fun part, my definition of digital media.

*Digital media is the process of delivering exceptional customer value through active listening.*

Sound familiar? Let me share with you my perspective. In my 25-year career I have launched hundreds of technologies to the marketplace. I have been awarded more than 30 patents by the U.S. Patent and Trademark Office. I have developed innovation strategies for some of the world's best corporations. I have literally lived in the trenches of innovation. And what I discovered could only be described as the secret to innovation success, and that secret is *communication*. So what is the connection between digital, social, new media, Web 2.0 and the term innovation? If innovation is about communication, and it is, then digital media is about innovation.

To add to my experience I researched the true thought leaders in digital media. And despite the fact that I researched a vastly different group of organizations large and small, public, private, and governmental, with incredibly different value propositions, the same themes kept popping up.

First, you have to have a great product and great customer service. In other words, good is out, exceptional is in. Yes, this may seem on the surface to have nothing to do with digital initiatives, but without it, any initiative is bound to fail. Because of this, the first several chapters of this book are dedicated to understanding the customer experience in this new environment. Then we move on to what the best organizations on the planet are doing to win at digital and new media.

In this book I talk about companies I call Innovation Superstars®. I introduced the Innovation Superstar concept, which highlights some of the country's leading innovators. This book has some amazing stars as well, leading the way in the digital innovation industry. And you might be surprised by who some of them are. But first, let me define the term for you, describing the anatomy of an Innovation Superstar.

What it means to be amazing:

- Superstars are consistently better than the rest.
- You can count on superstars to deliver.
- Superstars are role models; you want to be like them.

- Superstars are good in all aspects of the game, not just one part of it.
- Superstars usually have a balanced and accessible personality to go with their talent.
- Superstars are team players, and they make everyone else better.
- If superstars were a culture, you'd feel comfortable being part of that culture.

In this book we'll talk to Innovation Superstars like Southwest Airlines, a company that found an open digital culture to be a natural fit for its already quirky, friendly corporate personality. We'll talk to Kodak, which found the social web was an excellent platform to connect to their valued customers and to create what are, in my opinion, some of the best technologies in the world. Innovation Superstars include the U.S. Army, which found a way to connect its soldiers serving all over the world with friends, family, recruits, and more, despite the dangers one might think are inherent in the idea. We'll talk to NewTek about the digital video revolution and how desktop video democratized the world of video content. And IndyCar will explain how it connects its fans from all over the world in their common passion.

Here's a sneak peek of what's to come.

## This Book's Setup

This book has 13 chapters, and each chapter ends with a QR code so you can visit http://digitalinnovationplaybook.com for updates.

### Chapter 1: Mastering Digital Innovation

The former CEO of IBM once said if you can't write your idea on the back of a business card, you don't have an idea. To that I would add, if you can't write your definition of innovation on the back of a business card, you don't know innovation.

Innovation is the process of creating exceptional customer value through active listening.

In this chapter we talk about why the *exceptional* and *listening* portions of that definition are so important. We also talk about why focusing on failure drives failure. Risk management can also be defined as failure management.

Closed, risk-centric companies cannot deploy successful internal or external open innovation initiatives. But, with a philosophical shift towards openness, companies can tap into a wide range of digital solutions that allow organizations to become open. Today, innovators must become digital and new media experts.

## Chapter 2: The Digital Sandbox

We're all in this together. And despite the vast landscape of the World Wide Web, the digital space can start to resemble a preschool playground when you spend a lot of time there. In this chapter we talk about what I call the digital sandbox, which includes all the personalities and interactions you'll find in any preschool sandbox anywhere. Look for the bullies, the sand eaters, and the kids that play nice.

There are four components in the digital sandbox: *Play, Listen, Invent,* and *Deploy.* We'll talk about playing well with others, listening well by actively participating in the digital community, turning those listening observations into meaningful innovations, and then having an innovation strategy ready to deploy with great haste.

In this chapter we talk with the listening experts at Radian6, which trains companies to actively listen, communicate, and deploy innovations that result from the interactions.

You'll learn that there's a vast, untapped pool of naturally occurring conversations going on about your company that you need to listen to and, in many cases, join.

## Chapter 3: The Digital Enterprise

We've talked some, and will repeat throughout the book, about the importance of *playing, listening, inventing,* and *deploying* within the digital sandbox. Say you become an excellent listener, locating and joining in on the conversations going on throughout the web about your brand. How then do you cull the best information for you innovations from the masses of information streaming the web?

There are several systems out there that can do this, but companies must be extremely leery of instituting risk-centric systems that could potentially turn away the terrible with the brilliant in an equal fashion (all ideas can look alike in a system that focuses on risk, not on the ideas themselves). And systems must be customized to fit your individual needs.

Innovation Superstar Spigit was founded in 2007 by Paul Pluschkell and Padmanabh Dabke. The company has evolved even in its short lifetime, but the idea—which has remained the same—behind the concept was to create a platform that harnesses the wisdom of crowds to capture, refine, collaborate on, and select the best ideas for your individual needs.

"One of the problems with really large communities is that it's difficult to find what's relevant without massive overhead on the client's side," says Jim Heilig, Executive Vice President of Sales. "They need to spend their time listening to the right discussions, prompting the right dialogue, and getting value from the collaboration from their communities."

The Spigit platform uses social media tools like blogs, Facebook, and other platforms that allow these large communities to interact. Then using analytics, game theory, behavioral economics, workflow, and many other tools, the software gives companies the ability to identify the relevant content.

With Spigit, social triggers can be set to measure how many people are interested in the idea, or that can be determined by how many review and comment on the idea (the buzz percentile). Ideas can then be set to advance if they meet quality objectives, social objectives, or a combination of both.

What this does is save companies from the need for a huge team of workers moderating. It culls out the masses of information, spotlighting the ideas that are most important so companies can react quickly with new innovations.

### Chapters 4–8, Digital Innovation Superstars

These chapters provide concrete examples of companies that are leading the way in digital innovation. Each is unique in its approach to meeting its customers' needs by listening and learning, and leveraging this knowledge through digital media processes.

Chapter 4—NewTek

Chapter 5—Southwest Airlines

Chapter 6—Kodak

Chapter 7—U.S. Army

Chapter 8—IndyCar

**Chapter 4: Digital Video Revolution**    Before the digital and social revolution of the last decade or so began, producing professional-quality video was left mainly to the professionals. With the creation of technology like NewTek's TriCaster, the technology evolved to allow anyone and everyone to have the ability not only to create professional-grade video but also to distribute it to the masses.

These changes had a snowball effect, giving voice to the individual, which provided equal footing to television networks, large corporations, and the mom-and-pop businesses as well.

In this chapter I speak with Philip Nelson, Senior Vice President for Strategic Development at NewTek. Nelson talks about how live webcasts allow business to be conducted online, saving travel costs and maximizing efficiency; how live webcasts and recorded video at tradeshows are allowing companies to share their messages with the masses; and how live streaming video gets viewers to make an appointment to view content, thus increasing viewership and engagement of the participants.

You'll learn why the fascination of "getting behind the velvet ropes" drives viewers to participate in everything from *The Hills After Party* live webcast to a behind-the-scenes look at the Miss Universe Crowning Moment.

**Chapter 5: Flying High**    In this chapter you'll learn how a transition to the new digital community was a natural fit for Southwest Airlines, thanks to an already customer-first, open culture. Southwest Airlines' media specialist Christi McNeill will describe how the company embraced several social platforms including a video series, the corporate blog called *Nuts About Southwest*, Facebook, Twitter, and more.

This case example shows how an open platform provided a new way to dispel common myths about the company and share the experiences and enthusiasm of its employees on a daily basis.

Southwest Airlines' blog allowed the company to have a voice in the digital conversation. In the old days of PR, companies had to rely on the media to spread their messages to consumers.

"Now we actually have our own channel where we can put up video, share photos, get a statement out really quickly—a statement we prepared with all the facts," McNeill said. "That has been a huge benefit to us in some of the major news breaker situations we've been involved in. To be able to provide our statement for our customer and employees is very powerful. The blog has also created a great focus group for us. We can post a question to any of our online audiences—blog, Twitter, or Facebook—and get feedback instantly."

McNeil gives as an example the occasion when Southwest considered instituting a new method of assigning seats, and after mentioning the idea on the blog, the airline company heard an overwhelming "No!" And they had their answer. Southwest Airlines customers love the current policy; don't mess with it.

**Chapter 6: Picture Perfect Social Media**    Kodak is already a household name. But how does a company like Kodak, with its sheer size and well-entrenched culture make the change to be open, to be digital? With Kodak we talk about removing the internal silos found in so many old-line corporations in order to build a culture of openness necessary for success in the digital world.

The conversations about Kodak—or any other well known brand—are going on all over the web. Companies can't control those conversations, so it's important to get out there and be part of them.

In a long-standing company like Kodak, there can easily be an outdated public view. Kodak will share how the company permeated the web, giving people an up-close and personal look at today's company, as well as at the history of the technology and people running it.

In each chapter you'll see that the corporate website remains, but more and more often the social initiative sends companies branching out into the blogosphere, socializing on Facebook and Twitter, streaming on YouTube, and more.

In this chapter, I talk with Thomas Hoehn, director of Interactive Marketing and Convergence Media at Kodak.

People talk. And now there are so many platforms for those conversations. There's Twitter, Facebook, multitudes of blogs, community sites, chat rooms, Flickr, YouTube, and many others. People are sharing their experiences, asking questions, considering purchases, and comparing prices.

The digital community is out there, and if companies don't become part of these conversations they will, first, miss out on the opportunity to hear what's being said about their company, and second, have no say in the discussion.

"We quickly realized it was important for Kodak to be a digital player, which meant playing in the digital spaces," Hoehn said. "These conversations were happening about our brand—whether we wanted them to or not."

**Chapter 7: The Army Way**   I imagine this chapter will surprise many readers. The U.S. Army—an organization usually thought to be steeped in bureaucracy and closed-door secrecy—seems an unlikely social superstar. But think again.

The Army is one of the leaders in the industry, with a soldier-run blog and several other digital media endeavors. And how is this possible, you ask? I asked the same thing and found a fantastic tale of a strong, loyal relationship that goes both ways, resulting in an environment of trust and respect that allows the government organization to have an extremely open-door policy that gives prospective enlistees—and anyone else—a glimpse into this 200-plus-year-old organization's daily workings. The digital media world could learn a lot from the U.S. Army.

I met Army representatives at the 2010 Blog World Expo, where I learned about ArmyStrongStories.com, the Army's blog and story-sharing program. The site provides an online community for soldiers, families, friends, and supporters to share their Army stories. Through authentic perspectives on Army life and military service, the program provides those interested in learning more about the Army a platform to ask questions and interact with soldiers. This also provides the Army's first platform for soldiers to share stories, and for supporters to share their stories, leave comments, and ask questions.

I was blown away that this was even possible. And inspired that the Army, with soldiers facing life and death situations every day, was able to be so open and put such trust in its members and community.

In this chapter you'll learn about the Army's two-pronged digital campaign that includes soldier blogs, soldier networks, SMS mobile, and an instant messaging campaign. You'll learn why the genuine stories and communication from soldiers—not PR people—are so important to the community, which includes the soldiers, recruits, family, friends, and others.

We'll talk with Chief Marketing Officer Bruce Jasurda about the U.S. Army's journey to digital innovation superstardom—how it happened and why it had to happen.

The target audience for the Army's recruiting initiative is age 17 to 24. This age group is texting, listening to iPods, watching television, and Facebooking. The Army, like many other corporations before them, has found that they needed to *go* to their client base's conversations and speak in a genuine voice in order to connect in a real, productive way.

"It became painfully apparent, a blinding flash of the obvious, that we needed to look at both how our prospects were consuming information and where we were in our efforts to try to reach them and communicate with them," Jasurda said.

**Chapter 8: Winning the Digital Race**  No single digital strategy fits every business, and IndyCar is a good example of this. Mobile service, a digital camera company and video technology probably weren't big surprises in a book on digital innovation. But IndyCar? The story told here is one of a fast-track digital strategy that provides the ultimate experience for fans.

In this chapter I tell the story of how IndyCar has been able to utilize all the tools of the digital domain to drive customer connectivity, to support their customer community, and to provide significant and meaningful value-added resources by longer-play video and interactive experiences. The fact that they were able to take the one-dimensional media that really are digital media and to make them multi-dimensional and truly customer connected is amazing.

This is what it's all about—the ability to add more value and draw closer connections to our customers; in their case, it is a matter of industrial equilibrium in that they provide a tremendous value to their customers, an amazing resource to their advertisers and customers, and a way to build upon their brand and business.

Building on the "behind the velvet ropes" theory from the NewTek chapter, IndyCar uses the social web to provide its fans with an inside view of the unique experiences of the drivers and teams and their stories that occur throughout the season. The IZOD IndyCar Series will conduct 13 races in the United States, one in Canada, and one each in Japan and Brazil in 2011. And the lineup! Marco Andretti, Ryan Briscoe, Helio Castroneves, Scott Dixon, Dario Franchitti, Ryan Hunter-Reay, Tony Kanaan, Danica Patrick, Graham Rahal, and Dan Wheldon—leaders in the industry.

The IZOD IndyCar Series is the first racing series to power its Honda engines on 100 percent fuel-grade ethanol, a renewable and environmentally friendly fuel.

This is the IndyCar digital story. Each of these corporations has a story, and it's unique. But they're all front-runners in the digital race.

## *Chapter 9: Digital Direct*

Over the last 40 years a scientific form of marketing, direct response marketing or DR, has grown to consume more than half of all U.S. advertising dollars. This alternative to more traditional brand advertising uses rational arguments to elicit real-time responses from the consumer. DR's objective is simple: increase sales and profits by maximizing marketing return on investment, rather than by maximizing general audience awareness. One of the true thought leaders in digital direct marketing is Ken Robbins from Response Mine (www.responsemine.com). In this chapter I share with you what I have learned about the power of digital direct marketing from Ken.

The dawn of the Internet ushered in a new era of direct marketing. By combining the time-tested techniques of DR marketing with the speed and measurability of the Web, innovative companies can drastically increase their returns on marketing investment. In this chapter I'll show you how to use digital DR techniques to improve your own marketing ROI, get more customers, and increase profits.

In this chapter we explore the evolution of DR in the new digital world and how the effects of this tool can be maximized in new and hugely effective ways.

## *Chapter 10: RealOpen® Innovation*

There are more than 170 different so-called innovation management systems—at least that I've found. The reality is, of course, that most of these systems have two very basic problems. First, they're actually risk management, rather than innovation management systems; and next, they use a cookie-cutter approach that almost always results in failure.

Different processes work for different organizations, industries, and technologies. There is no grapefruit diet panacea solution that manages innovation. One size does not fit all.

Because of this, I've developed a framework called RealOpen®, which contains conceptual steps, and which your organization can use to develop the specific processes and measures to succeed.

In this chapter I describe how RealOpen provides a diagnostic chart for companies with its holistic innovation framework. RealOpen is designed to do three things: speed the process, provide results, and build profit. RealOpen accomplishes these things by creating an external innovation sourcing function that is manageable, which includes a filtration process to quickly decide which innovations should be acted upon.

RealOpen is ideally suited to the digital media innovation world that is opening up vast opportunities. RealOpen can help guide you and your company through this new world. Chapter 10 helps you realize this potential for RealOpen to lead you into digital and new media with a customer experience focus.

### Chapter 11: Creating a Digital Culture

This chapter's aim is to give some pointers on how to build a successful cultural base to support innovation. It also examines how to best incorporate what we're now coming to call *digital innovation* as a tool to sustain not only the innovation process but also the innovation culture.

In my last book, *The Innovation Playbook*, I devoted a chapter to *The Anatomy of an Innovation Superstar*. I defined three essential parts of the anatomy of the body of innovation: Customer, Process, and Culture. The Customer part was analogous to the head—containing the information and brains to decide what needs to be done in the interest of the customer. Process was compared to the torso, containing the vital parts necessary to keep the organization alive and functioning, while Culture was the legs, supporting the rest of the being and propelling it forward.

You'll learn why it's so important to have an externally focused company and why a predominantly internal focus with excessive risk management protocols is to blame for most failed innovation within corporations.

You'll learn the difference between Innovation Socialists and Innovation Capitalists—hint: You want to be a capitalist. Socialists are internally focused, slowing innovation or halting it altogether. In a digital world, the last thing you want is to be bogged down in processes or procedures.

The Innovation Pyramid, which pointedly shows just how much contact employees have with your most important resource—your customers—proves that a shake-up needs to take place, putting the top layers of the organization closer to, or even in direct contact with, the customers. Again, a new day of openness is upon us. No longer can we sit in corporate boardrooms. A culture of genuine openness is a necessity in the digital world we now live in.

## Chapter 12: Rules of Engagement

Throughout *The Digital Innovation Playbook*, I talk about the importance of creating digital resources that add value for the customer. These resources include everything from podcasts to vodcasts to full-duplex dialogue on a variety of social platforms. But whether your company is large or small, it's critical that you understand any potential legal pitfalls associated with using these tools, as well as the opportunities to monetize your digital innovations through intellectual properties protections.

In this chapter, Intellectual Property Counsel Robert (Bob) Siminski of the law firm Harness, Dickey & Pierrce, PLC, provides an overview of these issues and possibilities. Siminski looks at the rapid evolution of technology in recent years, as well as where we're heading in the future. If you're out in the digital world, this is an important chapter to read.

## Chapter 13: The Innovation Game Plan

In order to succeed at innovation you simply must define the term in a way that directly connects to your organizational mission. As you have already read in *The Digital Innovation Playbook*, I define innovation as the process of developing exceptional value through active listening.

In this chapter we recap the high points of becoming a digital innovator. Remember that innovation requires clearly identifying who it is that you serve. Most organizations define the people they serve as internal customers, or stakeholders, and external customers. Mapping those relationships will help you identify how best to serve them at all contact points.

Organizations rely heavily on their teams to identify new opportunities to add value to their customer community, but unfortunately most organizations do not properly train their stakeholders to be innovators. You should have a comprehensive innovation training program to be sure all members of your team are contributing profitable innovations to your enterprise.

In researching and writing *The Digital Innovation Playbook* I experienced an amazing journey and witnessed the transformation of many organizations who were taking advantage of the power of the digital universe to plug in to their customer community and provide exceptional levels of customer value. These leaders are reaping the amazing benefits of the digital universe.

## This Book Is Alive

The only thing we know for certain about change is that change is speeding up. Because the digital world is constantly evolving some of the content in this book will become less relevant. And in true digital innovation fashion I have created a living version of this book. This includes a QR code that can be scanned and a URL to allow you to instantly access updated information on statistics, innovation superstars, and relevant strategies and tactics.

The QR code appears along with the URL at the end of each chapter. Simply scan the QR code with your smart phone or other code reader for an instant update. If you're reading this book in its digital format you can simply click the hyperlinks. And if you're reading this book in its pulp format, simply enter in the URL for updated information on any given chapter, as directed at each chapter's end, at www.digitalinnovationplaybook.com.

 *The Digital Innovation Playbook* is a living book. We are constantly updating the book online so you can watch uploaded videos, read the latest best practice on digital media, and even participate in free ongoing webinars. For more information visit www.digitalinnovationplaybook.com.

To access this chapter's updated web page, please go to www.digitalinnovationplaybook.com/Intro.html or scan the QR code with your mobile device.

# CHAPTER 1

# Mastering Digital Innovation

## THE ROLE OF DIGITAL AND NEW MEDIA ON INNOVATION AND COMMERCIALIZATION

The former CEO of IBM Corporation once said, "If you can't write your ideas on the back of a business card, you don't have an idea."

How can you begin if you don't know what you're doing? The same holds true for innovation. In order to really understand the effect of the digital universe on innovation, you must first define innovation.

This seems like a simple enough concept, doesn't it? And yet, there are no two definitions alike. And most of them resemble dissertations—tough to fit on the back of a business card.

Needless to say, defining innovation has been a colossal challenge over the years, a disturbing reality to say the least. If you asked an ophthalmologist the definition of ophthalmology, he or she would quickly tell you it's the diagnosis and treatment of human eye disease—simple, clear, and short. No matter where you traveled around the world, you would get the same definition.

Like the ophthalmologist or an expert in any other field, innovators must first understand their job in order to reach excellence.

I have spent the past 25 years as a Certified Management Consultant in the area of innovation strategy. Over that time I've found great success as an inventor with more than 30 U.S. patents.

I also know the definition of innovation and here it is again—it's oh, so simple:

*Innovation is the process of creating exceptional customer value through active listening.*

## Breaking It Down: The Key Words Are 'Exceptional,' 'Value,' and 'Listening'

It's one sentence. You can put it on your business card if you'd like. But, despite the fact that it's a simple sentence, several words are heavy with importance. To truly understand innovation, and later learn to be a digital innovator, you must understand the three key words in this definition: *exceptional*, *value*, and *listening*. When I present this definition to my colleagues in the innovation space, they're often highly critical of its simplistic approach. But it includes all of the necessary ingredients of successful innovation.

Before I go on, I'd like to dispel a couple of common myths about innovation. Most people believe you must be creative to innovate. It's a common myth that we need more creativity in organizations.

Well, in the United States alone, there are 3,000 patents issued each and every week. That's a lot of creativity. But unfortunately, less than 2 percent of those wonderful, creative ideas are ever successful in the marketplace.

There are three reasons those examples of creativity did not succeed. Creativity in itself is not the answer. Those patents didn't succeed because:

1. They weren't *exceptional*.
2. They didn't add *value*.
3. The inventor or the organization wasn't truly *listening* to the customers.

If they were listening, they would be able to develop relevant technologies for their customers. We do not have a shortage of creativity in most organizations. What we have is a shortage of organizations or individuals who are creating exceptional value driven by active listening.

## Risky Business: Focusing on Failure Drives Failure

Another significant myth in the area of innovation has to do with controlling risk. Most organizations believe they can succeed at innovation if they can manage risk, or what I call *managing failure*. Because, after all, that's really what they're trying to do. Statistics do show that 95 percent of all consumer products fail in the marketplace. Scary stuff. But here's the catch: Of all the companies failing in the marketplace, 100 percent of them were using risk-management or failure-management systems. As it turns out:

*Managing failure breeds failure.*

So we lack creativity, we have a vague, complicated, and convoluted definition of innovation, and we assume we can fix everything through managing risk or through failure management. Turns out, all of this is wrong.

## The Open Innovation Myth: No Initiative Can Defeat a Closed Culture

*Open innovation is a colossal failure.*

Open innovation was a great idea. In fact, one could argue that it's an obvious solution. But here's another myth: Open innovation is a success.

When you look at the money invested in open innovation and then look at the return from open innovation, you see that, with very few exceptions, most organizations have failed. It's not because open innovation isn't a terrific idea. The problem is deployment.

When you have an organization with a closed culture that's compartmentalized, it's virtually impossible to deploy internal or external open innovation initiatives. The good news is there is a wide range of digital solutions that allow organizations to become both internally and externally *open*. You don't have to completely rearrange your organization to plug into the digital world. You do, however, have to make a philosophical shift toward openness.

## Jumping In with Both Feet: Digital Innovators Must Become Experts

Innovators must become digital and new media experts. This is something that has been met with a great deal of resistance. Unfortunately, it's inevitable. If your job function is in new business development, new product development, technology development, or in any area that manages innovation, you simply must become a real digital expert. But there's a catch. You can't do this fractionally.

It's much more than opening a Facebook fan page and starting a blog. In fact, those are probably the least interesting of all of the digital opportunities available to innovators. You need to understand all of the fibers of connectivity available for simplex, duplex, and full-duplex dialogue, a communications analogy that we will talk about throughout this book.

## A Walk through Your Digital Customer Community

Let's take a quick walk through your customer community. Facebook representatives say that 50 percent of active users log onto the site every day, which breaks down to about 175 million users every 24 hours. That's up from 120 million users just six months ago, according to a recent econsultancy.com article. Facebook currently has more than 350 million active users around the globe. Six months ago that number was 250 million. That's up 40 percent in half a year.

More than 35 million Facebook users update their status each day, an increase of 5 million when compared to the end of July, 2009. Photo uploads to Facebook have increased by more than 100 percent; there are about 2.5 billion uploads to the site every month, up from about 1 billion six months prior.

When it comes to Twitter, that same econsultancy.com article listed more than 75 million user accounts. Fifteen million are active users, using accounts on a regular basis. That is still a fair increase from the 6 to 10 million global users just a few months back. LinkedIn has more than 50 million members worldwide; it has added about 1 million members since July/August, 2009. Wikipedia has more than 14 million articles, which breaks down to 85,000 contributors having written nearly a million posts in the last six months.

Remember, your customers are talking and they're talking about you. There are more than 3.5 billion pieces of content—and that includes web links, news stories, blogs, posts, and so on—that are shared each week on Facebook alone. There are now 11 million LinkedIn users across Europe. At the end of 2009, the average number of tweets per day was more than 27.3 million. The average number of tweets per hour was around 1.3 million. More than 700,000 local businesses have active pages on Facebook. Purpose-built Facebook pages have created more than 5.3 billion fans. Seventy percent of bloggers are organically talking about brands on their blogs.

According to econsultancy.com, 38 percent of bloggers post brand and product reviews. More than 80,000 websites have implemented Facebook content since December, 2008. More than 60 million Facebook users engage with it across the internal sites each month. (Facebook statistics are from the Facebook press office.)

As we said, your customers are talking and they're talking about you. That's the good, the bad, and the ugly. If you are mediocre or even if you're good, you're not good enough. In Seth Godin's amazing book, *Purple Cow,* he talks about the importance of being exceptional. Exceptional is in; mediocre is out. If your product is just good, you've created an opportunistic environment for entrepreneurs and competitors alike to create the next big thing.

Exceptional is in; mediocre is out. If your product is just good, you've created an opportunistic environment for entrepreneurs and competitors alike to create the next big thing.

### Fans of Facebook

Take a look at Facebook facts. The average Facebook user has 130 friends. More than 25 billion pieces of content—from web links, news stories, blog posts, photo albums, and notes—are shared each month. More than 300,000 users have helped translate the sites through the translation application. More than 150 million people engage with Facebook on external websites every month. Two-thirds of comScore's top 100 U.S. websites and half of comScore's top 100 global websites have integrated with Facebook. There are more than 100 million active users currently accessing Facebook through their mobile devices. People who access Facebook via their mobile devices are twice as active as nonmobile users. The average Facebook user is connected to 60 pages, groups, and events. People spend more than 500 billion minutes a month on Facebook. There are more than 1 million entrepreneurs and developers in 180 countries on Facebook. (Statistics are from the Facebook press office.)

### Atwitter about Twitter

What about Twitter? Twitter gets more than 300,000 new users each day. That's incredible. There are currently 110 million users of Twitter services. Twitter receives 180 million unique visits each month. There are more than 600 million searches on Twitter every day. More than 60 percent of Twitter users are outside the United States. There are more than 50,000 third-party applications for Twitter and more than a third of Twitter users access it via their mobile devices. (Statistics are from Twitter and the Chirp Conference.)

### Linked on LinkedIn

LinkedIn is also a very powerful solution, especially business to business. There are more than 70 million users worldwide. Their membership comes from more than 200 companies from every continent. LinkedIn is available in six languages: English, French, German, Italian, Portuguese, and Spanish. About 80 percent of these companies use LinkedIn as a recruitment tool. A new member joins LinkedIn every second. LinkedIn receives almost 12 million unique visitors per day. Executives from all of the Fortune 500 companies are on LinkedIn. (Statistics are from the LinkedIn press center and SysComm International.)

### Touring the Blogosphere

More than 77 percent of Internet users read blogs. There are currently more than 133 million blogs listed on leading blog directories. About 60 percent of bloggers are between the ages of 18 and 44. One in five bloggers update their posts daily. Two-thirds of bloggers are male. Corporate blogging accounts for 14 percent of blogs. About 15 percent of bloggers spend 10 hours a week blogging. More than half of all bloggers are married and/or parents. More than 50 percent of the bloggers have more than one blog. Bloggers use an average of five different social sites to drive traffic to their blogs. (Statistics are from Technorati's State of the Blogosphere.)

## A Social Revolution: People Are Talking All the Time, All Over

Trust me, it's not a fad. In Erik Qualman's excellent book, *Socialnomics*, he proves the point that digital and social media are the "biggest shift since the Industrial Revolution" with a series of startling statistics.

In 2011, Generation Y will outnumber baby boomers. Ninety-six percent of them have joined a social network. Social media have overtaken pornography as the No. 1 activity on the web. One out of eight married couples has initially met on social media sites. And this is a really interesting set of statistics: years to reach 50 million users? Radio took 38 years; TV took 13 years; the Internet four years; iPod took three years; Facebook added 100 million users in less than nine months; iPhone applications hit 1 billion in nine months.

If Facebook was a country it would be the fourth largest in the world, with a population size between that of the United States and Indonesia. Some say China's QZone is the largest, with over 300 million using their services. comScore indicates Russia has the most socially engaged audience, with visitors spending 6.6 hours viewing 1,370 pages per month. A 2009 U.S. Department of Education study revealed that, on average, online students outperformed students receiving face-to-face instruction. One in six higher education students are enrolled in an online curriculum. Eighty percent of companies use LinkedIn primarily as a tool to find employees. The fastest growing segment is the 55- to 65-year-old female.

As you can see, we are extremely digitally connected. What all these statistics tell us is that all of our communities have become digital. Our customers, our internal stakeholders, everyone we will ever do business with is highly digitally connected. The Internet, Web 2.0, social media—whatever you'd like to call it—it's really about communication, the ability for our customer communities and also internal stakeholders to be able to communicate with one another. So it creates a tremendous opportunity, while at the same time posing a threat for mediocre technologies. Once again:

*Innovation is the process of creating exceptional value through active listening.*

## The Exceptional Layer: Defining Value Layer by Layer

If that's the case, then what does exceptional mean? Exceptional is really best described by what I call the Net Customer Value Strata (see Figure 1.1). The Net Customer Value Strata defines the *layers* of value. And remember that value is in the eye of the beholder, or in this case value is in the eye of the customer. Value is determined by the customer, not by the business. The best way to look at it is: Exceptional customer value is the difference between what someone expected versus what they got throughout the experience cycle.

> Exceptional customer value is the difference between what someone expected versus what they got throughout the experience cycle.

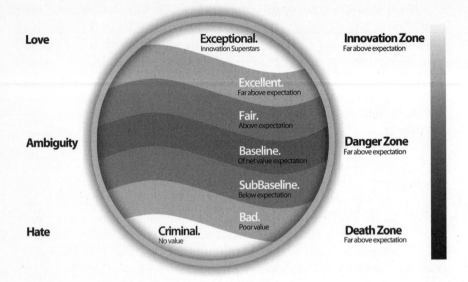

Figure 1.1    Net Customer Value Strata

## Criminal Behavior: Digital Disposes of Every Level below Exceptional

Let's take a look at the criminal layer. Criminal is when somebody takes your money and gives you nothing in return—or nothing good anyway. I think we've all gone to a bad restaurant where the service was poor and the food was terrible and it cost us money. We've all bought technologies that were absolutely in no way similar to what was advertised and cost us a lot of money. These are instances when you've experienced the criminal level of the value strata. The good news (or bad, if you're delivering that service) is: The digital community kills the criminal. It kills the bad companies and it kills the sub-baseliners. Unfortunately, many baseline companies are also destroyed by the baseline buzz. This is why you must be exceptional. You would assume companies that make good technologies would be on the right track. The problem is that when you are delivering at the baseline level of current expectation you are creating an opportunistic environment for inventors, entrepreneurs, and competitive companies to create technologies above that trajectory into the layer I call Innovation Superstardom, which is exceptional.

**I**nnovation is the process of creating exceptional customer value through active listening.

A great example of a baseline level product is the Kindle. The Kindle does exactly what it advertises. It's lightweight, it's inexpensive, and it has good battery life. You can store thousands of books on it. It's a tremendous value for buyers. If you bought a Kindle today, you'd expect to be able to read books on it, and that's exactly what would happen. But along came the iPad. When the iPad came out, it was instantly called the Kindle-killer. It had layers of value that can only be described as exceptional. It is an Innovation Superstar®.

## How You Can Become Exceptional: Manage Your Culture to Become a Listener

Can you now see why residing at exceptional is a much better place than the baseline level of expectation? If we want to be exceptional, we must be able to listen, which requires opening up. That concept creates a problem for most organizations because most organizations have a culture that is toxic. What is a culture? A culture is a symptom. The causality of a poor culture is focus.

So our organization develops a culture based on the collective daily focus of the people who come to work at our building each day. And that's really the best way to look at it. Culture isn't some ominous ether that flows throughout the building. It's nothing more than the collective focus of every member of your organizational team.

**C**ulture can be defined as the collective focus of every member of your organizational team.

## Are You Trapped in Analog? Comparing Digital Socialists to Digital Capitalists

There are digital cultures, and then there are analog cultures. By this I mean current cultures versus outdated cultures. There are successful cultures and dysfunctional cultures. Dysfunctional cultures often fall under the definition I call "innovation socialists." These are the old, closed, analog cultures that result in organizational and innovation failure. These groups look inward, focusing on their own needs, problems, and opportunities. They look at ways to control costs and increase efficiencies and mitigate risk. What are the psychographics of that cultural focus? They are internally focused—process focused rather than result oriented; risk centric rather than opportunity centric; and they are reactive rather than proactive. They are all about the next bright shiny object.

*Innovation capitalist*, or digitally ready companies, are customer focused. *Innovation socialists* are all about the blame. Innovation capitalists are about accountability. Take a look at these two different cultures and ask yourself, which culture describes my organization? And how can I make the transmutation from innovation analog socialist to an innovation capitalist, digital-ready company? See Figure 1.2.

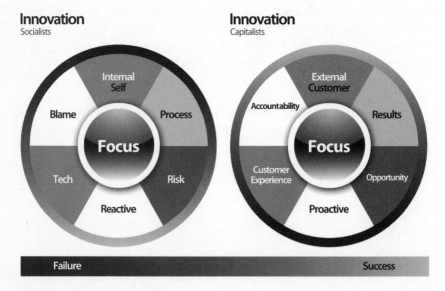

**Figure 1.2    Innovation Focus Model**

*Source:* Lassen Scientific, Inc. 2010. All rights reserved.

## Communication—The Key to Everything

Let's talk about what digital really means. Digital innovation is communication. It's that simple. It's a new way in which we can communicate with data-rich dialogue, in real time.

Now I'd like to describe it using radio terms. I call one form "digital simplex." This is how we broadcast information to our communities using platforms like Twitter and blog posts.

Once again, let's get back to the essence of digital innovation, which is communication. Communication in the digital universe most often comes in the form of "digital duplex" dialogue, which is a two-way, but not necessarily in real time, dialogue through platforms like Facebook, texting, and online forums. Then you have "digital full-duplex," which are live hosted events and other real time forums.

All of these forms of communication are important, but needless to say, the most important aspect of all digital innovation and digital communication is *listening*.

When bad products—and sometimes good products and services—are quickly destroyed through online communications, this is a byproduct of what I call *digital polarity*. Digital communication moves at the speed of light, which isn't a good thing for those that might not be at the best price point or providing the greatest value. For instance, price comparisons can now be found instantaneously as a result of embedded mobile devices that include Smartphone scanning. Scanning QR codes can instantly provide real information about features, benefits, and pricing and shopping alternatives. Never before has there been a more informed audience. With a click or two, your customer can find all sorts of information on the features, the value, and the reviews of your technology.

Feature benefit roundups and product forums are routinely reviewed during the buying process. Customer communities are quickly inventing the next best thing. The question is, are you listening? Yamaha, for example, through their Motifator website, has spent years listening to their synthesizer customers in order to discover where there are quality problems and opportunities to increase the value of their core technology. As a result, their latest synthesizer was a tremendous success because it was hardwired directly into the soul of their customers. That is, they truly co-created by listening.

## Full-Duplex Dialogue Takes the Win

Winners of digital innovation practice regular, full-duplex dialogue. Closed innovation cultures will retard digital growth. And the bottom line is most organizations will not make the full digital commitment. Most of them will never make a true commitment to an integrated digital strategy.

It's important to not only fully commit to a cross-organization or cross-enterprise digital strategy; you must also tie your digital listening to an innovation platform (see Figure 1.3). And that innovation platform will determine what's relevant in terms of what you should be listening for.

## Digital Innovation Best Practices: Commanding the Digital World

Digital strategy must be part of an integrated, open culture. Tear down the internal and external barriers. You cannot fix a closed

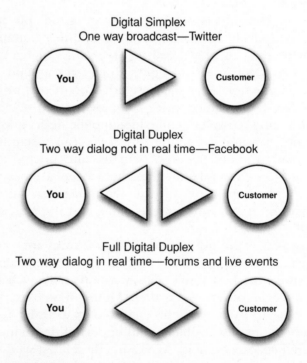

**Figure 1.3    Digital Dialog**

*Source:* Lassen Scientific, Inc. 2011. All rights reserved.

organization with digital strategy. One of the biggest mistakes many organizations make is they attempt to rule the day digitally without fixing their organizational culture and infrastructure. You must be digital ready before you begin if you are going to succeed at this.

The digital domain is the ultimate resource you can use to connect you to your customer. Companies that want to become fully connected must develop a digital command center that works as an air traffic control center for all things digital. About five months ago Dell Inc. became one of the first companies to launch a digital command center. The command center looks like NASA. They listen to over 27,000 key words related to their technologies. They listen to the Internet in 11 languages. They've trained 5,000 of their employees to be digital superstars. Now that's a company that's innovative. This digital command center will directly result in increased sales, reduced quality problems, improved profitability, brand building and brand protection, and the list goes on.

Use automated online submission portals that provide prefiltration that's directly tied to your innovation platform. Remember, never operate at the baseline level of expectation; always aim for the exceptional. By participating in online digital communities you drive customer co-creation.

Be very careful of what I call the bumper sticker syndrome. Many organizations have developed internal innovation systems that allow people to post ideas. This sounds like a great idea. The problem is that often the people with the most bumper stickers on their cars usually have the worst ideas. It's a phenomenon I think must be related to having a short attention span. It's not frequency and loudness that wins the innovation race; it's relevance to your innovation platform that matters. This is extremely important. Use your digital presence as a value added resource for all new products and services, not as a shortcut.

> It's not frequency and loudness that wins the innovation race; it's relevance to your innovation platform that matters.

## Creating Your Platform: Defining Wants Provides Filter Backdrop

It's incredibly important that you develop a well-defined innovation platform. We can't filter innovation ideas if we don't have something to filter them against. In other words, we need to know what we want before we go out listening to our digital communities. I recommend you develop 21 questions that, when answered, will prefilter online submissions. A ratio to live by in the online submission process is 80 percent filtration/20 percent evaluation. This will allow you to access incremental innovation and breakthrough innovations alike, but significantly increase your throughput by eliminating the time spent going through and evaluating technologies that should have never made it inside your building in the first place.

So, here's the playback:

- Launch an online innovation center with innovation submission portals.
- Develop a digital command center. Install and deploy fast-track methodologies in your NPD function.
- Avoid the pitfalls of the bumper sticker syndrome and commit to your innovation strategy at all levels of the organization.

## Value Layered Innovation: Invent at Each Point of Contact

Remember the customer value strata—once you have completed your innovation, make it better, and then better again, layering on the value. And also remember to invent to each point of contact, and by that I mean innovating where the customer buys the technology, the packaging, and the customer's experience with the technology. The entire innovation cycle must be addressed during your innovation process.

Most organizations do not invent at each point of customer contact. This is a colossal mistake, as each point of contact has its own unique and special opportunity to deliver layered value (see Figure 1.4). These experiences include:

*Pre-Touch or Brand Noise*—This is the impression that customers have of you prior to their first point of contact. Needless to say, your brand noise is driven by what your customers are

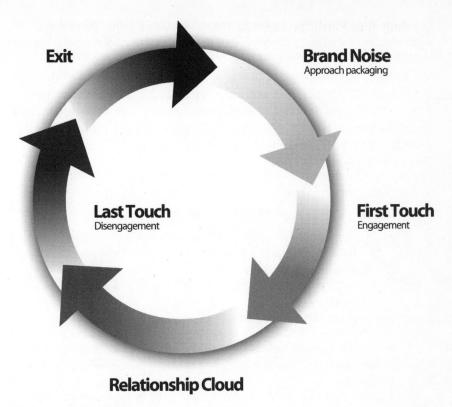

**Exit**

**Brand Noise**
Approach packaging

**Last Touch**
Disengagement

**First Touch**
Engagement

**Relationship Cloud**

**Figure 1.4    The Innovation Cycle**
*Source:* Lassen Scientific, Inc. 2010. All rights reserved.

saying about their experience with your product, service, or technology.

*First-Touch*—This first point of contact is extremely important and heavily weighted. Some experts suggest that 80 percent of a customer's lifetime opinion of you is based on the customer's first experience.

*The Cloud*—This is what a customer is experiencing while they're engaged with your product, technology, or service.

*Last-Touch*—This is the last impression you leave a customer with when disengaging with him or her.

*In-Touch*—This is how you remain customer connected in a way that serves the customer value.

As you can see, each one of these contact points affords you an opportunity to create layered exceptional value. Don't just invent technologies; invent exceptional customer experiences.

Lastly, own the digital domain. The only way you can do that is to commit 100 percent and develop a digital command center. I believe that if you deploy these simple systems within your innovation function, you will see colossal results. There's no better way to develop exceptional solutions than to hardwire to the soul of your customer through digital innovation.

## Chapter Takeaways

- To be a successful innovator, you must first define innovation, and it should be simple. I believe innovation is the process of creating exceptional customer value through active listening.
- The three active ingredients in that definition are exceptional, value, and listening.
- Managing failure results in more failure.
- Innovators must now become digital and new media experts.
- To fully connect with your customers, you need to understand all the fibers of connectivity including simplex, duplex, and full-duplex dialogue.
- The social revolution isn't a fad, as evidenced by the vast numbers on networks such as Facebook, Twitter, LinkedIn, and the thousands of blogs on the Web.

 *The Digital Innovation Playbook* is a living book. We are constantly updating the book online so you can watch uploaded videos, read the latest best practice on digital media and even participate in free ongoing webinars.

   To access this chapter's updated web page, please go to www.digitalinnovationplaybook.com/Chapter1.html or scan the QR code with your mobile device.

# CHAPTER 2

# The Digital Sandbox

## PLAY, LISTEN, INVENT, AND DEPLOY FOR A SUCCESSFUL STRATEGY

**W**e defined innovation and then discussed the basics of digital communication in Chapter 1, Mastering Digital Innovation. We know innovation is *the process of creating exceptional customer value through active listening*, with an emphasis on the vital words *exceptional, value,* and *listening*. We also know communication is king in the digital world, and a commitment to an open culture based on real-time, data-rich dialogue must tie into your innovation platform. Now let's talk strategy.

Is it possible that a single technique could facilitate a full and integrated digital strategy that succeeds every time? The answer is yes! The problem is most organizations have some degree of success in their digital initiatives. And because they're having some success, they're unaware that their digital strategy is incomplete, operating with a high level of inefficiency and ultimately delivering substandard results.

Because analogies can be so effective, I've often described the digital and social media world as the *Digital Sandbox* to clients. There are four components of the digital sandbox: *Play, Listen, Invent, and Deploy*. These four components must all be in play in order for your digital strategy to work. (See Figure 2.1.)

Let's start with *play*. The best way to look at play is to consider the fact that within the digital sandbox you're participating in play, having fun, and playing nicely with others. We have known ever since

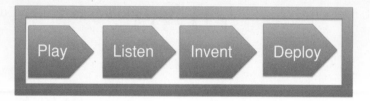

Figure 2.1    The Digital Sandbox

kindergarten that certain behavioral traits allow sandbox success to happen. First of all, you have to be amiable. That means you need to approach the sandbox with the idea that you'll be talking with—and playing with—a wide range of personality types, some of which are bullies, while others are extremely passive. But they're all different. Successful players know that it's okay for the other players to be different; they're not required to be the same. Even when they say mean and hurtful things, we still have to take it in stride, listen for relevance, and move on.

Successful players are amiable, but they are also very conscious. Living consciously is an extremely important ingredient in successful playing. Successful players are conscious of flying buckets. They're aware of their environment and they pay attention. That's how they have fun and remain safe.

And lastly, successful playing is about trust. It's not just about being trustworthy but also about trusting others. There's always risk associated with trust, but the fact of the matter is that it's just as important to be trusting as it is to be trustworthy.

Now if you're successfully playing in your community, both online and analog, you should be constantly *listening*, which is our second step. Listening is extremely important and part of listening is also living consciously. It means asking yourself, "How well am I participating in my community? Am I looking for opportunities to solve problems? Am I listening for opportunities to create new inventions? Am I listening for opportunities to improve the delivery of my service?"

It's really important to know what you're listening for. And that, of course, is why having a comprehensive innovation platform is so critical to your innovative digital strategy.

We know we need to play well while we're in the sandbox, and we need to listen for opportunities to find ways to meet needs, solve problems, and seize opportunities. And this brings us to the third step: *invent*. It's surprising to me to see how many great companies are out there with employees playing well in the digital sandbox and listening attentively to opportunities to solve problems, to meet needs, and to serve opportunities. But they haven't actually created a system to transmute those listening observations into meaningful innovations. So the work goes nowhere. I'm not just talking about products and technologies. Some of the best innovations are simply ways to improve the quality of service and/or product quality.

Some of the best things you'll learn and the best inventions you'll create will be completely intangible but will have meaningful and long-lasting organizational benefits. Make certain that you have systems that allow for regular ideation sessions that turn your observations into world-class technologies and solutions, and also give you the ability to seize emerging opportunities.

This leads us into the last component of the digital sandbox—and remember, the digital sandbox is the total integration of your digital strategies. The last component is what I call *deploy*. The three ingredients I've found to be required for successful deployment are *speed*, *relevance*, and *layering*.

Change is no longer a linear process. It's rapid and it's unpredictable. But there's one thing you can do about a varying speed in terms of technological development and market acceptance, and that is: Always *go fast*. If you always go fast, using conventional fast-track methodologies, you'll always be ahead.

Unfortunately, many organizations are so loosely connected to their customer community that they're deploying innovations that are irrelevant. Your product has to be meaningful and has to be relevant to your target. That may sound obvious, but when 95 percent of all consumer products fail in the marketplace, it's obvious many aren't fulfilling this requirement.

There's one more recommendation I have when it comes to your digital sandbox in your deploy stage, and that's *layering*. When you're done inventing your technology, or done inventing your new service or product, or done inventing your new delivery modality, you're still not done. You're only done when your product has reached the level of *exceptional*. Remember the Customer Value Strata? It's so important that you go way beyond the trajectory of the baseline level of customer expectation.

## A Walk through the Future of Mobile Technology: More and More Smart Connections

You can't talk digital and new media without looking at mobile technologies, where we've been and where we're going. There are many players in the digital sandbox who are utilizing mobile technology to access that very sandbox. Amazing things are happening in the mobile phone industry, and it's one more area in which companies are connecting with customers, innovating their services, and communicating in many ways.

A short four or five years ago, smartphone technology was just for business people and techies. Then, the iPhone hit the market and changed the industry with its simple infrastructure and connectivity. Now, you see 12-year-olds walking around with smartphones, digitally connected and communicating, along with stay-at-home moms, college students, business people, and everybody in between.

Here's the future as I see it: Connected devices are going to become more and more common until, at some point, anything with an electric current running through it will be "smart" and connected. The phone will probably stay the center of it all, but the actual talking on the phone portion of the technology will be only a small part of its capabilities and everyday usage.

### Evolving Before Our Eyes

We're seeing the evolution of mobile technology in the works right now with tablets, eReaders, and portable navigation devices. Developing, but less common as yet, are the connected auto and home technologies. As anyone with multiple technologies used on a daily basis will understand, connecting these devices with smart communicating technology will make our lives much more efficient. As noted in Chapter 4, The Digital Video Revolution, the multiple screens in our lives (TV, computer, cell) are merging. Many other technologies will merge as well.

How will this change how we innovate? In many ways. In Chapter 9, Digital Direct, we talk about direct marketing, something that is seeing a huge impact from the digital and new media revolution.

What's also happening is the boundaries of time and space that once existed between you and your customer are coming down. In the old days, any public correspondence was intensely vetted before a print submission was mailed, faxed, or more recently e-mailed to media or directly to customers. Any of these methods included a lag time. It's time to say goodbye to lag.

### Real-Time Marketing

Advancing mobile technology means real time. It means businesses can now communicate in real time, and both business and customer must be accessible 24/7. Some of this might seem a bit "big brother," but those walls coming down have changed the way we do business a great deal.

For instance, GPS technology has given businesses the ability to monitor potential customer whereabouts, so coupons and other incentives can be advertised on smartphone technology dependent upon the customer's location. You might walk into a Barnes & Noble, and if you then hop online onto your phone, you'll notice a 20-percent-off coupon for hardcover books at Barnes & Noble being advertised. That's no coincidence.

### It's Still All about the Customers

In researching this book, I worked with some of the leaders in the mobile technology industry. Here's what I've learned. The technology is advancing at such a rapid pace that those who wish to stay in the game must focus on two key factors: When you're developing technologies or solutions in this space, you must first focus on delivering customer value (don't get caught up in the technical aspect), and then, you must keep it simple and usable.

No matter how cool the apps or other capabilities are, if you can't figure out how to access them, they might as well not exist. After years of launching products at Lassen Innovation, and also inventing many of my own, I've learned the lesson that the technology needs to disappear for the customer. No matter how complicated the device may be for those in the know, to the customer it should seem as simple and natural as breathing.

### Layering on the Value

In addition to the product's simplicity, true innovators will add layer after layer of value until the product reaches the level of exceptional, as discussed earlier. Remember, in Chapter 1, Mastering Digital

Innovation, we talked about the iPad? When it first came out, it was called the Kindle-killer because it does everything the Amazon Kindle does, but also includes many additional layers of customer value. Despite these many more layers, the technology is incredibly simple and accessible.

There's a lesson to be learned here when you're developing your technologies, be they products or services. As we discussed toward the end of Chapter 1, it's not just the software or device that's important. It's the entire customer experience, from the time they begin thinking about purchasing your product, to buying it, using it, and caring for it—all of the aspects of that customer's life with that product. To be successful in the space of technology and innovation, you'd better be prepared to think of it that way.

Remember, the contact point innovation process is about delivering layered value by innovating at each contact point a customer experiences.

- Pre-Touch or Brand Noise is what customers have heard before contact.
- First-Touch is your first point of contact.
- The Cloud is the customer's experience when they're engaged with the product.
- Last-Touch is the impression a customer will be left with.
- In-Touch is how you remain connected, allowing continued service.

## Back to the Basics: Input and Output

When we look at mobile connected devices, I think we can visualize the technology in its simplest form—inputs and outputs. Leaders in the industry are now looking at new and exciting ways to input into the smart, connected device and output in exciting ways. From hard-monitored devices that are sending wirelessly via blue tooth data to a smartphone that's being used as a health care diagnostic tool, there's a lot of really exciting stuff going on that still falls back on the simple input/output process.

It's really limitless, what can be done with computing, consumer electronics, health care, automotive, and more. With the emergence of each new technology, companies must first evaluate it from a customer's perspective. How can this increase the customer experience? How will it be used in an everyday fashion? What can be done to add value?

In my opinion, mobile technology, and really all of the social and new media technology we discuss in this book, come down to being more connected than ever before. Connected with friends, family, customers, businesses, employees . . . you name it. The ability to communicate—effectively, genuinely, and with the right focus—is more important now than it has ever been. The opportunities are tremendous for those who are willing to evolve with the times and take advantage of these new tools.

And an important reminder for those who are utilizing these great tools—don't forget speed. All of the technologies mentioned—mobile phones already, and blogs and listening technology to come—are great tools, but each must be used with speed and wisdom. Throughout *The Digital Innovation Playbook* I will be talking about the power of *speed*. To help drive speed you should be digitizing your innovation portfolio. Great companies like Planview can make it easy. Planview solutions combine enterprise software and proven best practices to help you react to change, develop and execute strategies, and dynamically balance money and people to help you meet your strategic goals. You can optimize business opportunities, guide business processes, and deliver value as you drive performance and innovation across your organization. For more on this great solution visit www.planview.com.

## Blogs: The Foundation for the Social Web

### Balancing the Playing Field

Blogs truly do fuel the world of social media. Whether they're maintained from a desktop, mobile phone, tablet, or any of the multiple screens, thousands of blogs run by individuals and corporations are updated with thoughts and opinions every minute of the day.

I'd like to share with you the details of two conversations I had with two leaders in the social industry: Rick Calvert, CEO and co-founder of Blog World and New Media Expo, and Marcel Le-brun, CEO of Radian6. Calvert talked blogging and Lebrun talked about listening to the conversations on blogs and the many other web platforms out there.

After attending Blog World in 2010, I was able to connect with Calvert, which was a great thing. You just can't talk social media without talking about blogs, which fuel the social web.

"Blogging, social media, allows small businesses to appear big and big businesses to appear small," Calvert, said.

That was one of the statements Calvert made that most stood out to me. What an amazing advantage for companies at both ends of the spectrum. Blogs not only provide a great platform for companies to connect with both customers and potential customers, but they also equalize the playing field. Big companies like Ford, Sony, or McDonalds get a bad rap, whether deserved or not.

"It's fun to hate the big guy," Calvert said.

And I agree. It's not just fun, it's easy because usually you can assume it's a big, faceless corporation that doesn't deserve your love or attention.

In Chapter 5, Flying High, you'll read about a big guy who is doing it right. Southwest Airlines is a huge company that makes its customers feel like they're friends, like they've got the inside track to the best deals and they're on a friendly, first-name basis with everyone in the company, from the person handing out boarding passes to the pilots.

"They're a big company, but they feel like our friends," Calvert said. "The flight attendants are funny and friendly. The pilots that operate the airline are friendly. And their blog is friendly."

All of these things feed into an image of goodwill and good feelings that customers connect with. Blogging (and an open, customer-centered culture) reinforces that positive brand image. It allows people to feel they know the company in a personal way—something that isn't usually possible with traditional marketing media like direct mail.

"I'll give you the perfect example," Calvert said. "Microsoft is a company everybody loves to hate. They're a gigantic business. And we hate them because we have to buy their product and we all have our little gripes and complaints."

One day Robert Scoble, who used to be one of Microsoft's top bloggers, went around Microsoft with a little handheld camera creating what basically amounted to a series of mini-documentaries. He talked to employees all over the company, getting names, job descriptions, and painting a more personal picture of what goes on behind the walls of one of the biggest software companies in the world.

"He changed it into a company full of individuals that are easy to like," Calvert said. "You see how smart Joe is, what a nice guy Joe is, and how hard Joe is working to make this product better for the customer at the end of the day."

This personal connection changed the brand image of Microsoft completely. Adjusting brand image in such a way allows customers to feel personally and emotionally attached to your company. Improving your SEO capability or positioning your brand as an expert—the individuals within your brand—provides value for your customers before they make a buying decision and thereby influences that eventual buying decision.

But in order to connect to that customer base in a real and lasting manner, all communications, both in person and online, must be genuine. And this is why blogs must be real. Posts must be chronological and allow for honest conversation.

"I firmly believe the definition of a blog is posting content in reverse chronological order that allows comments," Calvert said. "Some people don't, and I don't think that's really blogging. It has to be a two-way conversation, where you post content, people respond to it, and you react to the response. Otherwise, the connection is lost."

## Learning to Listen with Radian6: Helping Companies Communicate and Deploy

Another listening expert in the digital community is Radian6. I spoke with Marcel Lebrun, the CEO of Radian6, about the vast power of digital listening.

As you may recall from my last book, *The Innovation Playbook,* I coined the term *digital command center.* I was very surprised and pleased when I recently heard an announcement from Dell that they had actually deployed a digital command center. Radian6 worked with Dell on the project.

For those of you who might not be familiar with Radian6, the organization helps companies distribute and scale up their listening capabilities throughout the enterprise. They've worked with companies such as Intuit, the U.S. Army (see Chapter 7, The Army Way), and Dell. Radian6 then helps companies tie that information into the various processes going on within the corporation.

"Our platform, similar in some ways to a Google crawler, finds all the conversations, whether they're on Twitter, Facebook, YouTube, blogs, even the little news groups—all the places people have conversations—and we identify all of those things that relate to the subjects you care about," Lebrun said. "We help analyze those conversations, process those that need a response or engagement, and then help turn that information into insight about your enterprise."

A far step beyond the traditional focus groups or research surveys, this type of listening tells companies what their customers like or dislike about the products or services. You learn about issues they may be having or what your competitors might be doing better.

"We have a variety of tools that are like insight dashboards, or we have another product called an 'engagement console,'" Lebrun said. "These are the types of tools that sit in the digital command center at Dell."

Listening is really what powers social strategies across the enterprise. But then the data or knowledge gained from that digital ear needs to translate to the next step: *action*. Remember *play*, *listen*, *invent*, and *deploy*? Just listening isn't enough. So Radian6 ties that information into its clients' systems, which then track the information to assure that the problem is resolved or the idea now lies in the right hands.

"If someone has a complaint, they may need to open a trouble ticket, and it would be processed as would any other case," Lebrun said. "Companies can keep track of the issues and resolutions. We also do a lot of analysis around things like advocacy and influence. Let's say you're Tylenol and you want to study the arthritis conversations. We answer questions such as: Who are the influential voices in arthritis? Who is everybody listening to and who should you be building relationships with if you want to understand and connect with this community?"

The social web isn't just a medium with words; it's a medium with action. As people interact with content, they leave behind bread crumbs that are indicative of attention. When people Tweet things or comment or link or "like" them on Facebook or "star" them on YouTube, all of these things are indicators of importance to these people.

"The Radian6 platform crawls not just content but also social metrics, and those social metrics help you understand relevance of conversations so you know what's really important today, what's really buzzing," Lebrun said.

## Conversations: A Previously Untapped Resource, But Are You Listening?

There's a huge pool of unsolicited, naturally occurring conversations that companies can tap into. Think about how companies previously gathered information—the surveys and focus groups and so on. I've often joked about the fact that surveys are a great way to gather the thoughts of people who don't value their time. If someone's going to take 15 minutes and answer your call and all your questions, what is their time worth? Are you really getting at any sort of real truth in that conversation?

Most people are more motivated to share ideas if they believe that knowledge may actually result in some sort of action. That's the difference between data gathering and *listening*. The purpose of listening is learning. So when I listen, I'm telling someone they're worth my time. And the investment of that time eventually translates into trust. When you have that foundation of trust, you gain the type of information you wouldn't normally get.

> **W**hen I listen, I'm telling someone they're worth my time. And the investment of that time eventually translates into trust.

Marcel Lebrun gave an example from his early days of working with Dell. There was an issue with an audio chip on some products with the Windows Vista driver. Customers were calling Dell a flack of the recording industry association because the driver issue wasn't allowing people to rip their CDs. The bug in the system was soon found and, to compensate customers, Dell offered a warranty to fix the machines over a certain period of time.

Throughout this process, Dell's chief blogger was talking to people, explaining what happened, answering questions, and walking people through the process.

"I remember seeing people responding to the blog," Lebrun said. "The blogger was their champion of truth; they trusted him. They stuck with him all the way through it."

These customers were upset by what happened, but even in their frustration, there was a connection, a trust that was built with that face of Dell.

Brands have an opportunity to listen and engage in a wider conversation. Take aspirin, or any branded pain reliever, for example. If you go to the brand's website, you'll see there are different topics they address. They'll talk about arthritis, for example. I'm sure they have marketing folks who target topics such as the five big uses for such-and-such an arthritis drug. This may be useful information to some, but it's a one-sided conversation. They aren't really listening.

If you think about the brand and what people are saying about the brand, you now have an opportunity to listen—in real time—to what people with arthritis are talking about every day. What do people with arthritis talk about right now? What are the issues? What do they care about? You had no way to do that before, but now you can. Now you can listen to that industry conversation in real time and let that guide your marketing, your messaging, your product, your initiatives. If you find that they're all talking about this certain angle, you look at how you as a brand can add value to that—even if it's not your product—and then you grow as an insider in that conversation. It's a very powerful tool, being an insider in these conversations. It's a far better way to tap into the shifting tides of opinion, more so than all the traditional vehicles we've been using.

## The Sandbox Mentality: Learning to Play, Listen, Invent, and Deploy

In researching this book and in the drama of understanding all things digital, I found that the simultaneously complex and simple concept of digital was best broken down into the categories mentioned earlier: play, listen, invent, and deploy.

Usually, when I hear the term *best practice*, it's more like *bad practice*. The concept is usually eight years old. The key to this seems to be that you first have to be willing to play. The two parties need to participate in full-duplex dialogue. The two-way conversation has to be genuine. It can't be faked.

The other part of the equation is *listening*. You aren't listening if someone has a technical complaint and you refer them to cubicle eight in sector nine. You need to get the story, see what the customer sees.

Most companies who are failing at this transition to open, digital cultures don't understand that it's all about a holistic customer experience. You must listen, invent, and then deploy.

Dell uses the phrase "Listen, engage and act," which is a similar policy. Be prepared to play, but understand that others within the sandbox may be different from you. You must be willing to engage in these digital conversations despite these differences. That's definitely the first step. And listening is a process that involves getting an organization to build the processes and the culture that will allow true *listening*. It's training and cultures and processes because you have to be systematic about it so things don't fall through the cracks.

## Playing Nice in the Sandbox: Be Aware and Share the Space

When I think of the sandbox analogy, I think of the many personalities in a playground sandbox. There are the authoritarian bullies, the shy pacifist, and all kids of different psychodynamics in play. So when you're in the sandbox, you need to be conscious and you have to be amiable. You need to let go of the controls and simply listen.

This idea of letting go also translates into allowing employees to be the face of your company. Many companies keep employees out of the sandbox, or provide so many rules for conduct that they're sure to be ostracized.

Lebrun told the story of how he used to tease one of the marketing managers at Dell for wearing a cowboy hat. The marketer was one of the very active conversationalists on the web and, as he became more and more known, his personal brand, his style, began to merge with Dell's.

"He started to color it," Lebrun said. "Dell starts to mean something different to me because I know him and that's a good thing."

People trust people, not big faceless corporations. You've probably seen studies on trust. At this time, organizational trust and institutional trust are hugely in decline. As a brand you're trying to grow your institutional trust, not stunt it. People trust people. So why not let your people be known?

One of the best things about social networking is it averages the scales. Michael Dell is out there and accessible on Twitter, right along with thousands of others, known or unknown. He may not have time to chit-chat constantly, but he's there. If someone sends him a message with a question, there's a process in place that assures the question will be answered. It's important to be sure those processes are in place.

## Giving Employees a Voice: Sharing the Brand to Make It Stronger

Allowing employees to participate and be part of the brand is one of those letting go things. There's an illusion of control companies are still hanging onto with tooth and nail. Marketers need to realize that we never had the control we thought we had over our brands and how they're perceived. So, let's accept that we're a participant in the conversations. We are an equal participant with our customers, so let's engage.

One of the things I've found over time is you have people who are really good at delivering good products, and you have people who are really good at delivering great service, but there aren't a lot of companies that deliver both great service and good products consistently. So when a lot of organizations make this transformation from analog to digital—from being closed to being open—and start this new discussion, it's interesting that, for a while, they're in denial about what the customer community says about their defects. Once they start to open up and participate in communicating, they spend the first part of their transition into this space denying what they hear. They need to learn to listen and accept what the customer is saying, evaluate it, and interact in a way that is meaningful to the customer and the company.

## Learning New Communication: Traditional Media No More

At Lassen Innovation we have a program called RealOpen® (See Chapter 10, RealOpen Innovation). We work with clients to develop online innovation submission portals, which have aperture settings

speed.results.profit

Figure 2.2    RealOpen Innovation Management Framework

that allow the outside world to communicate, to submit ideas or comments, and then that commentary is pre-vetted against the client's innovation platforms. They can actually pre-vet ideas so they don't have to just send people away. It's a delicate balance that many companies face. (See Figure 2.2.)

## A Paradigm Shift: From Listening to Engagement

Even as recently as a few years back, many companies were starting to listen in on digital conversations. But engagement was still a distant concept. We've been trained to be closed for so many years because the traditional media were something to be managed.

Anyone allowed to speak externally had to go through extensive media training. For a long time that careful behavior has been embedded in our psyche.

When this new social communications style came along, everything changed. Now we actually want to be transparent. We want to admit to occasional mistakes, then apologize, and make improvements. That's a fundamental transformation for many companies. Two years ago I think it was more difficult.

Today, more and more brands are seeing the benefits of that kind of transparency. There are many more case studies proving this point, and companies are finally seeing the value.

## The New Digital Multipliers: Real People Create Real Loyalty

Let's talk digital multipliers. If you have one person who is upset with you, that person will tell anyone who will listen. People who are happy will also share their experience, but not with the same veracity. Now you can multiply those numbers by the fans and friends on Facebook, blogs, Twitter, and other socialscapes, and you've got a massive outpouring.

At Lassen Innovation, we do a lot in the health care field. I find it interesting that the incidence of malpractice suits has almost nothing to do with clinical efficacy; it mostly has to do with whether the plaintiff hates the doctor or not. If the patient goes to the doctor and has a bad experience, suddenly he or she didn't get clinically efficacious treatment and therefore files suit.

This mentality often transfers to customer service in any retail chain. If I have a problem but I actually like the person who provided the customer service, I'm probably not going to complain. People complain when they feel they have no other recourse. Then they spread that anger on the social web and everybody else hears about it. This is exactly why engagement is so important. When the brand responds with, "sorry to hear that," then customers feel they've been heard and may still retain some sense of loyalty to the brand.

Take this engagement one step further and you can create super fans. Companies should also engage those speaking positively about the brand and thanking company advocates.

"When someone recommends your brand and you show up to thank them it can be an amazing thing," Lebrun said. "Xbox is an interesting case study on that. They have the Xbox Elite Tweet Fleet. They basically have a bunch of people, gamers who know the gamer community, and they're basically there to simply hang out. Someone will say, 'Hey I got this cool new Xbox thing . . .' and they'll actually engage in that and people will say, 'Whoa! Xbox actually talked to me!' They're blown away that Xbox was out there listening."

That's where the real loyalty lies. A lot of times we focus on the crises, but what about nurturing the community and the brand?

## Gaining Customer Credit by Being in the Conversation, Not Just Problem Solving

Now we've established that reaching out proactively, before anything has gone wrong, is a great idea. Take this concept to the big picture level. A lot of companies put massive resources out there to protect their brand after the products are already out the gate. But what's really important is making good products and providing good service in the first instance. If you're good from the start, you'll have already built up credibility with your customers. Even if customers have a problem, they're not as inclined to go out and tell everybody they hate the brand. They'll trust that they can go to you and get an active listening ear.

## A Theory of Relativity: Weighing "What You Get" versus "What You Expected"

To me the biggest takeaway for this entire book is that really bad things can happen with mediocre or baseline products too. As we discussed in Chapter 1, at the end of the day the difference between good and bad customer service is the difference between what you get and what you expected to get. It's all relative when you evaluate the customer experience compared with the customer's expectation.

Remember when color monitors first came out? They were amazing. Everyone had these huge color computer monitors. Now, if you gave someone a monitor, they'd be upset. Things change over time from amazing to baseline expectation. Marshall McLuhan once famously said, "The medium is the message."

What he meant is that the medium itself actually has a social impact on society; it changes things. For instance, television was destined to shrink the globe no matter what we sent over its signals. So when you think about the social web and the things it is driving in society, it's good. It's forcing an equal voice, and so the guy who can afford the Super Bowl ad is not the only one able to get his message out. The social web has allowed these remarkable stories to flow more freely. So we found the Susan Boyles of the world.

"The social digital world has democratized things," Lebrun said. "The Web itself is changing society."

## No. 251?! No More Lines

On the customer service side—this is my expectation—people now expect businesses to line up for them. In the old days, we'd wait our turn for attention. We'd sit on hold, waiting for the next free representative, or we'd pull our little number, waiting our turn.

Now we are connected anytime and anywhere, which means customers are telling companies I'll complain when and where I choose, and then you will have to find me to resolve my issue at my convenience.

What's good about this is that it's actually more cost effective when the customers do exactly that. Rather than staffing huge call centers, complaints are monitored and responders don't need to stick with a constrictive response plan. But because of this shift, customers are becoming less and less patient with traditional, cost-saving customer service methods found in many companies.

Lebrun agreed. He used automated phone services as an example.

"When I call in and I hear, 'Thank you for calling; your call is important to us,' what I'm really hearing is, 'Your call is important to us, but not as important as the efficient utilization of our resources,'" Lebrun said. "Because otherwise, we would wait for you, not have you wait for us. But that's an expensive model where I have to have people on standby waiting for you to call."

## A Social Shift in Customer Service: Cost Effective with Power Going to the People

But with this social web communication, everything is different. We can multitask and everything is quick, but it doesn't have to be real time.

When I make a complaint over the web, I don't expect an instant reply within seconds. I do expect a response within a few hours, but not in real time. I expect the company to come find me, which is a big change in the customer/customer service dynamics seen in recent years.

There are a tremendous amount of tools available to improve customer service, but if your principal goal is to reduce cost, you almost never hit your target. As they tell a race car driver, "If you go into a spin on the track, don't look at the wall because if you do, you're going to go right into the wall." We move toward what we focus on. If your focus is on efficiency and cost control, that is not going to improve customer service.

After all my years of innovating and launching new technologies, one thing I've learned about innovation is: You really have to focus on the right thing. I spent a lot of time and money making mistakes in order to learn that lesson, which is why it's so deeply imbedded. You really have to focus on a holistic customer experience if you want to get this right. (For how this works, see Figure 2.3.)

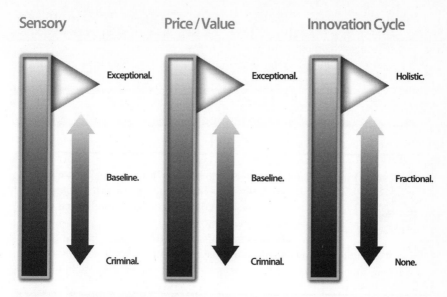

**Figure 2.3    Experiential Sliders**

## Chapter Takeaways

- Organizations that experience some degree of success are often un-aware that their digital strategy is incomplete and operates with a high level of inefficiency that ultimately delivers substandard results.
- There are four components of the digital sandbox: *Play, Listen, Invent, and Deploy*.
- Play well in the digital sandbox, despite the fact that many other players will have very different personalities. Listen actively so you can hear innovations that don't necessarily have to be product related. Some of the best innovations focus on service.
- Have a process in place so you can deploy rapidly when innovations arise.
- The social web has balanced the playing field, making big companies appear small, and small companies big.
- Change is no longer linear, and it's happening at lightning speed. The only way companies can expect to compete is to always move quickly.
- When you listen, you're telling someone they're worth your time. The investment of that time eventually translates into trust. And when you

have that foundation of trust, you gain the type of information you wouldn't normally get.

- People complain about a brand when they feel they have no other recourse. Listen and respond to gain trust and loyalty, even when there are problems.

 *The Digital Innovation Playbook* is a living book. We are constantly updating the book online so you can watch uploaded videos, read the latest best practice on digital media, and even participate in free ongoing webinars.

To access this chapter's updated web page, please go to www.digitalinnovationplaybook.com/Chapter2.html or scan the QR code with your mobile device.

# CHAPTER 3

# The Digital Enterprise

## HARNESSING SOCIAL MEDIA
## INTELLIGENCE, SMARTLY

We've talked some, and will repeat throughout the book, about the importance of *playing*, *listening*, *inventing*, and *deploying* within the digital sandbox. Say you become an excellent listener, locating and joining in on the conversations going on throughout the web about your brand. How then do you cull the best information for you innovations from the masses of information streaming the web?

There are several systems that can do this, but companies must be extremely leery of instituting either risk-centric systems that could potentially turn away the terrible with the brilliant in an equal fashion (all ideas can look alike in a system that focuses on risk, not on the ideas themselves), or systems that aren't customized to fit your individual needs.

We talk more about this concept in Chapter 10, RealOpen Innovation, but in this chapter I'd like to introduce you to another company I've found to be a leader in this space. Innovation Superstar Spigit was founded in 2007 by Paul Pluschkell and Padmanabh Dabke. The company has evolved even in its short lifetime, but the idea—which has remained the same—behind the concept was to create a platform that harnesses the wisdom of crowds to capture, refine, collaborate on, and select the best ideas for your individual needs.

In this book and the first in the series, *The Innovation Playbook*, I've talked about both the greatness and the inherent dangers in crowd sourcing. Harnessing the collective intelligence of a crowd—be it internal at a corporation or open to the entire world—can be a beautiful thing, if it's done properly. Companies must be truly committed to an open culture that gives participants the inside track to what that company's wants and needs are if they're to understand what will be successful in that playing field.

## The Spigit Community

I talked in depth about this concept with Jim Heilig, executive vice president of sales at Spigit. He described the amazing tools that are now available to harness social media in a smart way to innovate your company.

Here's how Spigit is a little different from many other crowd sourcing sites. Spigit creates networks of ideas. It's not about a user submitting an idea and seeing if management likes it enough for it to be implemented. Instead, the ideas are both created and filtered through the community. People contribute to others' ideas and they share their opinions. These contributions and opinions help ideas to progress along a gradation path to selection—or they can hold ideas back, filtering out those that aren't good or simply not right for your company's purposes.

"One of the problems with really large communities is that it's difficult to find what's relevant without massive overhead on the client's side," Heilig said. "They need to spend their time listening to the right discussions, prompting the right dialogue, and getting value from the collaboration from their communities."

### A Customized Approach

An organization using Spigit will first set the criteria for what they consider a good idea, and then set stages for graduation. These stages or triggers are set according to the organization's culture, markets, objectives, and so on. This is where it's important that your culture is healthy. You also need to truly understand who your customers are and what they want, in order to add the greatest value to your products and services.

The Spigit platform uses social media tools like blogs, Facebook, and other platforms that allow these large communities to interact.

Then using analytics, game theory, behavioral economics, work flow, and many other tools, the software gives companies the ability to identify the relevant content.

With Spigit, social triggers can be set to measure how many people are interested in the idea, or they can be determined by how many review and comment on the idea (the buzz percentile). Ideas can then be set to advance if they meet quality objectives, social objectives, or a combination of both.

What this does is save companies from the need for a huge team of workers moderating. It culls out the masses of information, spotlighting the ideas that are most important so companies can react quickly with new innovations.

## Automating the Heavy Lifting of Enterprise Collaboration

Organizers who strive for enterprise collaboration are often disappointed. They buy the software and yes, they may get some interesting conversations going, but at the end of the day it's hard to determine where the value actually lies in these discussions. The problem is that generic collaboration platforms have no structure to manage the ideas. And they have no incentive to entice participants to continue submitting ideas and stay active within the community. So what happens? Community members lose interest.

## Rewarding a Common Focus

We discuss this incentive idea frequently throughout this book. Employees and those participating in programs like this must have some sort of incentive in order to motivate them to not only strive for improvement, but also to feel loyalty to the brand, which furthers commitment. I recommend a rewards program such as the Innovation Superstar system I use that spotlights those making a real impact on customer and company value.

Spigit rewards its community members with the advancement process. Good ideas move forward as other members like them or add improvements and everyone benefits.

Rather than enabling random conversations, Spigit has a structure that guides the users to a common objective—submitting ideas and solving problems. Think of it as the difference between employees going into the lunch room to communicate and employees going into a meeting to solve a problem. You're going to have a much different mindset in different settings.

### Crowdsourcing from Several Avenues

The benefit a system like Spigit provides its clients is the fact that it utilizes the crowdsourcing concept from so many communities: employees, customers, partners, and even strangers. Employees can provide valuable feedback about creating better products or services and they should—in theory—be able to do it more efficiently.

But that's not always the case because, in many systems, employees are working in organizational silos.

"We often hear how multiple departments within a single company are not able to reach out across groups to collaborate around a subject, but realize the value if they could," Heilig said.

A system like Spigit helps to break down organizational or departmental silos so employee groups can work more closely together within a new idea management community.

Initially, most companies utilized this idea pool internally, with employees only submitting ideas, voting on ideas, and interacting within the community.

"You want to leverage the scale of your organization," Heilig said. "But now, more and more we're seeing an internal discussion but you're inviting customers into it. Retailers will bring their supply chain in. We're seeing more groups bringing outside people in."

### Your Most Important Asset: The Customer

Customers can provide huge insight into how to create more marketable products or services they want to buy. They can tell you what the most important features are and where other products out on the market are missing the mark. The funny thing is that these potential customers want to tell someone these things. They want to share information about other brands and they want to tell you what can be improved specifically on your brand. Even those who haven't experienced your particular product can tell you what they like via social media tools such as Facebook, Twitter, or many others. You just have to be there to collect that data.

**C**ustomers want to tell someone what they think. They want to share information about brands and tell you how your brands can be improved. This happens every day on social media tools like Facebook and Twitter. You just have to be there to collect the data.

## A "Gap" in Judgment: Followers Cry Out for Old Logo

Just ask clothing retailer Gap how valuable it is to reach beyond their employees to ask customers about certain changes. In October 2010, after much design work and money spent, they swapped the old Gap logo for a more contemporary design. What they didn't expect were their followers on Facebook and Twitter to become upset and make it very clear that they preferred the old logo. It was switched back after one week, and Gap learned a very valuable lesson about better understanding what their community of customers is thinking.

There are many other examples of this type of innovative listening, in which organizations reached out to the public to solve problems and generate ideas. Take the Cisco I-Prize case study.

## Cisco Looks to the Public: Widening the Idea Net

Cisco was looking for their next billion-dollar idea and was willing to pay $250,000 for it. So they created a global contest website that tracked user ideas, facilitated collaboration, and increased customer engagement. Because they cast such a wide net, they needed to implement a software platform to manage submissions and automatically surface the best ideas using more in-depth factors than just popularity.

The idea was to employ a more intelligent approach than just simple "post & vote" functionality, and create a community that can easily scale to accommodate two million users and incorporate multimedia to showcase Cisco products. To do this, Cisco approached Spigit.

Spigit designed and implemented an external Cisco I-Prize community that included voting, comments, and an idea market to identify the billion-dollar idea.

Spigit's innovation management platform in combination with Cisco's collaboration tools, served as the platform by which entrepreneurs submitted, shared, and built on their ideas with fellow innovators. The platform included functionality for reputation scores via RepURank algorithms to assign value to an idea based on several factors such as the idea generator's reputation, role within an organization, level of expertise, number of votes, and the 360-degree feedback given by the community.

The Cisco I-Prize for 2010 had a total of 2,900 participants representing more than 156 countries, who submitted 824 ideas to the competition. The prize was awarded in mid-2010 to a team of five researchers based in Mexico that proposed creating a physical and virtual platform that would facilitate connectivity along with smart objects, people, and information.

## AAA Looks to Gen Y: Spigit Creates Innovation Community

The innovation group at AAA was recently asked to develop new products and services for members that would promote AAA's message of safety and security, while also looking for new ways to increase the company's relevance among new markets, namely the Gen Y segment.

The executives are asking for new products and/or services that would be more appealing to people who are not in the core demographic group of 55 years and older. The target themes for innovation included discounts, marketing to members, green transportation, and all things related to transportation (automotive, travel, etc.).

AAA chose Spigit to create an innovation community called Idea Garage for their employees across club boundaries. AAA is set up as a franchise model with the national office overseeing the brand, but each region has its own product offerings, pricing, and so on.

With the creation of the Spigit-powered community, AAA finally had a tool that allowed its employees from across the nation to share ideas around common issues that all of its members deal with. For example, some of the best ideas have come from colleagues in Florida and have been built upon by employees in Arizona.

The product development teams at AAA will also be using the new SpigitFusion product to manage the movement of ideas to concepts and ultimately new products and services. Remember, companies must have a system in place to move on to the deploy function mentioned in Chapter 2.

SpigitFusion will be providing the AAA product development teams with transparency to the idea authors that work is being done on their idea.

AAA has indicated one of the challenges they have in managing the Idea Garage is the constant question of "so what has happened to my idea?" SpigitFusion gave the community the tools they needed to see how ideas are progressing along their gradation paths.

## A Need to Stand Out: Veridian Credit Union Pulls in Collective Intelligence of Employees on the Front Lines

With a tough economy and an even tougher financial industry, Veridian Credit Union recognized a need to differentiate from competitors. The bank needed to capture their customers' attention and drive more revenue. So they unleashed a companywide initiative, deciding that innovation would be their path to success and the best way to stand out from their competitors in an industry that has been branded as stale, old school, and noninventive.

To do this Veridian decided to tap into the collective intelligence of the source closest to their customers—their front line employees.

"Spigit stood out because it was more than a project management tool with the term 'innovation' slapped on it," said Paul Farmer, Innovation Officer at Veridian Credit Union, about how the company chose Spigit. "It develops ideas and allows users to rate and grow them according to their relevance and worth to the company's objectives through conversations, discussion threads, and blogs."

Veridian launched Spigit internally in the summer of 2010. They created internal buzz around the initiative and Spigit itself by developing a unique, creative, and impactful presentation that simplified the idea management process.

The company had more than 70 percent of their 500 employees joining in and testing out the system very soon after launch. They launched a scavenger hunt where employees were encouraged to navigate the Spigit system and were eligible for prizes after completion.

"After six months of deployment, upwards of 85 percent of the employees were entering ideas, voting on their favorites, and graduating them into action," Farmer said. "With the Spigit system, Veridian can now measure and report on net dollars saved or earned based on ideas produced or implemented. It is really the driving force behind organizing and driving our innovative ideas."

Veridian reported a savings of $115,000 in the first six months by polling members and quickly implementing the best ideas. The bulk of the savings was cutting the daily courier services at 26 branches down to two days per week and installing automatic light switches to save energy. Adding bike racks outside of branches also made commuting more convenient for employees and members.

The success at Veridian was so great the company has continued to work with Spigit and has set new goals for 2011. Corporate incentive programs are in place to drive participation, and innovation workshops have been set up to further promote the new culture of innovation gained with the successes.

## Innovating with Collective Intelligence: Taking the Ideas and Running with Them

In this chapter we looked at organizing the flow of internal and external ideas. The information is out there for the taking and companies like Spigit and RealOpen can customize the flow to fit organizational needs, maximizing idea potential. In the next few chapters we look at the technology out there innovating how we communicate with both customers and employees.

### Chapter Takeaways

- When it comes to culling through innovative ideas, companies must be extremely leery of instituting risk-centric systems that could potentially turn away the terrible with the brilliant in an equal fashion.
- Companies must also be careful information flow systems are customized to fit individual needs.
- Crowdsourcing, harnessing the power of collective intelligence, can be a beautiful thing if—and only if—it's done properly.
- Customers can provide huge insight into how to create more marketable products or services they want to buy.
- Customer opinions are already out there on the social network highways; you just have to be there to collect them.

- A system like Spigit helps to break down organizational or departmental silos so employee groups can work more closely together within a new idea management community.
- Companies like Gap that have used social avenues to test new concepts will tell you: Just ask and you'll hear what your customers really want.

 *The Digital Innovation Playbook* is a living book. We are constantly updating the book online so you can watch uploaded videos, read the latest best practice on digital media, and even participate in free ongoing webinars.

To access this chapter's updated web page, please go to www.digitalinnovationplaybook.com/Chapter3.html or scan the QR code with your mobile device.

# The Digital Video Revolution

## DIGITAL TECHNOLOGY GIVES ANYONE THE ABILITY TO MAKE A QUALITY TELEVISION SHOW

**W**e spent the last chapter talking ideas and innovation. Now it's time to look at some of the amazing technology that is revolutionizing the digital industry.

In researching *The Digital Innovation Playbook* I had the sincere pleasure of interviewing some of the true thought leaders in the areas of digital and new media. And I discovered some very important trends that should be known to anyone committed to promoting their innovations via new media.

The first major change occurring with breakneck speed is that of micro video production. That is, the ability for small entrepreneurial organizations to create exquisite, high-production value video. We're talking television-quality videos. The second thing I discovered is the fact that video distribution is no longer a monopoly and that any smart organization with a good digital strategy can build buzz around their video and use it to build both sales and brand value.

Another important trend is the melding of the screens; mobile devices, desktops, and home television sets are now sharing the same micro-produced content. No longer do cable and satellite networks *own* the cable to your customer's home television set, or better yet, the screen on your mobile device or computer. The digital conduit of the Internet provides a way for great content to earn its way onto small, medium, and large screens.

As champions of digital media, we can no longer look at mobile devices, desktops, and televisions as separate platforms. They are now, and will continue to be, a single homogeneous medium.

I recently had the privilege of speaking with Philip Nelson from NewTek, which is always on the leading edge of trends within the digital media space.

## Philip Nelson on NewTek: Revolutionizing Desktop Video

Philip Nelson is the Senior Vice President for Strategic Development at NewTek, creators of the TriCaster, the latest and greatest in HD portable live video production. In addition to his years of digital video experience, Nelson brings a great deal of passion for the amateur video creator to the table. In his words, he'll explain how NewTek revolutionized the desktop video industry, allowing anyone from garage band members to corporation CEOs to create quality video available for all to see.

In the mid-1980s, the founder of NewTek, Tim Jenison, was quoted as saying, "In the next 20 years your favorite television show will be made by you or someone you know." He foresaw the democratization of television.

### Passing the Power of Video to You and Me

The technology has evolved to allow anyone and everyone to have the ability to not only create professional-grade video but also to distribute it to the masses. Before the desktop video revolution in the early 1990s, power was in the hands of a select few executives at television networks. The average guy had no chance of making a television show.

A few years down the road NewTek created the desktop video technology called the Video Toaster. It was the first of its kind and, according to NewTek, signaled the start of the desktop video revolution. For the first time in history, anyone could make a television show.

"It wasn't just people with millions of dollars in equipment; truly anyone could make a TV show," Nelson said.

However, the gatekeeper television networks still ran the show as far as who got to see that content. So people could make their own shows, but since television networks controlled air time, there still weren't many options for distributing that content.

Fast forward to the Internet television revolution, which is where we are now, in the early phases of it. With the proliferation of broadband and the availability of free, or practically free, live streaming, there is no gatekeeper. Now the power is in the hands of the producer and the consumer of that content. It's up to the producers to make the shows they dreamed of making, and it's up to the consumer to determine if those shows have value.

"And when it has value, the currency is the consumer's time," Nelson said. "It is so exciting now because shows and ideas that would never have seen the light of day are being made. Shows that don't have a million-viewer potential can find an audience on the Internet. A show with a thousand viewers could be successful depending on the audience."

"Shows that don't have a million-viewer potential can find an audience on the Internet," said Philip Nelson of NewTek. "A show with a thousand viewers could be successful depending on the audience."

### Doing Away with the Gatekeeper: Brightcove Provides Access to All

We've all heard of YouTube, which provides a free platform for anything and everything a person might want to share with the world. But other, more professional quality on-demand software platforms for video, platforms used by media and marketing professionals, began emerging around the same time. Brightcove is one such platform used by media companies and marketers with tremendous success.

Brightcove has more than 1,800 customers in 58 countries that operate video across nearly 10,000 websites, including many of the most popular news and entertainment destinations on the Web.

Another great resource is TubeMogul, an online video analytics and advertising platform that processes billions of video streams every month from the Internet's top publishers. More than 200,000 users rely on TubeMogul's distribution and analytics, and hundreds of marketing agencies and brand advertisers are among the company's clients.

Brightcove and TubeMogul teamed up to develop a new online video index and quarterly research report that identifies the leading industry trends. In reviewing the finds of the second quarter, it's obvious that the viewing and creating of digital video are growing at an explosive rate. Here's the latest:

## Online Video Stream

- In Q2 of 2010, broadcast networks and pure-play web media properties remained in the top two positions among media industry verticals for overall video stream growth.
- Online video streams from newspaper websites surged in Q2 by more than 65 percent. This can be attributed to the sustained coverage of the BP oil disaster in the Gulf of Mexico, which started April 20, 2010 and ran through May and June.
- Video stream growth slowed among magazine website properties, as well as music label and artist websites in Q2.

## Engagement

- The volume of unique viewers accessing online video grew across all media verticals in Q2 of 2010 by an average of 2.8 percent per month compared to .05 percent month-over-month growth in Q1.
- Viewers watched 11.8 percent more videos per month in Q2 than last quarter.
- In Q2, across media verticals, the average viewing time per video stream was two minutes.
- Broadcast networks and magazine websites saw an increase in the average length of viewing time per video in Q2 by 3.1 percent and 2.1 percent, respectively.
- The online video content of media companies has an average completion rate of 38 percent per video view. Magazine and pure-play web media properties had the highest overall completion rates per video view.

### Discovery

- Google continues to generate the highest volume of traffic to online video content, followed by Yahoo!, Facebook, Bing, and Twitter.
- Referral traffic from Facebook and Twitter is growing faster than traditional search engines as a source of video views. At current rates, Facebook will surpass Yahoo! within the year to be second only to Google in referral traffic to online video content for media companies.

There are a lot more of these findings, but let's first return to NewTek.

## Chasing the Elusive Dollar: How Do Companies Monetize Their Video Efforts?

One question on the mind of every company is, how do we monetize our efforts and create value? The answer is there are many ways video can create value for a company.

Content created by enterprise clients, including marketing content where they're making an investment to create buzz around a product or service or an idea, can provide value by pulling in sheer numbers. The company may not be looking at making money on the webcast itself, but they use it as a marketing tool. Enterprise clients may be using the webcast to distribute ideas to a larger internal audience. Rather than flying people in for a meeting, the company saves money by creating a virtual meeting and allowing people to participate online.

NewTek has clients, such as the U.S. Department of Homeland Security Science & Technology Directorate, that use live webcasts to broadcast their science and technology director and stakeholder conferences.

According to Nelson, the agency recently added an online component to ensure that their information is distributed to a wider audience. If a first responder cannot attend, that person can now attend online.

Then there are also the entertainment-type webcasts and events, which sell sponsorships and create revenue from advertising. There are a variety of different ways large corporations, small corporations, and everyone in between can create value or benefit from live stream-ing video.

## Wallets Open Thanks to Social Media

Bazaarvoice, an industry research company, recently posted a great social commerce statistics case study entitled *Power of Word of Mouth*[1] that had some very telling statistics. In this study, it was stated that 53 percent of people on Twitter recommended companies and/or products in their Tweets, with 48 percent of them delivering on their intention to buy the product.[2] It was also found that 44 percent of moms use social media for brand/product recommendations and 73 percent trust online community recommendations.[3] More than half (51 percent) of consumers are using the Internet before mak-ing a purchase in shops, educating themselves on the best deals out there.[4] And, most pertinent to this conversation, nearly 64 percent of respondents had watched a user-generated video review, and more than three-quarters of that group said it helped them make a pur-chase decision. Of that group 81 percent listed the ability to see the product in action as their favorite thing about video reviews. This idea is not new to NewTek.

## Moving Customers to the Full Online Purchasing Experience

"When you think of online sales, first ask yourself, why does someone buy from a brick and mortar store?" Nelson asked. "Because they can touch it, feel it, smell it, try it on. . . . So the more that a com-pany can do to walk that buyer through the funnel of buying, the better."

And he's right. One of the biggest reasons people go to a brick and mortar store is for the tactile experience. So for online initiatives to be truly successful, you need to give the online version of a tactile experience. Say a person is looking for a camera. He or she will want to pick up the camera, look through the viewfinder, scroll through the menu, experience the weight of it, and so on.

---

[1] www.bazaarvoice.com/resources/stats.
[2] ROI Research for Performance, June 2010.
[3] BabyCenter LLC, July 2009.
[4] Verdict Research, May 2009.

For online initiatives to be truly successful, you need to give the online version of the tactile experience. This is why many retailers are turning to video.

Online retailers are trying to give that same information, but obviously it needs to come in a different format than that of an in-person experience. Many make the mistake of listing pages of content and, while information is important, lists and bullet points aren't enough anymore.

This is why retailers are turning to video. Watching someone experience the technology is the next best thing to experiencing it yourself. And it may be even better since, while watching video, consumers also have miles of information, comparisons, and competing pricing information at their fingertips.

"It's the equivalent of a demo in the store," Nelson said. "In fact it's even better than a demo in the store because the streaming video delivers a consistent message and doesn't rely on a sales person to remember the key benefits of the product."

## Video to Tell and Sell

In 2008, 18 percent of retailers used video. Today that number is 68 percent. In more and more cases, retailers and other companies are realizing the power of video to tell a story and sell. It has also been said that people remember about 20 percent of what they hear or read, but with video they retain about 80 percent of what they hear and see. We know that memory and being driven emotively can create a higher impact and increase the opportunity to sell. Not only does NewTek provide an opportunity for this increase in sales for its user, the company fully embraces the concept in its own sales.

"We created the TriCaster, which has really powered this live Internet television revolution," Nelson said. "But what's neat for us is that not only do we sell this gear, we also use it. We do so many live webinar demos, because how much would it cost for me to fly and meet with 50 different clients all over the country? A lot of money would be spent on that travel. So if I can take a TriCaster and a couple of cameras and do a demo for 300 or 400 people watching online, that's a huge cost reduction."

### Expanding the Trade Show Audience

In addition to direct selling, you also have trade shows. How much money do companies spend creating a trade show experience? Millions and millions of dollars. And how many people see that booth? If you are a trade show exhibitor, you want to put as many people in those trade show seats as you can.

Enter live streaming video. Live streaming trade shows have allowed people take their show experience to a worldwide audience.

"When we stream our booth presentations at NewTek, we may have 100 people sitting in our booth watching a demo, and another 400 or 500 people online watching that same demo," Nelson said. "And a lot of times at these trade shows, the person you may want to reach isn't at the trade show. It's their boss back at the office. A quick call back to the office to say, 'Hey they're streaming this great presentation, watch this,' and you've reached the person you want to sell to."

So live streaming video has allowed individuals, small businesses, and massive corporations to expand the reach of anything they do. It's allowed them to take an idea or presentation and share it with the world.

You're not geographically limited anymore, or limited by the time and space it takes to jump on a plane and fly to meet someone. You can reach many people, at many locations, all at the same time.

> **Y**ou're not geographically limited anymore, or limited by the time and space it takes to jump on a plane and fly to meet someone. You can reach many people, at many locations, all at the same time.

## Lasting Value Creates Durability

The terms durability and accumulation pop up often in this industry and they are both often associated (in a very positive light) with digital video. Picture this: If you were to send out a press release for your trade show, it would probably show up in a few locations online. But if you set up the video and send it online, it creates a durable value. Because it's educational, it begins to rank higher and higher in the search engines, increasing its durability online. It's there forever. In fact, it's been found that you're 53 percent more likely to rank at the top of search results with a video when compared with using text. So you have the durability of that trade show message, and you have the predominance on search engine traffic, which accumulates more and more sharing among social media sites.

## Taking It Live: Going Live Gets People to Plan to View

As important as on demand video is, real opportunity lies in live events and there are several reasons for this. Promoting an upcoming live event makes people make an appointment to be there, which increases viewership and viewer engagement. And, more people tune in for live simply because it's live and you never know what might happen.

"One of the reasons people like live is because of the unknown," Nelson said. "Are they going to make mistakes? Are they going to slip something? Are they going to show something they weren't supposed to show?"

In some cases, like trade shows, you can enjoy the best of both worlds, scheduling live coverage that will leave you with on demand content after the fact. And to enhance that content, technology like NewTek's allows viewers to include live chat options that can be enjoyed by watchers and used in presentations and real-time discussions.

In another example from the Department of Homeland Security Science & Technology Directorate, Nelson explained how the agency included a live chat section on their live video feed. People are now able to chat online live about what they see happening on the stage. This live chat option incorporates one of the benefits of going to a trade show—the dialogue, meeting, and interacting with people, discussing technology, and asking questions.

As a company, if you're doing a presentation and have people asking questions online and in person, those questions or observations can be worked into the live event. You can have questions coming in from the Internet and be tweaking your live presentation based on the reaction online.

Another benefit of a live event is that you can be streaming live and gathering the content. Then at the end of the event you now have master video of the show that's been edited live. So now, instead of having to take all your cameras back to the edit room, digitize your tapes, or ingest your footage, at the live show you pretty much just upload and go. Or you can cut down highlights or cut certain pieces you want to make available, then use those on YouTube to drive more traffic to your web page.

"There are so many benefits to that live video component," Nelson said. "So, many times people talk about on-demand content because that's what is easy in their minds. But live is almost easier because once the show's over, it's done. You don't spend three days editing your show."

### Going Live to Drive

"Live to drive" is a phrase coined by NewTek," Nelson said. "If you have a live event and you want to record it, you can do so because the TriCaster actually archives the video right to the hard disk as you film live. So now that show can be used in so many different ways. It creates this dynamic content that increases your search engine rankings and retains the viewers and all those other benefits. And it just makes it easier to create."

## From Airwaves to the Screen: Radio Goes Digital

Radio—an industry that's seen multiple industry overhauls—has been a huge growth market for live streaming.

"Radio is an interesting industry because they survived the invention of television," Nelson said. "Their world was turned upside down and they survived. They went from doing soap operas and drama to music and other formats. They reinvented themselves and what we've seen here and in the Internet revolution is that they're one of the leaders in moving to that content delivery."

Radio talk show hosts are adding value to their shows by doing live streaming video online, so the content is now accessible. In the past, when a listener arrived at the office in the morning, the radio went off and the connection was lost. Now, that same listener can launch the video player at his or her desk and catch the rest of his or her favorite talk show host as they live stream to the Web.

Radio stations no longer lose those listeners. They now watch and listen at work. The radio stations are able to utilize the video as a new revenue source because they're selling paid subscriptions.

## Live Streaming Expands Brand Potential: MTV and *The Hills*

Brands are always looking for ways to reach a larger audience. NewTek has seen some interesting new uses for its technology with some of its larger clients.

"One that I've worked with a lot is MTV. They were one of the very early adopters of live streaming and one of the first projects they did was *The Hills After Show* party," Nelson said. "Because *The Hills* was one of the top shows on MTV, they were looking at ways to bring the viewers to the website after the show. One of the executives at MTV had the idea to do a live webcast and call it an after show party. So at the last commercial break, watchers were told to log onto *The Hills* website at mtv.com. They had a host and three girls sitting on the couch and basically for 15 minutes they discussed the show, and then one of the cast members took questions from people who sent messages via social media. They had millions of viewers log in for this webcast."

Catering to a different crowd, Nelson also told the story of how the Miss Universe Pageant decided to live stream the "Crowning Moment" for viewers, imagining it could be something fun and interesting.

"It's one of the most-watched television events . . . up there with Super Bowl and World Cup because you have so much interest from all the countries with contestants," Nelson said of the pageant. "They said, 'Let's show the world what it's like during the first 30 minutes of being crowned Miss Universe.' So Miss Universe is crowned, they announce it's Miss Mexico, she takes the walk down the runway, waves, cries, the girls crowd in to congratulate her, and the credits role."

We're all curious what goes on backstage, behind the curtains. So that's what the webcast was all about.

"We set up multiple cameras, set up a TriCaster next to the stage, plugged it into the Internet and did a live half-hour webcast showing the frenzy of the press," Nelson said. "The photographers were going crazy. Donald Trump comes in to congratulate her, and all the celebrity judges come in, and they are getting their pictures made with Miss Universe, and she's just trying to take it all in. And hundreds of thousands of viewers log in to watch."

## Getting Behind the Velvet Ropes: People Like the Inside Scoop

The content created with this technology is continuously evolving. It's allowing shows and content to be created that you'd never roll in a live TV truck for, but that content can still have great value.

You aren't going to spend a hundred thousand dollars producing a *Crowning Moment* webcast or *The Hills After Party*. But with technology like the TriCaster, you can spend a couple of thousand dollars, use a couple of cameras and an Internet connection, and you have live television content for the web, for TV, for on-demand, for whatever you want to use it for, all at a fraction of the cost of what you would spend with traditional television equipment.

In another example, MTV had hundreds of thousands of viewers tune into a live red-carpet and backstage webcast of the MTV video music awards.

"What I like to say is people like to get behind the velvet rope," Nelson said. "They can't get enough of that VIP access to whatever they're interested in, be it the Super Bowl or the NBA Development League, the Miss Universe beauty pageant, or the MTV music video awards. If you're a fan, there's this insatiable demand for access, for information. And that's what we're allowing—for an affordable price that information can be created, distributed, and developed into a program that has value."

## The End of the Dorm Room Video: Video Makers Gain Credibility with the Advent of TV-Quality Production

A company that has spent millions developing a brand needs to appear credible. *Any* company that wants to be successful must appear credible to its customers.

"We live in a day of television experts," Nelson said. "My 9-year-old daughter and 12-year-old son know what television looks like. It's critical that when someone's doing online video, it must look like broadcast television."

Those companies that have spent money and time working to ensure their brand is presented in the right way need to be sure that same care goes into their video production as well. A common mistake among companies is developing video content that looks like a dorm room video.

"So many times I've seen companies say, 'Oh, we wanted it to look like the web,'" Nelson said. "It's crazy to think they want it to look worse than television. The idea is that the Internet television revolution has left us with this ability to make videos that look like television. There has to be that television production value so you have that credibility for the message you're going to distribute on the web."

### Adding Polish

The TriCaster technology gives users the ability to add graphics, pre-roll video, an introduction, and all the other good stuff found on television networks that give the look of polish. With a few cameras, now anyone can achieve the same look for their Web show, which gives brands that needed credibility.

The technology also allows the user to film in a virtual set—rather than a television studio's million-dollar set that may have cost $100,000. So again, this technology—like that of many others now found on the social web—has democratized content creation, distribution, and availability.

This technology—like that of many others now found on the social web—has democratized content creation, distribution, and availability.

"What that means is with a simple green screen—whether it's a cloth you buy at Wal-Mart or a pan of paint you get from Home Depot—you can sit in front of a green wall and we make it look like you're on a million-dollar sound stage," Nelson said. "And what that does is add credibility to your message because you aren't distracting the viewer with low production value; you're giving them what they expect to see from a professional television production."

If you're doing a brochure, you're not going to print it out in black and white. You're going to do a nice quality piece you can distribute that adds credibility to your message and brand. The same goes for live online video on demand.

"I think the days of this 'should look like the web' are gone," Nelson said. "Unless it's a viral video and you want it to look like a 12-year-old shot it on a camcorder, then make it look like TV. That's the important differentiation between professional value and dorm room antics."

### Setting the Stage for Delivery

The average person may not realize how simple it is to create a set with a green screen. A swath of fabric and a few props and you can have a professional stage that appears to be straight off the television screen.

This is where technology is going. Not only will anyone be able to create great content, even in niche areas, but that content can now easily be delivered anywhere. Earlier we talked about the Internet television revolution and how there used to be a gatekeeper. With the proliferation of broadband in the home and the availability of free or low-cost live streaming distribution sites like Livestream.com or Ustream.tv or the high-end levels like Akamai, you can buy bandwidth or use a free service, and with the click of a single button you can be live on the web, and once it's created you can be on demand as well.

> **N**ot only will anyone be able to create great content, even in niche areas, but that content can now easily be delivered anywhere.

### Shrinking Needs

If you've been to a sporting event and seen the TV trucks, you know how much equipment goes into those live television broadcasts. Now you can create a broadcast that looks similar using a box that's table-top sized. Technology like the TriCaster can roll in graphics, video clips with commercials, sponsors or pre-edited news segments.

"The TriCaster allows you to take all of that and bring it together in a single show and distribute to three outlets—live to digital signage (closed circuit TV in a company, or LED video screens or Jumbotron)," Nelson said. "Next, you could go live to broadcast television or there's the live streaming video option. These three options are why it's called TriCaster; you can reach your audience three ways at once. A fourth option would be live to drive; it can then be made available on demand or on DVD or in clips to clients."

## Melding of the Screens: From Television to Cell Phones, It's All about the Content

Everyone currently in the digital space is trying to understand the five-year projectory for this technology and its evolving usage. It's often called the melding of the screens, meaning the screen of the TV in your living room, the screens on your laptop, in your iPad, your cell phone, and any other Internet-connected technology are melding.

In fact, we might take a note from the newest generation, which views much of the current technology in a different light from that of their parents or grandparents.

"My 12-year-old son does not see a TV, computer screen, and mobile device," Nelson said. "He sees a large screen, medium, or small screen. This is normal to his generation; it isn't a new development. They don't differentiate between a television show and a YouTube video. They'll just watch it wherever it's convenient. Sometimes my son will watch a video on my iPhone, sometimes the iPad, and sometimes on the laptop."

There's an increasingly blurred line between TV, radio, and video. More and more, it's really about content. It's important that a producer makes the content available and makes it accessible.

The recent decline in cable subscriptions? It's not necessarily due to people not watching cable; they're finding a new way to watch and doing it where it's convenient. Broadcasters and cable networks are looking for ways to keep those viewers in their world. Newspapers are doing the same thing.

"*USA Today* bought a TriCaster and brought it to the Olympics," Nelson said. "They did *USA Today at the Olympics* live. They had a picture of Vancouver on the set. It was great. They shot live in front of a virtual set. It looked like they were in a giant studio."

The *New York Times* has also purchased a TriCaster and they are streaming daily video coverage of the news.

"Some newspapers are doing fantasy sports shows," Nelson said. "They're looking for ways to deliver more content online. Good content gets created and finds its audience."

## The Next Five Years

We started off this discussion with a quote from the founder of NewTek, made back in the mid-1980s: "In the next 20 years your favorite TV show will be created by you or someone you know." That's where we're going and we're nearly there.

With the availability and accessibility of social media, not only are content creators making great shows, they're finding an audience, and they're building relationships with their viewers. It's not a one-way street anymore, it's two-way communication, a concept I mention repeatedly in this book—*full-duplex dialogue*.

"Say you're a fan of Patrick Norton and the show he does for Revision3," Nelson said. "With online media and social media and the accessibility people have now through technology like Twitter, you can now follow Patrick Norton, you can know Leo Laporte, or others and become part of an exciting two-way dialogue."

And that's where it gets really exciting. Not only is the technology available, but now you have this relationship between the show producer and viewer. That's where the excitement happens, in the two-way full-duplex dialogue. It's not a boob-tube any longer. It's real-time dialogue that's beneficial to both parties.

### Finding Your Niche

When radio and television personality Adam Carolla took over the Howard Stern show, he had a huge fan base. When that show ended he created the Adam Corolla podcast (see Figure 4.1).

"No longer was he limited by the fans that could get through his radio signal," Nelson said. "He could reach his fans all over the world through his podcast. Now they're adding the video component so

Figure 4.1    TriCaster Powers a Live Webcast of the Adam Carolla Podcast

when he has cool, crazy guests you can see it. He's basically creating his own network."

This is happening all over. And it's not just celebrities.

"There's a guy in L.A. named Mike Rotman, he was a writer on South Park and politically incorrect for Bill Maher, he wrote for Greg Kinnear and Leno. He's a comedy guy," Nelson said. "He got a TriCaster, enclosed his garage, purchased some cameras, and created a network called *The Streaming Garage*. He has multiple shows, including a movie review show called *Stupid For Movies*. Every week 50,000 viewers watch. He has a show each week with Tears for Fears' Kurt Smith called *Stripped Down Live* with emerging artists; they play some music and talk about it. He has a niche show called *Stupid for Dexter* and he has two girls that come on the show and talk about *Dexter*. And they're building an audience. That's when you see long-tail TV really happening and it's not only television creating it. Rotman is a television writer who wanted to create his own network."

Who's to say you can't too?

## Chapter Takeaways

- Before the desktop video revolution in 1990, power was in the hands of a select few executives at television networks. Now, anyone can create TV-quality video and deliver it to its intended audience.
- We're in the early phases of the Internet television revolution. With the proliferation of broadband and the availability of free, or practically free, live streaming, there is no gatekeeper, so not only can anyone produce quality video; it can be viewed by anyone.
- Many companies have added an online component to live events such as tradeshows to ensure that their information is distributed to a wider audience. If a first responder can't attend, that person can now attend online.
- You can give the buyer a lot more information through a simple video than through pages and pages of written word. That's why both creators and consumers are going to video.
- There's a lot of value in live events because not only will people tune in thanks to an unknown factor—will there be any surprises? Something we weren't supposed to see?—it also forces them to make an appointment to tune in and view.
- Markets like radio that were turned upside down by the video revolution are embracing it and capturing listeners—who become viewers—with live videocasts or podcasts that continue even after the listener arrives at work.
- Niche has found its niche. The digital television revolution made it possible for anyone to use video to reach an audience.

*The Digital Innovation Playbook* is a living book. We are constantly updating the book online so you can watch uploaded videos, read the latest best practice on digital media, and even participate in free ongoing webinars.

To access this chapter's updated web page, please go to www.digitalinnovationplaybook.com/Chapter4.html or scan the QR code with your mobile device.

# 5

# Flying High

## AN OPEN CULTURE KEEPS AN AIRLINE COMPANY ON TOP OF THE COMPETITION

When Southwest Airlines made its first venture into the digital world, it utilized video—a medium discussed in the last chapter that has revolutionized the social web. Video was a great jumping off point for the company, but Southwest Airlines' success is best noted when looking at the broader picture—a culture that fits the evolution of digital and new media innovation like a glove.

As I've mentioned throughout this book, the key to successful digital and new media strategies is an organizational culture that fosters openness and customer connectivity. Many organizations are afraid of the idea of allowing their customers to connect to the employees at various levels within the organization. Their fear is primarily based on the fact that many organizations don't have happy employees that, frankly, don't do a good job of delivering good customer experiences.

The foundation, then, for a great new media strategy is a functional organization, that is, an organization that communicates freely, that has torn down the organization silos, and has created an company comprised of employees that have a central focus on delivering customer value. I know that in large organizations with a lot of bureaucracy and massive numbers of employees, such a culture can seem almost impossible. Yet it does happen.

Southwest Airlines is one of the largest airlines in the world. They operate in one of the world's most problematic and stressful environments. Yet somehow they have prevailed in exceptional customer experience on- and off-line. They are truly pioneers of digital media, and their strategy is as simple as extending their long-time positive culture onto the digital highways. They have transposed their open, customer-centered values onto digital media with tremendous success. Recently, I had the tremendous honor of interviewing Christi McNeill. In this interview, she shared with me the secrets to Southwest's exceptional success with their digital new media strategies.

## First Taste of Social Media: Video Series Ends, New Communications Begin

Southwest Airlines' first venture into the social media world was with an online video series called *Airline*, which ended in 2005. The video was treated much the same as a blog, telling stories of daily life at the airlines in short, friendly bits. The show was a success, but after it reached a natural conclusion, the airline giant had to figure out what to do next.

As with many other Innovation Superstars spotlighted in this book, a blog was one of the airline's first ventures into the social web world. For Southwest Airlines, with its quirky, friendly style, a blog was destined to be a good fit because it gave the company a platform to share that personality with a larger audience in a more personable way, and it opened the doors to two-way dialogue in a way the video series couldn't.

"So we developed our corporate blog, which is *Nuts About Southwest*," McNeill said. "The blog was built in 2006 and it was initially managed by our team. It was one of the first corporate blogs—definitely the first airline blog."

At that time there weren't many corporate blogs. You'll find when reading further that many of the Innovation Superstars mentioned were also forging new social trails with the first corporate blogs.

In Southwest Airlines' case, the company had about 30 contributors who updated the blog on a daily basis. It was open for comments, which gave the company the means to continue the conversations begun with the video series.

"We posted stories about new boarding processes we were testing, about our peanuts, about what it's like for mechanics who work on an aircraft, and more," McNeill said. "We were able to showcase all those kinds of fun stories about working for an airline on the blog."

Because the idea of open, genuine communications—even allowing complaints and mistakes to be viewed by the public—is such a foreign concept to many large, well established corporations, many companies both then and now make only a token effort at social communications. They carefully craft blogs or videos in much the same fashion as those of traditional media. They don't allow comments, or they edit them to such a strict degree as to prevent anything negative from appearing. As you've already begun to see in the previous chapters, this attitude will no longer cut it in a digital world. And this is not the route innovation superstar Southwest Airlines went.

As the blog gathered a larger following, Southwest made the natural progression to other social channels as well.

"During the 2006 to 2007 timeframe we started communicating on Facebook, Twitter, and YouTube," McNeill said. "Those channels have grown immensely now, so company-wide we now have three employees focused solely on our social media channels, but our entire communications and marketing teams are responsible for feeding content through all our different channels."

While writing this book, Southwest Airlines was a frequent flyer in the media for wear and tear found the same in some of its older equipment. The airlines embarked on an investigation with the National Transportation Safety Board to be sure all flights were safe for its employees and customers.

While this investigation was completed, the airplanes that could have similar fatigue wear were grounded and Southwest set out to answer any questions or concerns on the company blog and through Twitter.

What I found impressive about these interactions was just that, the high level of *interaction*. This wasn't a one-way e-mail blast with a corporate spiel. This was *people* talking to other *people* about any issues or worries, with real answers that provided a level of assurance that allowed customers to stick with a favorite airline even through a tough time.

## Content Controls: Editor Approves Comments with Moderation

Despite the need for open, honest communication, moderating social communication is still a necessity. A moderator may remove profanity, threats, and other unproductive content, as well as organizing content in the most fitting fashion to make clear timelines, or making sure that pertinent information is grouped in the best fashion.

"We have an employee that acts as our blog editor," McNeill said. "He controls the content, timing, and management of the blog. We also use a department-wide editorial calendar. If any of our contributors have a story they would like to post to the blog, they have a very small editorial process they must go through to get their content online."

So yes, the content is organized, but the communication is open and honest.

## An Open Culture: How Tough Is It Showing the Good, the Bad, and the Ugly?

Most people don't know how airlines work. We know what it's like to book a ticket, board a plane, be a passenger. But we don't know what goes on behind the scenes—what it takes to schedule flight patterns, securely load and unload luggage, manage the massive pool of multi-leveled employees, and the myriad of other things that take place on a daily basis at Southwest Airlines.

"Many folks don't really understand how an airline operates unless they've worked in the industry," McNeill said. "The videos we create, and our social media interaction, have helped dispel many myths about airlines. These channels show the kind of experiences our employees have on a daily basis."

Employees are the face of a company. Because they're on the frontlines every day, they usually know the most about the customers they serve—a situation many companies need to rectify. I have a concept I call the *Innovation Pyramid* or the *Inverted Pyramid*, which shows why the current, common set-up with employees most often touching customers and higher-level executives having next to no contact, is the opposite of how corporations should be organized.

With the inverted pyramid—or "inverted pyramid syndrome"— companies have their executives at the highest levels—the top of the pyramid—making most decisions about new product and service offerings, yet they have the least amount of contact with actual customers. Conversely, front-end people—the customer service representatives, service technicians that have high levels of customer connectivity—usually have virtually no voice in the products and service offerings available to the valued customers. So the first thing that has to happen is that people really involved in the decision making need to get out to see where the opportunities are—take an innovation safari, another concept I talk about in more detail in Chapter 10, RealOpen Innovation.

Employees on the front lines are going to be faced with a variety of unique situations, some a bit stickier than others. Read further to see how Southwest Airlines uses the ultimate combination of personality, training, and experience to prepare its employees for any situation.

"They receive a ton of training for dealing with those situations, but each situation is very unique," McNeill said of Southwest Airlines' employees. "On our Facebook or Twitter channels we may see somebody wanting to propose to a girlfriend on a flight or someone wondering why their flight is late. This gives us a platform to easily address those questions."

## Direct Line to Customers

Before social networking, companies had to rely on the media to get messages out to customers. The power no longer lies within traditional media now that companies can create their own personalized channels for video, photos, or getting statements out—prepared by the company itself with all facts listed correctly.

> Before social networking, companies had to rely on the media to get messages out to customers. The power no longer lies within traditional media now that companies can create their own personalized channels for video, photos, or getting statements out—prepared by the company itself with all facts listed correctly.

"That has been a huge benefit to us in some of the major situations we've been involved in," McNeill said. "To be able to provide our statement for our customer and employees is very powerful. The blog has also created a great focus group for us. We can post a question to any of our online audiences—blog, Twitter, or Facebook—and get feedback instantly."

Southwest Airlines found this to be true when the company decided in 2007 to test the idea of assigning seats. Southwest's unassigned seating policy was an established fact, something the company would soon find was well liked by the long-time customers. To experiment with the idea of instead assigning seats, the CEO wrote a blog explaining that the company would be testing assigned seating in certain markets, but that it was only a test.

"We had an overwhelming number of commenters go to the blog and say, 'Leave it the way it is!' or 'We love Southwest because you don't assign seats' or 'If it ain't broke don't fix it,' " McNeill said. "It was really overwhelming to us, the amount of positive responses we got for our nonassigned seats."

Southwest Airlines has a variety of followers, but the most loyal of them are the aviation enthusiasts.

"These are people who want the deeper story or the behind-the-scenes look," McNeill said. "These are the people who have worked for an airline or worked for an airport and just have a huge passion for aviation. So we affectionately call them the 'airline geeks' or the 'aviation geeks.' They're looking for the deeper story and our blog allows us to provide that for them."

## Making Friends on Facebook

Southwest Airlines joined Facebook in 2007 and it's been a channel that has grown and changed quite a bit over the years. The company now has more than one million fans.

"The dialogue or conversations that take place on that channel are pretty unique," McNeill said. "It's a mix of people sharing their great experiences, even down to mentioning their flight attendant's name, employee number, and photo, and posting on the Facebook page to make sure that flight attendant is recognized. Some really touching stories have been shared, as well as some not-so-great situations that we've been able to take a deeper look at and assure the situation has been addressed. It's great place for community and dialogue."

## Responses for All: Yes, You'll Get Some Crazies, But It's Important to Respond to Good and Bad

In any public avenue of conversation you're going to get some crazies. These are the people who get their kicks out of harassing people, writing inflammatory statements, and generally being obnoxious. This isn't to say there aren't valid complaints that a company should address immediately. But sometimes there's no validity to the complaint and it's a waste of company time and resources.

"We get our fair share of those," McNeill said. "We read every single comment that comes into our Facebook page, blog, or Twitter account. We do get people who fly by and leave nasty comments on our Facebook page or maybe aren't fans of ours and let us know that. You just have to understand that when we carry as many people as we do, you're going to have those people that didn't have a great experience and that's another reason why we have the Facebook page. We need to see if there's something we can do to resolve it."

It's equally important to respond to both the negative and the positive. While it may be impossible to respond to every single commenter, in a good community the conversations can take place among readers as well.

"The people who love us and share photos or blog posts—we want to acknowledge them and reach out to them and say thank you for sharing your photos and thank you for flying us today," McNeill said. "You don't want to just send out a ton of Twitter messages that say 'Thank you for flying us' and 'Thanks for your time.' You want every engagement to be authentic and unique. So that's the tricky part."

Southwest founder Herb Kelleher is famous for saying, and I'm paraphrasing here, "Here's the employee manual, feel free to break any rules in there as long as it's for the customer." It's so important in the digital media world to maintain a culture of openness, but how do you manage that openness with the customer community and, at the same time, have reasonable policies that protect the company?

This is where Southwest Airlines shines. The airline gives its employees all the tools necessary to project a united front to the customer community.

"Whether they're sitting behind a computer like me, Tweeting, or they're helping a customer book a ticket, or they are a flight attendant addressing a cabin full of people, we expect all our people to communicate the Southwest way," McNeill said. "And that means you have a fun-loving attitude, warrior spirit, and a servant's heart."

Addressing the needs of each and every customer in the same fashion is something employees are taught from day one. And the company is very peculiar about the people hired to fill those shoes.

"We get a ton of resumes every year and only hire a small percentage of people because we're looking for specific folks that fit that bill, that we can trust to communicate on behalf of our brand all the time," McNeill said.

## Putting in the Time: Listening and Understanding the Feedback

One of the things a lot of our pioneers in new media and digital media have learned is that there's another level of analysis that you can't automate. Doing this right requires some heavy lifting. You have to put in the necessary time required to really get your head into that online community to listen to the dialogue as a way of driving new product and service innovation.

> You have to put in the necessary time required to really get your head into that online community to listen to the dialogue as a way of driving new product and service innovation.

When you're in there listening, you can not only pick up new product ideas, you can also find new ways to innovate your service.

"A good example that comes to mind is this: We started selling ad space on our boarding passes a while back," McNeill said. "So when our customers would print out their boarding pass it would have ads for some of our partners. When that program first launched, it was a revenue generator for us, but on the customer side of things, somehow those boarding passes were set to print color all the time."

Southwest began receiving complaints that the boarding passes were wasting expensive color ink. There wasn't any way for people to default to black and white.

"We were able to make a quick change on the technology side of things so it would automatically default to black and white and the problem was quickly solved," McNeill said. "That was a big win for us and a great example of being able to listen to our customers and make changes effectively."

Listening in on big news announcements also gives companies like Southwest Airlines the ability to see what questions arise and then to pass that knowledge on to the front line employees as well.

"We see what kind of themes are showing up in those communications so we can pass those on to the frontline employees," McNeill said. "We address those questions with our employees so if they get asked those questions, they have the answers."

## Keeping Up with the Changes; Southwest Finds a Natural Fit with Already-Open Culture of Communication

The changes in communication for organizations have been rapid and great over a short period of time—as talked about in Chapter 1, Mastering Digital Innovation. Many companies seem to be floundering, but Southwest Airlines doesn't seem to miss a beat.

The reason for this is culture. The employees are carefully chosen and extensive training gives each and every person—from top to bottom—the right attitude for the ultimate customer experience.

"I think for Southwest it's more of a natural fit than maybe for some other companies," McNeill said. "We've always been a really offbeat, chatty, quirky company. This style of communication really works for us and works in our favor because this is how we communicate with our customers and how we've communicated with them for 40 years now."

But the means with which companies communicate that style and personality is evolving rapidly, as McNeill has seen in her four years with the company.

"Even in my time, it's changed really drastically since the day I started," she said. "The amount of time we spend creating content to share online and in the traditional media is overwhelming."

## Lessons from Southwest

### First, Be Authentic

People know when they're being manipulated. In the social channels on platforms such as Facebook, Twitter, and others, the conversations must be genuine.

"Be authentic," McNeill said. "Make sure that you know your company's core values and be sure you're communicating those. I think that even we get stuck in the trap sometimes of trying to craft a message that appears how we want it to appear, but I think in time we always stick to the core value of being ourselves and being authentic and speaking in that Southwest voice."

### Next, Find Passion

Passion makes for genuine communication. It also drives innovation. Be sure to find people within your organization that are really passionate about communicating to man your communication center. And be sure these people are passionate about the brand.

"At Southwest we tried to find people for our social media group that really reflect who the brand is," McNeill said. "These people will go to bat for the brand even if it's on the weekend or holiday."

When you get a loyal following online, even those who aren't on the company's payroll will go to bat for the brand on the weekends and holidays.

"A group like that is online all the time watching what's being said," McNeill said. "If they find anything questionable, they know who their contacts are and they'll get in touch. Finding those excited employees and really embracing them is crucial."

### Step Up the Speed

Also very important: Be responsive and be quick. Speed, really more than anything in the social media world, is one of the most important things. The more time you spend thinking about how to word that message, or what word goes where, the more that negative message spins out of control. You lose critical time in responding. In these audiences it's speed—not punctuation—that matters.

> **S**peed, really more than anything in the social media world, is one of the most important things.

## Video at Southwest: Vital Communication with Employees and Customers

As we've heard, Southwest Airlines has been on YouTube since 2007 and has been using video for anything from news announcements to responding to media to really capturing what it is the employees do on a daily basis. The company has had a flexible video strategy and it's worked really well. Since 2007, the company's digital strategies have become more sophisticated. There is now a live studio at the

Southwest headquarters that allows for a quick turnaround when announcements are needed. The studio is also used for a weekly news series that goes out to employees and highlights new things that have been going on throughout the week.

"Using video to communicate with our employees has been a huge success because we use different anchors each week and they like to see themselves on the computer screen," McNeill said. "The employees then share the video and it creates an enormous amount of employee engagement."

## The Pits: What to Avoid in the Social Media World

A common mistake companies make is a lack of planning for their social communications. It's important to tackle one platform at a time and be sure you're giving the best possible value before moving on to the next. In Southwest Airlines' case, the company began with video, then moved onto the blog, then began moving into Facebook, Twitter, and other social platforms. It was a natural progression made at a pace that allowed the company to provide real net value.

"I see companies who spread themselves too thin, across Facebook, YouTube, Flickr, and Twitter and they end up with really weak content," McNeill said. "Make sure you focus your attention on the channels you think you can really build and maintain."

It's also important to review social actions to be sure each scenario has been handled well. Learn from successes and mistakes to continue growing social communications.

Learn from successes and mistakes to continue growing social communications.

"Almost everything we come out of, whether it's an event or a new city opening or something in the media, our team has a debrief where we ask if we tackled it the right way, if our messaging was correct, and if there was something we could have done better," McNeill said. "Our team has the mentality that nothing is done perfectly and everything can always be done better. It's a huge learning process and the cool thing about social media is that it is such an early practice.

We're writing the rules as we go. Anyone who says they've got this new media down pat, that they're an expert or guru—they're still learning, just like the rest of us."

### People Make Up the Company

Because the people within a company make or break that company, it's so incredibly important to not only provide those employees with the tools for success but to appreciate what they do.

"In the early days of Southwest, it was determined that the employees come first," McNeill said. "If you have happy employees, you have happy customers. If you have happy customers, you have happy shareholders. I think that's the mentality we have every day. Working at Southwest is like working with my family every day."

The environment is warm, friendly, and fun. At Southwest, the HR department is called the People Department. There's a reason for that: It's all about the people.

"It sounds cheesy but it's the truth," McNeill said. "Southwest Airlines is the nation's largest carrier in terms of originating domestic passengers boarded, but we haven't lost that core value of how to treat people and following the Golden Rule."

## The Next Five Years: Keep Creating Content and Finding the Best Channels

Social media is still an evolving art. There are new channels popping up all the time.

"At Southwest we kind of look at all the new channels that come about and we study them in order to create our own voices within these channels," McNeill said. "By that I mean, we are the content creators and we are the storytellers. So whatever channel that's on, I think our consumers want to hear directly from us. And that's the shift we're seeing in communications and I think we'll see over the next five years that will become even more intense. They'll want information all the time."

### Flexibility Is the Key

"I think we have done a pretty great job of being very flexible and responding to the changes within our organization and within the online audiences as well," McNeill said. "I hear a lot of companies talk about organizational charts and structure, and where does social media live, but I think here at Southwest, we've really tried to evolve our team to working outside of our personal silos and working with other departments on projects."

And that's what social media communications is all about: working together within the company and outside it to evolve with the changing media landscape.

Social media communications is about working together within the company and outside it to evolve with the changing media landscape.

### Chapter Takeaways

- The foundation, then, for a great new media strategy is a functional organization, that is, an organization that communicates freely, that has torn down the organization silos, and has created a company comprised of employees that have a central focus on delivering customer value.
- Despite the need for open, honest communication, moderating social communication is still a necessity. A moderator may remove profanity, threats, and other unproductive content, as well as organizing content in the most fitting fashion to make clear timelines, or making sure that pertinent information is grouped in the best fashion.
- It's equally important to respond to both the negative and the positive commenters. While it may be impossible to respond to every single commenter, in a good community the conversations can take place among readers as well.
- Listening in on big news announcements gives the ability to see what questions arise and then that knowledge can be passed on to the front line employees as well.
- Passion makes for genuine communications. It also drives innovation. Be sure to find people within your organization that are really passionate about communicating.

*The Digital Innovation Playbook* is a living book. We are constantly updating the book online so you can watch uploaded videos, read the latest best practice on digital media, and even participate in free ongoing webinars.

To access this chapter's updated web page, please go to www.digitalinnovationplaybook.com/Chapter5.html or scan the QR code with your mobile device.

# Picture Perfect Social Media

## HOW KODAK GOT SOCIAL MEDIA RIGHT

In researching *The Digital Innovation Playbook* I looked at literally hundreds of companies in an attempt to find Innovation Superstars. As you can already see so far, I found some amazing companies doing incredible things in the digital and new media landscape. Southwest Airlines was a great example of a company with a healthy culture that has flowed seamlessly into the social web scene.

Now we're going to look at Kodak, which is a perfect Innovation Superstar example. In fact, I will even go on record by saying that:

*I believe that Kodak is one of the most innovative companies in the world.*

I would like to substantiate that comment by once again stating my definition of innovation: *Innovation is the process of delivering exceptional customer value through active listening.* When I think of Kodak, those three important ingredients in that definition mentioned earlier come to mind: *exceptional, value,* and *listening.* In this chapter you'll learn how one of the United States' best companies is building its business and brand by connecting to its customer communities.

Imagine your business is your automobile. You're the driver, which means you are in charge of adjusting your mirrors so you have the view you want; you set the speed—slowing or speeding up when necessary; you set air conditioning comfort levels, and you set the tone with your choice of rock, country, classics, or talk radio.

Then, one day, a bunch of unruly passengers start lowering the rear windows when you already had the air set at a comfortable 68 degrees. They launch their iPod playlists on your stereo, and then try to yank the wheel for an off-road experience you aren't even remotely prepared for.

Now imagine this—the best thing for your traveling experience is not only to let those backseat drivers have some say in your trip; it's to make them use their own cars.

Most companies—especially the older, more firmly entrenched ones—are closed organizations. Once upon a time, that was probably okay. But today, there's no locking out those upstart drivers, not without causing a pileup of epic proportions.

In some of the other chapters in this book, and within this one, we learn that whether you want it or not, people are going to talk about your business. The average Joe now has an open platform on the digital superhighway and everyone's connected to it. In the past, information was limited and businesses could control the message and persona they wished to project. Now there are drivers everywhere—too many cooks in the kitchen, or whatever metaphor you may wish to use.

In order to protect your brand, provide your current and potential customers the greatest value and continue learning and growing, you need those other drivers. You can no longer do it alone.

This doesn't mean you completely let go of the wheel. No, you find the best and the brightest who fit your company well—see the fantastic stories in the Southwest Airlines chapter. You train, train, train these family members, as Southwest puts it. And you give them the power to be the many faces of your company.

In this chapter we'll talk with Thomas Hoehn, director of Interactive Marketing and Convergence Media at Kodak. Kodak found the digital evolution a natural one and quickly emerged as an Innovation Superstar. Not only did the technology within the company evolve and grow with the times, but the company's culture of openness and social awareness did as well.

Over the last decade there has been an aggressive movement toward so-called open innovation and open cultures. A great number of books have been written on the topic of understanding how to create an open culture, but it's not an easy transition.

Similar to social interplay, an open culture can't be faked and it can't be automated. Being open means really connecting to your community through full-duplex dialogue and through various fibers of connectivity, such as social media and other digital forums.

A lot of companies are struggling with this concept of openness. These companies have competitors to worry about. In the case of the U.S. Army, the Innovation Superstar showcased in Chapter 7, competitors are actual life-and-death enemies. Other organizations have trade secrets and they want to protect the trajectory of their innovations and developments. These privacy concepts are understandable, but in this fast-paced digital world where we are now living, companies *must* tear down not only the walls protecting them from their customer communities but also their internal silos. Despite the fact that we've been talking about this concept since the 1980s, it's now become absolutely critical that we knock down these silos in order to have a unified front within the digital community.

In this chapter we look at imaging giant Kodak and how this iconic company has transitioned into the twenty-first century with all of its digital possibilities. I spoke with Thomas Hoehn about many of the issues facing companies today.

## Finding a Digital Culture: Kodak Finds a Voice to Join the Conversations

People talk. And now there are so many platforms for those conversations. There's Twitter, Facebook, multitudes of blogs, community sites, chat rooms, Flickr, YouTube, and many others. People are sharing their experiences, asking questions, considering purchases, price comparing, and more.

The digital community is out there, and if companies don't become part of these conversations they will miss out on the opportunity to hear what's being said about their company, and they will have no say in the discussion.

> The digital community is out there and if companies don't become part of these conversations they will miss out on the opportunity to hear what's being said about their company, and they will have no say in the discussion.

"We quickly realized it was important for Kodak to be a digital player, which meant playing in the digital spaces," Hoehn said. "These conversations were happening about our brand, whether we wanted them to or not."

The days when Kodak, or any other company, controlled brand messages, shaping what people thought of products or service with carefully crafted messages, are over.

"That horse has left the barn," Hoehn agreed. "A little over four years ago we recognized this fact as part of our digital transformation."

While the social media world grew and evolved around Kodak, the company itself was innovating new digital technology. It soon became apparent that these processes and changes were enormous and there was a story that needed to be told.

"All of these things were changing simultaneously and the changes weren't getting communicated properly to the world," Hoehn said. "We realized we had a big stake in this and should probably tell this story ourselves. So we decided to start a blog."

Like many of the other Innovation Superstars highlighted in this book, a blog was the company's first foray into the social media world. It was a platform for storytelling that also allowed direct communication between readers and storytellers. Real-time dialogue was established, giving two-fold results: Kodak was able to share many of the new, exciting technologies and innovations going on as well as the stories and personalities of its employees. And the company was able to get direct feedback from customers and would-be customers who began following the blog.

During this time frame, mid-2006, corporate bloggers were still pretty few and far between.

"Only 3 percent of Fortune companies were doing blogs," Hoehn said. "So we decided that even though these types of blogs were new it was important to tell our story. We wanted to get out there and dispel some myths we were finding. For instance, many people thought we were late to digital, but we invented the digital camera in 1976 and have all the original patents. We're very proud of that."

## Behind the Brand: Kodak Connects by Sharing Stories and Correcting Misconceptions

Many long-standing companies like Kodak have a similar problem. Yes, people know their name, but they generally think of the companies in terms of outdated personas. These mammoth corporations become faceless entities and, over time, the world has begun to see the traditional branding techniques of these companies as so much white noise.

"People understood what Kodak was, but they didn't understand what Kodak is," Hoehn said. "They didn't understand a lot of the innovations Kodak has done in the digital space. Many of the sensors and the high-end digital cameras are made by Kodak. The way image sensors see light and color actually comes from Kodak technology from years past, and from current development. More than half our revenue comes from commercial businesses, a fact that isn't commonly known. It was about bringing our story directly to the people."

So Kodak began telling the story of its evolution to the company it is today. As these stories were told, windows began emerging; giving customers a glimpse into the inner workings of a corporation they had previously viewed in a very different light. But this change required a true commitment to openness, something that wasn't always easy.

"We wanted to bring those kinds of stories directly to the people, while sharing information on Kodak innovations. We needed to become open in order to make people understand what we do," Hoehn said. "But this openness didn't sit easily with a lot of people."

When Hoehn originally pitched the blog idea, he did it in the form of a carefully crafted white paper on blogs. The concept was still new, so he described what blogs were, explained the risks and rewards inherent in the project and gave examples of some other blogs from that time. When the white paper was completed he shared it with top levels of management. Not surprisingly, he was met with some wariness. Think in the context of the time. These ideas of openness and honesty were pretty foreign to companies that routinely held massive vetting processes for every little public communication.

The response to Hoehn's blog pitch was pretty supportive but there were valid concerns about trade secrets and other privacy issues. However, Hoehn was given the go-ahead to speak with the company lawyers about putting the idea into play.

That conversation started with a bit of a speed bump.

"At first, the conversation started with listing the things we wouldn't want to talk about . . . and there were a lot of them! Our legal counsel is world class and it was their job to point out these issues. We teamed together on this journey to explore this new era of openness and direct engagement with people to the benefit of our business."

The risk would be worth the reward. So Hoehn agreed to put the company bloggers through training prior to launch. He reviewed the training materials with the legal team to ensure the views he had negotiated were expressed and he included them in those initial sessions. In the end, Kodak trusted their people—these blog contributors—to do the right thing while being transparent and genuine.

These content creators were excited about their projects and ready to share with the world. A communications team is the face your social community is going to connect with, so it's an extremely important one. Another good example of this is Southwest Airlines (Chapter 5), which handpicks its team from top to bottom, assuring the friendly, fun persona of the airlines is there at every touch point.

Kodak carefully chose its team and gave them a short training course that included information about image rights and claims, and that satisfied the legal team. Now, after more than four years of blogging and use of other social channels, there have never been any legal issues.

Hoehn listened to the concerns about divulging trade secrets or floods of support calls that couldn't be addressed, but those issues never materialized. Support or technology questions that did appear were resolved, which was a good thing. It allowed the company to fine tune its processes and follow up on potential innovations in products and services.

## What Are the Opportunities, What's in It for Us, and How Do We Create Value for Them?

The first step in engaging in social media outreach is listening. When Kodak began its social initiative, the company first thought about what it wanted to get out of it. It was an educational process.

"We saw how Kodak was being portrayed on social media channels," Hoehn said.

In the beginning the Kodak brand mostly appeared on blog platforms. Then in 2009, the brand began popping up on Twitter. In

2010 there were more than 500 million impressions for the term "Kodak" on Twitter alone. When the team at Kodak saw the sheer number of mentions, light bulbs started going off: There is opportunity for us here! They realized it was time for a fully engaged digital initiative.

"We realized, 'Wow, we had better pay attention to this,'" Hoehn said. "But before jumping in with both feet, we asked ourselves, 'What is the smart way, the best way, to engage?'"

Despite the need for speed in the digital world, this pause for reflection was a smart one. The web is spattered with casualties, companies that haphazardly jumped in without first considering their customer base, what followers wanted to learn, and how they liked to be engaged. Remember, creating value and providing the ultimate customer experience are your goals—not creating a fancy new web program. The digital initiative is just another tool to further those goals.

> The web is spattered with casualties, companies that haphazardly jumped in without first considering their customer base, what followers wanted to learn, and how they liked to be engaged. Remember, creating value and providing the ultimate customer experience are your goals.

"It isn't about doing it because everyone else is," Hoehn said. "It's important for us to be there for our customers in a way that adds value to those conversations. It's about articulating the information in a prudent, meticulous fashion. It's not about doing it because others are; it's about helping our business grow. I see this as a competitive advantage."

As the positive response grew, Kodak's digital programs grew as well.

"We started with the one blog, and then as Facebook and other social channels gained in popularity, such as Twitter and YouTube we added those as well," Hoehn said.

## An Open, Active Ear: Kodak Staffs Chief Listener Position

Because many companies find they hit a speed bump in the legal department when it comes to opening up to the digital world, I have devoted a chapter to the issue. Chapter 12, Rules of Engagement, was put together by Harness, Dickey & Pierce, one of the top intellectual property (IP) firms in the country. Each of the Innovation Superstars profiled in this book hit similar speed bumps, but all have deployed excellent digital strategies with great success.

Once past that bump in the road, it's time to start listening. But there's more to this than simply putting an ear to the ground. Companies need to establish listening posts, become actively engaged listeners in those conversations, and have a system in place to create and validate new innovations that emerge as a result of that listening.

> Companies need to establish listening posts, become actively engaged listeners in those conversations, and have a system in place to create and validate new innovations that emerge as a result of that listening.

In some cases, companies are devoting that ear-to-the-ground job to one important person who filters and manages all of that incoming information. Kodak is one of the first companies to create this position. Dell created such a position as well.

"We believe so much in the importance of listening to these ongoing social conversations that last year we staffed a role called 'Chief Listener,'" Hoehn said. "I believe we created the first Chief Listener position."

There are a variety of digital listening tools in the market, both free and fee based. Despite the fact that Kodak is a $7-plus billion company, the free, simple software was used first. The digital communications team was small and evolved with the times.

"We're small but really nimble and productive," Hoehn said. "We started out with a number of free listening tools such as Google

Alerts and Twitter APIs like TweetDeck and Seesmic. We used very basic things like that just to get the pulse of the conversations that were happening. This provided us with a good sense of what was being said about our category, brand, and products. It also gave us insight into who was saying it—customers, fans, advocates, and even competitors."

After proving the worth of that information, Kodak moved on to some of the more sophisticated listening tools that can sift out unrelated information, thus streamlining the process.

### Being Prepared to Act upon Information

When you're in the social space listening and engaging in the conversations about your brand, you're going to come across some good information. The key is being prepared to act upon that information. Kodak has a good example of just how profitable this scenario can be.

"When we came out with our pocket video camera, called the Zi6, people loved it. From the very beginning we saw things on Twitter like, 'Should I get the Kodak or X model?' " Hoehn said.

By this time, Kodak had a good grasp on how to interact with potential customers in a real, genuine way. Remember the profiles on Innovation Superstars Spigit and Radian6? These companies had other examples of how to engage participants in ways that provide the best value and experience, ensuring loyalty in a way no pop-up coupon or link to a corporate webpage ever will.

"The right thing to do is go in there and add value in a smart way," Hoehn said. "We were seeing those kinds of questions popping up on different sites every 30 to 45 minutes. So we found four or five side-by-side comparison reviews regular people had done on these cameras, sharing their insights. They weren't all glowing reviews, but they said, 'I like this about this one better . . . we fared very well with this . . . and we like that.'"

After finding those reviews, Kodak popped into conversations, where appropriate, with messages such as, 'Hey, this is Jenny, chief blogger from Kodak and we found these reviews. I hope you'll find them helpful.' Kodak would then share a link to a blog post that contained these comparison reviews. They used the single blog post in this manner over and over again.

The responses were very positive. Whether those people went on to buy the product or not, Kodak was still adding value to their conversations and that has a lasting effect.

"Knowing when to jump in and when not to jump in—a tough skill to learn—is really important," Hoehn said.

After participating in this interplay for a while, Kodak listeners began noticing a trend. People were talking about the camera and a few suggestions kept surfacing. Most liked the camera, but issues with three items kept coming up: a need for an external microphone jack, a flexible USB port, and image stabilization.

This information went to Kodak's commercialization team, which rapidly came out with the next version of the product that included those three innovations—the Zi8.

"At the time we could not make those cameras fast enough," Hoehn said. "They were flying off the shelves. That was a year ago now and they're the benchmark in that space. It really was a wonderful thing and it came from listening and having agile, talented people in the business group."

This information simply came from listening to the information that was already out there. It didn't involve focus groups or surveys. Kodak didn't invest a lot of money in traditional media to gain and act upon the information. It was done with user generated, public relations, and social media efforts.

"Really engaging in these conversations is now the primary way we make people aware of these products," Hoehn said. "And then we arm our ambassadors with the right assets, like great pictures, reviews, sample videos, and so on. We give them great content or the tools to make their own so they can tell these stories as well."

## Making Your Customers Blue: Recognizing Actionable Listening Moments

Over the years I've looked at a lot of businesses and learned how they use digital platforms as a way to drive innovation. It's always interesting to me that, in so many cases, people brag about the size of their digital community, but first they don't listen well, and then they don't do post-listening ideation.

Here's an example: A few years back I watched the flip video wave go by. There was a community of flip users—me included—demanding audio input at every outlet. And what was the response to this demand? They changed the color of the flip and re-released it. It was such a disappointment. I called this type of response "painting it blue and calling it new" in the first book in this series, *The Innovation Playbook.*

Kodak's response to the customer clamor was exactly right. Customers weren't asking for the camera in a different color; they had specific needs and wants they vocalized. Kodak heard, made a quick turnabout, and is now reaping the rewards for their innovation with huge sales and a happy customer base.

The difference between this story of success and others of failure has to do with commitment throughput. It's something many organizations have a tough time with. When I'm speaking on the subject, I often use this example of signing up for a gym membership: 80 percent of Americans will never *sign up* to go to a gym. Of those who do, 80 percent will not *show up* more than six times. Of those who sign up and show up, 80 percent will never *stand up*, meaning they go to the gym, drink coffee, work out for five minutes, and leave. So if you look at the process in a digital commitment, you really have to have that commitment across the organization, from the top down. And then when you do commit to the digital strategy, you need to do something with what you find. This commitment throughput failure is a common pattern with universities and their intellectual property portfolios. They have 20,000 patents and yet they have virtually no market success. Having a community in which you aren't delivering any value or extrapolating new ways to add additional value almost seems like that digital community isn't worth having.

Extracting and acting upon that knowledge must be part of your digital strategy. And that's why many companies are now devoting staff resources to it. At Kodak, this job falls to Hoehn and his team.

"I live and breathe this social marketing stuff every day," he said. "Marketers and product development people have many issues they deal with on a daily basis to run their business. It is incumbent on me to show them how they can best use these assets and create value."

Hoehn recalls similar conversations in the mid-1990s when leaders in the industry were trying to make sense of how the Internet was changing their worlds in so many ways.

"You can just replace *social media* with *Internet,*" Hoehn recalled. "I heard many of the same complaints: 'It's just for kids . . . it's not for business . . . it's a fad.' So it became our duty to show them how to use these great tools and resources. Today you wouldn't think of doing business without an element of the Internet—it is like oxygen. Social is delivering on those promises of community, commerce, and content made during those heady days of the 1990s."

And Kodak, like many of the other success stories is strategic in their digital initiatives. As evidenced in the stories told so far, it's not a matter of ham-handedly groping through the web barging in on conversations or spamming the world with flashy ads. It's understanding your product and customer base and engaging them in a way that's satisfying to both parties and adds value to the experience.

> It's not a matter of ham-handedly groping through the web barging in on conversations or spamming the world with flashy ads. It's understanding your product and customer base and engaging them in a way that's satisfying to both parties and adds value to the experience.

When someone asks, "Do I need a Facebook page?" the answer isn't simply yes or no. First, you need to think about what you're trying to do, then think about the customer demographic. Think about what conversations are already out there. Who are the influencers in your space? Traditional media still have their place; they just have a different role now, and social and traditional need to work together.

"There may be other influencers you haven't even heard about and you need to know how they are talking about your products," Hoehn said, "And then you make them aware of you and engage with them in a meaningful way."

## Active Listening: Air Traffic Controller for Those Insights

Gathering the data from these communities is one thing. Having a plan for using that data is another thing altogether. A large corporation like Kodak is going to have a huge, steady influx of information coming in that will include a wide range of data that may be hugely important, not important at all, or good for some later date. How do you sort through it all and then act upon the information accordingly?

In most cases there's a system set up that works in a way similar to an air traffic controller. Information is gleaned, insights are passed on to customer support, product development, or corporate communications, and then those departments act accordingly.

"We are growing in our maturity in these digital initiatives," Hoehn said. "We have the processes outlined. For instance, if it's a support issue—someone has made a comment about one of the Kodak-owned media properties and they've never had a support interaction with us—we'll send them to our website. There is tons of support information there and you can chat online."

Of course, not all mentions on the social web are happy. In most cases, there's a different process for the complaints. And within those processes, a company needs to have the capability to react on a dime if it's something that's going to hurt the brand in a big way. Kodak had a great example of this.

Early one bright morning in November the Kodak team noticed that there was misinformation being spread on the web that Kodak had pulled its ads from the Teen Nickelodeon show *Degrassi*. A small group protesting the content on *Degrassi* had published a false statement claiming Kodak had succumbed to pressure from them and pulled its ads from the show. At the time Kodak was running a new campaign with music industry stars Rhianna, Drake, Trey Songz, and Pitbull.

"It was really new, different, and fresh for us," Hoehn said. "The misinformation stated that our ads were pulled from the show. But what they were seeing was a normal pause in the media schedule. We were dark with media just before the holiday season kicked in earnest."

This error in the facts first appeared on the web at 8:00 A.M. on Veteran's Day.

"*Degrassi* audience skews younger and those kids were off from school that day. They got wind of this and were really negative against Kodak," Hoehn said. "There were posts like, 'Kodak how could you do this?' and, 'You're so ignorant, you're homophobes,' and 'We should boycott Kodak.'"

Kodak got to work responding immediately, sharing the facts and assuring *Degrassi* fans that Kodak did not pull the ads.

"We crafted a message and started responding to these individual Tweeters with things like, 'Hey this is Beth, Chief Listener from Kodak. This is just a normal pause in our schedule, we'll be back on next week, including on *Degrassi*,' " Hoehn said.

In a situation like this, there isn't time for internal silos, long planning meetings, or anything of the sort. Kodak handled it well. Hoehn's team was able to simply walk over to the media purchasing group and the communications team (they sit in the same building) to get he facts straight and align their engagement.

"We also reached out to five *Degrassi* fan site bloggers and said, 'Hello, this is Beth, Chief Listener at Kodak . . .' telling them the same story," Hoehn said. "They were impressed that Kodak was listening and glad to hear the rumors were in fact just that, rumors."

Kodak monitored the situation for another day, but it soon died down. The communications team got in touch with Teen Nick to let them know what had happened and they generously offered two spots on *Degrassi* that evening to help rid the public of the poor impression.

"By literally 28 hours later, this issue had gone away," Hoehn said. "It could have been a terrible, terrible thing. We are proud of our company's support of diversity and the GLBT community and the perception being conveyed was the exact opposite of that. We said, 'Let's engage directly with these Tweeters, bloggers, and on Facebook. Let's reach out as a person from Kodak, not just a faceless corporation.' And it worked."

## A Story with a Moral: Kodak Learns Fast Action and Personal Response Avert Disaster

The moral of the Kodak story is it's crucial to listen to that digital chatter. And, participating in that dialogue has real business deliverables. You ignore that information at your peril. People are talking about your brand, whether you're listening or not. To ignore it is bad business.

And because there's so much out there, businesses must be aggressive about setting up a variety of listening posts and be prepared to quickly—by dropping those organizational silos—have those connections to all the various departments to provide action to whatever may happen out in the digital world.

"The media is full of stories like this where people did not respond either correctly, or in time," Hoehn said. "And by the time
they do respond, it's over and they are dredging it back up again,
which can be even worse. So you need to be alert and know how to
respond, and then know how to engage the other group."

## The Flavors of Communication: Learn Which to Use and When

In the beginning of this book I talked about digital polarity. To me,
the single word that describes the digital community is *communication*.
Communication, just like radio communication, comes in three fla-
vors. There's *simplex* dialogue where we speak to somebody—one
way. Then there's *duplex* dialogue, which is a two-way exchange, but
it's not typically in real time. And then there's *full-duplex* dialogue—a
real-time, ongoing discussion.

I've talked about Yamaha a few times in this book, although it isn't
one of the companies studied in depth. I really like Yamaha's fan website, Motifator, which is an online space for digital synthesizer users.
And they're very passionate about this product. In many cases this
product is how the community members make their livelihood. Part
of what I find so interesting about Yamaha's website is the fact that
people within their community are allowed to say some bad things
about Yamaha. Those comments aren't removed. The second thing
they allow to happen—which has been very fortuitous to them—is
that they allow users to solve technical problems.

A great deal of their technical support has happened in these
micro-communities. Many of the community topics are very specific;
they're relatively small in the digital scheme of things. But they draw
the super fans that are among the most loyal to the brand.

## A Product That Stands on Its Own: Allowing the Community to Discuss Your Brand

Handing over the reins to discussion of your brand isn't easy. Yes,
you'll have those super fans out there—if your product and services are outstanding—but you're also going to have people saying
bad things. But, as mentioned multiple times already, they're going to say those things whether you're listening or not. If you're

involved in the social conversations, at least you've got the platform to respond.

"Wouldn't you rather have them do this in a place where you can do something about it?" Hoehn asked. "I always tell my team members, 'You really have to have a thick skin.' Most people are reasonable. If somebody is just 'F-bomb this' and 'GD Kodak' that . . . and if you reach out to them as a person (our avatars have pictures on them as well as the Kodak name), most people will immediately step off the ledge. Most will say, "Wow, I'm just really mad.' We'll then say, 'Tell me about it.' "

This is all true—unless your products or services or innovations really are terrible. Products must be able to stand on their own or there's no point in initiating any sort of digital strategy at all. No digital initiative can save a bad business. It will only spotlight the problems. But if you do have the products to stand upon and you still find those tough cases out there, sometimes you just have to let it go.

"Some people will never turn around," Hoehn said. "For those people, you just have to say, 'We gave it our shot and it's time to move on.' You want to make sure, obviously, that you don't have a lot of bad stuff occurring, but it's going to happen. And if you decide you absolutely don't want to see anything bad about your company, you shut all your media channels down, then it's simply going to show up somewhere else."

Kodak and the other Innovation Superstars spotlighted in this book all share a common belief in open communication—no matter what shows up out there. Like many others, the company doesn't remove negative posts on its blogs or Facebook pages or other platforms. This doesn't mean it's a free-for-all; most companies, including Kodak, do have exceptions for profanities or personal attacks. But for the most part, it's an open and honest dialogue without any edits.

And they find a great benefit to this honesty: A loyal customer base will defend the brand for you.

**W**hen you're honest, a loyal customer base will defend the brand for you.

"If you're regularly engaged, you'll find other people come to your defense," Hoehn said. "It's the best of both worlds. If you have something negative happen, and other people stand up for you or the product, that's great! Sometimes that voice can be stronger than the one coming from the company as far as credibility and validation."

## A Matter of Trust

So now we've seen how Kodak truly listens to its customers and is brave and open enough to let them discuss the good and bad with equal freedom, providing an arena of information open to all, and creating an opportunity for innovation in both products and service. This open attitude has also created loyal followers who advocate for the company, which is the best of both worlds for the innovative photography giant.

In the next chapter we look at an organization that's taken this concept of trust to a whole new level. The U.S. Army, an old agency steeped in tradition and bureaucracy, has turned the new media world on its head with incredibly open social media programs that have given soldiers and their families a worldwide voice, while allowing potential enlistees to learn the real stories of service from real soldiers on the front lines. Read on to learn why an open culture is possible for *anyone*.

### Chapter Takeaways

- First, know who and where your customers are. They are already out there talking, sharing, and relating their experiences.
- Be part of the conversations. Your customers will look to you for a level of authority and value. Be genuine and people will give you credit for it.
- Jumping into the social media world without a plan is a huge mistake. First find the customers, hear the tone, locate the influencers, and think about how you can add value.
- At the end of the day, it's all about being in touch with your customers at a high level.
- Digital and new media are not a fad. They are about better customer engagement and using the tools to your business advantage.

*The Digital Innovation Playbook* is a living book. We are constantly updating the book online so you can watch uploaded videos, read the latest best practice on digital media, and even participate in free ongoing webinars.

To access this chapter's updated web page, please go to www.digitalinnovationplaybook.com/Chapter6.html or scan the QR code with your mobile device.

CHAPTER

# The Army Way

## DIGITAL LEADERSHIP FROM
## A SURPRISING SOURCE

As your organization endeavors to rule the day in the digital environment, think about what you have at stake. If a blogger lets slip a trade secret, will anyone lose their life? If a commenter says something nasty about your business, could that endanger the security of the nation? In most cases, the answer would be no. But for the U.S. Army, a government organization usually thought to be steeped in bureaucracy and closed-door secrecy, the idea of social networking soldiers should seem ludicrous. Yet the Army is one of the leaders in the industry with a soldier-run blog and several other digital media endeavors. And how is this possible, you ask? I asked the same thing and found a fantastic tale of a strong, loyal relationship that goes both ways, resulting in an environment of trust and respect that allows the government organization to have an extremely open-door policy giving prospective enlistees—and anyone else—a glimpse into this 200-plus-year-old organization's daily workings. The digital media world could learn a lot from the U.S. Army.

### Eye-Opener at Blog World

I'll never forget walking through the trade show at Blog World Expo in Las Vegas. I saw the companies I would expect to see that are mastering the digital domain—Ford, PepsiCo, Southwest Airlines, Google, Yahoo!, and all the rest. Seeing them there made perfect sense and it was great to see the enthusiasm with which these organizations were using all of the new media options to deliver amazing customer value. But as I turned the corner, I looked up and saw a tradeshow booth from a surprising source: the U.S. Army. Wow, I thought. The Army's at Blog World Expo? Like most people, I've always had a very positive view of our military, but as an old organization that is usually surrounded by secrecy—in order to protect soldiers. It seemed unusual that the Army could be open in this fashion, a necessity that is the fueling force of digital strategy. It seemed doubtful that the organization could truly be open enough for this sort of digital strategy. But after talking to the booth representatives, I began to realize this was a sincere effort, a really genuine desire to create digital soldier communities.

### Army Strong Stories

The Army representatives were at the Blog World Expo talking about ArmyStrongStories.com, the Army's blog and story-sharing program. The site provides an online community for soldiers, families, friends, and supporters to share their Army stories. Through authentic perspectives on Army life and military service, the program provides those interested in learning more about the Army a platform to ask questions and interact with soldiers. This also provides the Army's first platform for soldiers to share stories, and for supporters to share their stories, leave comments, and ask questions.

There are a lot of secondary benefits in this online community for the Army, but the real goal was to allow their soldiers to communicate and to create a community where they can share their experiences. The positive benefits of this are almost immeasurable, but what's most important, and frankly impressive, is the fact that the Army could do this in the first place. After my one-hour discussion with the lieutenant colonel at the booth, I walked away thinking, "Wow, our country is in good hands. This is an impressive group of individuals sincerely committed to their missions. But more important, they are sincerely committed to the individuals." I don't want to go on preaching about the U.S. Army, but I just about enlisted after the experience. That's how strongly I felt about their message. It's a great organization doing some amazing things.

### A Worthwhile Mission

Let's take a look at their mission. Their stated mission is to increase the U.S. Army's social media engagement, including the opportunity to humanize the Army, build trust, and foster two-way communications between the Army and its online recruiting audience. The mission itself is obviously very impressive. But let's set the stage here. This is the U.S. military. They have enemies all around the world that are digitally connected. To use social media as a listening post to understand tactics and strategies could put soldiers at risk. When I interviewed the lieutenant colonel he shared with me that if he can trust a soldier with a machine gun, he can trust him with a laptop. That's impressive. And that makes an incredible point for the average organization. If the U.S. military, which has serious life and death risks, can become digitally connected, then can't your organization?

It's incredible to me that often, when I interview large companies, they talk about all the reasons why they have to maintain a closed organization that doesn't allow for full-duplex dialogue with their valued customers. I love the Army Strong Stories, because it shows an organization that literally has soldiers' lives at stake, but is still able to do the right things to create openness. Soldiers have rules of conduct, and those rules mandate that they may not share information that could be potentially dangerous. When you have hundreds of thousands of soldiers in the field, the chances that things could go wrong are real. But it was deemed that the advantages to the soldier, the community, and to their missions were far greater than that potential risk. I would argue that your organization's mission is going to be driven by your willingness to become an open innovator that truly embraces and demands the utilization of a smart digital strategy.

> **Y**our organization's mission is going to be driven by your willingness to become an open innovator that truly embraces and demands the utilization of a smart digital strategy.

## A Two-Pronged Campaign

What are the various digital campaigns used by the U.S. Army? The Army utilizes a variety of platforms, initiatives, and creative executions including soldier blogs, soldier networks, SMS mobile, and an instant messaging campaign. They also identify new trends, issues and leverage new marketing mediums with daily monitoring. These campaigns are important since they provide a variety of advantages for the soldiers and for the Army. The goal is to provide listening posts to understand how they can provide additional value to their soldiers and to create genuine open dialogue so that soldiers can share with one another their Army experience. The online community is comprised of two main features—the soldier blog and Army stories. While the soldier blog is exclusive to soldiers, cadets, veterans, and Army civilians, anyone can share video or written submissions through Army Strong Stories.

Soldiers of nearly every rank, background, and career path participate in the blog. It provides an open forum for any individual to ask the soldiers questions. Topics range from deployment and basic training to career opportunities and events in their personal lives. Army Strong Stories is where supporters come together to connect with fellow soldiers, recruits, family, friends, and others. Army stories can be written or video submissions, and users can post one or several.

## Hands Off! Let Go or Lose It All

I have found after looking at hundreds of different organizational online communities that the companies and other organizations that succeed at this are those who take a hands-off approach. Organizations who try to be legalistic and controlling with their digital communities fail with *mathematical certainty*. People don't want to participate in interoffice memos. They want to discuss their shared interest in a product or service or organization. This approach is critical. When you create your digital communities, follow the lead of the Army. Yamaha is another example of a company that has created an open environment that allows people to talk freely about their experiences.

### The Good and the Bad

Now here's the caveat, and it's a big one for most companies. You have to be willing to allow community members to say derogatory things about you. Ouch. That's hard for most companies. After all, your job is to promote your brand, not to allow people to destroy it. But allowing sincere, genuine openness in your digital communities is the only way to achieve your organizational results. If you produce a product or service, you must allow people to talk about the goodness and the badness. The reason this is important? Every bad comment amplifies the significance of the good comments. Despite its counterintuitive nature, the strategy of allowing derogatory comments to be posted for all to see is a good one. These comments actually drive the positive comments. Now, if the overwhelming majority of the comments posted in your digital community are negative, that may mean you need some internal analysis to determine if you're failing at the delivery of your product or service.

Socialmediatoday said this about the U.S. Army's digital initiative: "Well, the U.S. Army seems to get it. They need young men and women to join them and help protect our country, and they know that these young people are spending their time on the social web. The star of the Army's social media efforts on display at BlogWorld was ArmyStrongStories.com, a blogging system that allows anyone in the Army to post to the blog."

### Even the Ugly

Another very important point I must make is this: You don't control the Internet. Let me repeat that: You *do not* control the Internet. Now, because you don't control the Internet, the more you try to *close* your digital community, the more you try to *control* your digital community, the more likely it is that certain individuals will create other communities that you have absolutely no control over whatsoever. The goal is to create a great community supported by you that provides real open and honest dialogue. This open and honest dialogue is important and I talk about it throughout this book. Digital communication isn't about broadcasting our message in a simplex way; it's about full-duplex, real time dialogue. It's about the ability for our community to help us co-create amazing innovations, and the ability for our community to share with one another good and bad experiences so that we can use that community as a listening post to find ways to add additional value for our customers.

### "If It's Good Enough for the Army . . ."—Despite the Risks, the Military Creates a Real Community

This is an amazing story: The U.S. military, the Army, is taking control of the digital media platform to build its brand and to drive other organizational missions. This project was a risk for the Army; there's no question about that. It's always important to be sure there's a proportional reward for any risk we take. So what were the results of this initiative? It positioned the Army's recruiting program as a social media thought leader in the media, at events, and through word of mouth. It successfully built, launched, and managed the U.S. Army's first ever soldier blog, including—get this—450,000 site visits. It launched an instant messaging program that reached more than 5.2 million users in four months. It built the Army Strong Stories to YouTube channels, boasting more than 171,000 total views. It fostered a content program for Go Army's Facebook channel, reaching 25,000 fans, and Go Army MySpace channel, reaching over 90,000 friends. Did it work? Absolutely. One of the biggest challenges for the Army is recruiting. A great deal of money is invested in recruiting the very best candidates. This unbelievable success story drove recruiting and all their other organizational missions in a way that couldn't have been done otherwise. See Figure 7.1.

NBC News said this about the Army Strong Stories community: "From West Point to the front lines, soldiers are now armed with a new weapon (Army Strong Stories) that would seem in many ways outside the parameters of the traditional Army. . . . The Army is fully engaged now in the realm of social media. There are now more than 81 soldier bloggers and ArmyStrongStories.com is the first and only official Army blog open to every soldier, an outlet you won't find in any other branch of the military."

### Free Speaking

So what can a 235-year-old military organization teach your business? You must let go. In order to control your message, you need to let go of control. Real customer and organizational communities are comprised of individuals that are allowed to speak freely even if their comments are derogatory toward your brand. The best way to build positive dialogue is to create great products and services, not to manipulate the responses.

iMedia Connection said this about the Army's digital community: "Bloggers are encouraged to share both the good and bad about their unique experiences, giving the site a tremendous level of authenticity and transparency. Visitors are exposed to the raw and personal side of the Army in a way that traditional media rarely provides."

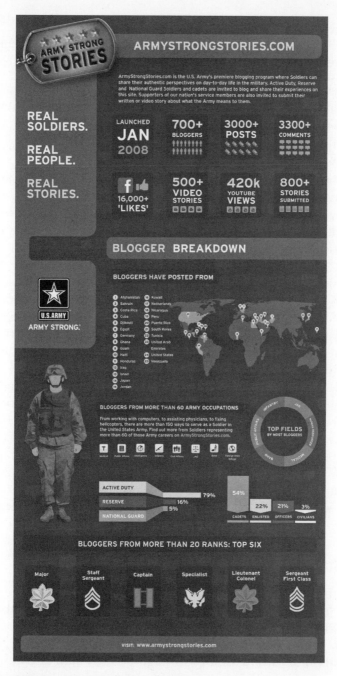

Figure 7.1     Breakdown of Army Strong Stories Blogging
*Source:* Courtesy of the U.S. Army.

Remember, the best way to build positive dialogue is to create great products and services, not to manipulate the responses.

### Open Up to the Possibilities

Real digital communities provide the ultimate forum of listening posts to identify ways to create new customer innovations and value. The digital and new media are not a battleground. They are a playground. Come play. Open innovation and open culture require risk taking.

I'd like to make a very personal observation about my former relationship to the military. I have spent my whole life as a serial entrepreneur, and when I think of the military or the military industrial complex, I can't help but think that in many ways it represents the exact opposite of everything I've always stood for—fluidity, freedom, the ability to take risks, try new things, capitalism, all the stuff that I think makes up real businesses. It turns out that I'm wrong.

The Army is really about the same thing—doing amazing things, delivering extreme value, being innovative and creative, and developing communities that allow all of their soldiers to share. I have to say that putting together this chapter was one of the most exciting and interesting experiences of my lifetime. I hope that you take away the powerful message that no matter how large your organization is or what you do, you simply must develop an open culture that takes advantage of the digital media to build communities in order to grow and prosper with your brand.

## Army Strong Stories: A Matter of Trust and Respect

I had the distinct pleasure of talking with Chief Marketing Officer Bruce Jasurda sometime after the Blog World Expo trip about the evolution of the Army Strong Stories community. One of the first questions I asked was the one I found most perplexing. From a political point of view, how did you go up the chain of command in this huge, bureaucratic organization and say this community that will be open for all the world to see is a good idea?

"If you go back two years ago in our marketing program, there was sort of a watershed moment when we realized that the old media way of doing things just wasn't appropriate for our target audience and their media consumption habits," Jasurda said. "Our target audience of 17 to 24 is texting, they are listening to their iPods, they're watching television, and they're on the computer, probably doing Facebook. It became painfully apparent, a blinding flash of the obvious, that we needed to look at both how our prospects were consuming information and where we were in our efforts to try to reach them and communicate with them."

## A Flash of Insight

The Army—like many other Innovation Superstars highlighted in this book—realized soon after venturing into social media communications that the target audience for its communications is absolutely bombarded with media messages from brands of all kinds. So what those readers valued most was an honest discussion, not being preached at or sold to.

"Once we understood this, we knew where we needed to go," Jasurda said. "So we conducted a wealth of proprietary research; we know our prospects inside and out. It was very apparent to us that we needed to be in the digital domain in order to be relevant and be in this conversation."

These prospects have become tone deaf to corporate voices over time. And in listening to the ongoing conversations about the Army, it soon became apparent that the Army, and its 235-year history, was sorely misunderstood.

"The days when the judge would say would you like to go to jail or go to the Army are over," Jasurda said. "But that perception is still out there even though it hasn't been a reality in over a decade."

## An Outdated Perception

Awareness isn't a problem for the Army. Our nation has been at war now for 10 years in two different theaters, which is the longest armed conflict in U.S. history. So awareness isn't an issue, but perception is. And an even bigger problem facing the Army is that, on average, only 3 in 10 people in the 17-to-24-age group are eligible to serve in the Army.

"The reality of it is, if the young man or woman has made some bad choices in his or her past, if they have major misdemeanors or any kind of felony, we're not going to talk to them," Jasurda said. "If they don't have a high school diploma, we're not going to talk to them. If they're overweight, we're not going to talk to them. If they sign up in the delayed entry status and say they're going to come in six months from now when they finish high school, and then they don't complete the mandatory things they have to do in that future soldier training program, we're not going to induct them into the Army."

### A Needle in a Needle Stack

So finding those 3 people in every 10 that are qualified is like finding a "needle in a stack of needles," as Jasurda put it. "We're looking for young men and women who fit the scholar, athlete, leader profile. If you think about it logically, kids who are joiners and who have shown some desire to finish something—whether it's a church group, scouts, band, a sports team, cheerleading, a charitable organization, or something else—simply better assimilate into the Army."

As described in Chapter 5, Flying High, selecting the right people for the job is half the job. Training comes next. So in the Army's case, if these potential candidates show some propensity to complete something, their odds of being successful rise a great deal.

"So the question is then, how do you honestly communicate with these young folks?" Jasurda asked. "This is the ultimate considered purchase. This is a very difficult decision. This isn't something that's a disposable. It's not even just life changing. It could be life threatening. We internally kind of consider it the ultimate considered purchase."

### A Life-and-Death Commitment

"At the end of the day, we know we're not selling soda or cars," Jasurda said. "We're acutely conscious of the very sober, very serious nature of what we do. The young people we're talking to are very savvy and very media savvy."

Because of this, the Army had to assess the best possible way to communicate. It seemed obvious they needed to educate these candidates, explain what the Army was all about, but not in a corporate voice. It soon became clear that those who had been out there on the front lines would have the most genuine voice and would have the experiences necessary to communicate these important messages.

"I'll give you some examples," Jasurda said. "We've all seen these perceptual images of the Army through movies and television and they portray basic training as something that's unbearable. Wouldn't you worry about those conditions? Are drill sergeants really as horrible as they sound?"

Army Strong Stories puts soldiers, including drill sergeants, out there to tell their stories, answer questions, and generally paint a picture of daily life and experiences.

"A lot of those barriers come down," Jasurda said.

### Listening to the Good and the Bad

As I've said repeatedly, I find it really interesting that some of the best, most digitally connected companies allow blog, Facebook, and Twitter participants to post very derogative things about them. I've seen how this can actually be a smart move. But most companies still don't get this concept. When I asked the Army about this policy, I was told that as long as what commenters are posting is just an opinion and they aren't abusive to another member of the community, the comments stay because for every one of them, there are 500 positive posts. It's been found that in terms of creating the digital community landscape, those negative posts were almost a necessary ingredient.

### An Authentic Conversation

Look at some of the less savvy corporate posts on a variety of websites and you'll find plenty of examples of how *not* to participate in these communications. For example, you may visit a packaged goods website and you'll find a long list of comments that say things like, "I love this yogurt. My family likes this yogurt. I tried a different yogurt but this one is much better. I'm going to go buy more of this yogurt."

It's a transparent attempt at bolstering public opinion in a way that's not going to fool anyone.

"These kids are so savvy, they see right through that kind of talk," Jasurda said. "And if they can see right through it with consumable goods—and again this is a life and death decision in some cases, in some measure—then there's no excuse for not being absolutely authentic with them on Army Strong Stories."

So in the Army's case, if someone asks, "Are you afraid in combat in Afghanistan?" the right and real answer is going to be "Yes." Of course the answer will be yes. But now, that person can also ask, "How do you deal with that fear?" And the responder will answer with details about how you would feel a little more secure in that environment after training and working with others.

"These are the conversational questions that need to occur on this site, because the people answering are those who have been there," Jasurda said. "And, often, the people responding on the site are similar in age to those asking the questions. The authenticity of the voice makes a lot of difference."

### The Bottom Line

Many of the corporations—the ones getting it right—have a very similar policy. So with Army Strong Stories, the deliverable to the community participant is pure level dialogue that's authentic and real and not planted, not part of your driven message. It's genuine, obviously compartmentalized in your web property, but the dialogue is factual. It's not moderated where derogatory things aren't allowed to be posted. So the deliverable to the perspective enlistee is a genuine perspective of what the landscape is all about.

"We have these things we not only espouse when we talk to young men and women thinking about joining the Army, but also Army values," Jasurda said. "And it is a very short list of things you might expect—respect and trust—those kinds of things. If we live those values, really believe in them, then why wouldn't we follow them in our marketing? If that authentic, genuine voice is important to us—you asked the question earlier how does the decision get made by this 235-year-old, reputedly bureaucratic organization to say, 'Go forth young men and women and blog?' "

### The Common Denominator

"It's a very simple precept," Jasurda said. "We have this fundamental core belief that we will always trust the judgment and the values of a soldier. If we can't, the whole thing breaks down and doesn't work."

Everyone in the Army is a soldier, regardless of rank and responsibilities. So the Army believes that—with the exception of things that are inappropriate, or profane, or violate some sort of Army security protocol—there pretty much are no restrictions.

"There are plenty of negative comments," Jasurda said. "Every day there are comments that say, 'This sucks, this needs to be fixed.' But in most cases, it's also these soldiers who spotlight what's wrong and invariably, these are the soldiers who have a big hand in fixing them."

The young men and women who join the Army must leave their families, live with a bunch of strangers, and go through basic training. Within a week after they join, they are sent down range with a rifle and live ammunition, and then they may get deployed to Iraq or Afghanistan and have to make life and death decisions.

"If we can trust them with all that, we feel very comfortable they'll do well on Army Strong Stories," Jasurda said. "They'll do the honorable thing. Our culture—in war and in peace—is predicated on trusting the person on the right and left of you."

## Learning from the Army

The Army's story is one of my favorites in this book. The main reason is that, as a management consultant that specializes in innovation strategy, I can tell you one of the biggest challenges in business today is that organizations are so closed that they are risk-centric. The reason I love the Army's story so much is that so many American corporations could benefit from their ideology.

"I think they could if they had a workforce they respected as much as we do ours," Jasurda said.

But since most corporations aren't involved in any life-or-death situation, the concept has probably never been couched to them in this way. I remember visiting Blog World and talking to the U.S. Army colonel running the booth and being bewildered. I've worked with many of the Fortune 50 companies and suddenly I find it's the Army doing what American companies need to do if they want to reconnect to the customer community. They need to be willing to trust their employees to be open to communicate with their own customer communities.

"I recently read an article that said something to the effect of corporations are finding the new best selling tool—employees," Jasurda said. "It's like its back in style again. Our affinity with soldiers isn't something new. This isn't a revelation to us. Soldiers are men and women, all races and creeds and colors, all ranks. If we can't respect those folks we depend on to make life and death decisions, to do this responsibly, then there's something fundamentally wrong with our marketing. And our Army."

## The Benefits

This seems like a bouquet of solutions. The Army provides a resource where potential enlistees get to talk to their peers and understand on a deeper level, in real time, the landscape of the actual Army experience. They can actually pretest the experience by talking to people. It seems like it solves problems because right off the bat you have educated your potential enlistees about the selection criteria.

"I am frequently asked, 'Is this about increasing contracts?' No. 'Is this about decreasing the lead time to close the sale?' No. Those questions go on and on; usually they are the types of questions you'd imagine an efficiency expert would ask," Jasurda said. "At the end of the day we do this for two reasons: First, we do it because the only thing that works is that authentic feedback from someone who went through an identical experience we're asking you to think about. Secondly, this is an education process. Potential candidates can ask what opportunities are available and gather the information needed to determine if this is the right course for them. "

So while efficiency might be a natural byproduct of the Army's digital strategies, that's not what they are trying to achieve. Recruiters are already out there providing information to prospects; the Web presence simply gives candidates another avenue for that education.

Aside from Army Strong Stories, the Army has its corporate website. Like IndyCar in Chapter 8, Winning the Digital Race, the corporate space is a great jumping off point that houses much of the information on all the many avenues of the large organization.

"We have 150 different skills just on the enlisted side," Jasurda said. "That menu of possibilities and opportunities and options for you is pretty robust in the Army, so we do need that repository where people can actually go and select: This is what interests me. For us, it is a bouquet, but it's a bouquet that kind of evolved and is organized in a way that we've learned they like to receive information."

## Process without Fear

When I looked at companies for this book, most were pretty underwhelming, but there's a handful out there that, like the Army, are doing some amazing things. IndyCar and Southwest Airlines both have great stories. One of the things I've noticed a lot is that these companies are developing processes—not risk-centric processes that stall or halt all innovation, but processes that allow them to formalize data planning, formalize the community as a resource. These processes create listening posts that can be used to gather opportunities for additional value.

The Army doesn't monitor or censor, but they do learn. Education is not optional in the Army, it's mandatory.

"If that's fundamentally the culture of who we are, and it is, we practice what we preach," Jasurda said. "As marketers we learn from what we hear. If we get seven comments a day for several months that say, 'People are concerned about the quality of health care at an Army hospital,' as a for instance, then we would have to see there's some type of misperception on this subject or we're not communicating this information correctly. And we will go fix it in our communications."

The Army tries to learn from those comments, not refute them. The community is so loyal, it's been found that they will often police themselves.

"We don't see those comments in particular because the health care is so good and the facilities are so great," Jasurda said. "But if we did get some comments like that, then we would learn from them and look in all of our communications. We wouldn't have seven guys go and blog about how good Army health care is. We would never do that. The community will police itself. But we would learn that maybe there are some perceptual issues out there that perhaps we need to focus on. So we're lifelong learners."

## A Learning Process

Here's a major turning point in media strategies: It's not about controlling the messages, it's about learning from them. That's a key mindset that has evolved a great deal from the old days of communications.

"We learn from this and take those observations and use those as a way to provide additional values," Jasurda said. "I think the worst thing we could do after listening in is to say, 'Hey everybody, we've been listening so . . .' But what we can do is learn from those observations and be sure they're addressed in future communications within the organization."

## An Educated Decision

There are many benefits to an open portal like that of Army Strong Stories, on both sides of the equation. Prospective soldiers get a real glimpse into military life, Army recruiters have this great tool that educates, and soldiers have an outlet to talk about their daily experiences.

"The benefit on the Army side is that the recruiter or professor of military science at a university may have less to do in order to communicate what Army service is like since so much of the information is now out there," Jasurda said. "It's sort of a head start."

Think about how people now buy cars. No one just walks in cold anymore. People go online and price shop. They do some research.

"It's the same with the U.S. Army," Jasurda said. "They've already researched it. Another reason we do things the way we do is that only 1 percent of the whole U.S. population has ever served in any branch of the U.S. military. Because such a small population has ever served, it's easy to understand why there are so many misconceptions about the organization."

And, as more and more bases close, people have even less exposure to Army folks. Jasurda used to work at Ft. Sheridan, Illinois, in the northern suburbs of Chicago. That's now a private neighborhood. The fort is closed and it's gone. That's about to happen at Ft. Monroe, Virginia, and in five other places across the United States, thanks to legislation. Because of these closures, people have less and less exposure, less face-to-face contact with the Army. So then, the obligation is on Army communications to get the message out through mediums like Army Strong Stories to expose them to what the army is really like.

"We get asked questions every day on Goarmy.com," Jasurda said. Things like, 'If I get hurt, will the Army take care of me? Will I have to live in barracks like my dad did that are wooden with bunk beds, and share toilets? Can I be married and be in the Army? Can I have a dog and be in the Army?'"

These questions were being asked 30 years ago and the Army is still answering them today. The Army is also a public trust. It's 100 percent funded by taxpayer money.

"That also speaks to the need to be authentic," Jasurda said.

## A Real Commitment to Communication: Openness Is the Driving Force behind Innovations

I'd like to close this chapter by sharing with you why I have spent so much time driving home the Army message. One thing is clear to me as someone who has spent two decades working as a management consultant with both large and small corporations: Organizations tend to look at their enterprise in a fractional way and as a result of that, they create organizational silos. Historically, these organizational silos were really more of an internal problem. But now with our need to be able to communicate in real time through full-duplex dialogue with our customer communities, the need to be open has never been more obvious.

> Historically, organizations have tended to look at their enterprise in a fractional way and as a result, have created organizational silos. In today's fast-paced world, the need to be open has never been move obvious.

### No More Silos

Openness is the driving force of all successful digital innovation initiatives. Let me repeat that, because it is important. Openness is the fueling force of all successful digital media initiatives. Here is a very important point: If you want to succeed at digital media, you have to be willing to succeed at openness. And that means tearing down the organizational silos and creating true cross-departmental communication. But more important, you must create true collective efforts with your entire organization to tear down the walls and to open up to your customer community. Without succeeding at openness you will never succeed at digital and new media innovation.

## The Army Can, and You Can Too

The Army shows us that organizations that have a life and death requirement to be secretive and closed are still able to be open in order to serve their organizational mandates. I would argue to you that if the U.S. Army, an old and bureaucratic organization, with a need to be secretive and a need to be closed, can be open and create true customer communities, I believe you can too.

Now it's time to go from the trenches to the auto racetrack.

## Chapter Takeaways

- The Army's goal was to allow their soldiers to communicate and to create a community where they can share their experiences. The positive benefits of this are almost immeasurable.
- Army Strong Stories provides those interested in learning more about the Army a platform to ask questions and interact with soldiers. This also provides the Army's first platform for soldiers to share stories, and for supporters to share their stories, leave comments, and ask questions.
- According to the Army mentality, if you can trust a soldier with a machine gun, he or she can be trusted with a laptop. This makes an incredible point for the average organization. If the U.S. military, which has serious life and death risks, can become digitally connected, then can't your organization?
- In most of the organizations doing this right, negative comments are left posted for all to see, as are the positive because this paints an accurate portrait of the digital landscape. And most often, the community polices those comments just fine on its own.
- For a long-standing organization like the Army, opening its doors to the public has allowed it to do away with unrealistic prejudices and perceptions and make clear how daily life in the military really works.
- If you want to succeed at digital media, you have to be willing to succeed at openness.

*The Digital Innovation Playbook* is a living book. We are constantly updating the book online so you can watch uploaded videos, read the latest best practice on digital media, and even participate in free ongoing webinars.

To access this chapter's updated web page, please go to www.digitalinnovationplaybook.com/Chapter7.html or scan the QR code with your mobile device.

# CHAPTER 8

# Winning the Digital Race

## INDYCAR CREATES THE ULTIMATE BRAND FORUM WITH ITS STRATEGIC MULTIMEDIA APPROACH

In writing *The Digital Innovation Playbook* I wanted to create a book that provides a true road map for businesses so that they can grow and prosper in the digital age. The problem is not that one digital strategy fits all. Companies, products, industries, and organizations themselves are very, very different. I've often said that cookie-cutter approaches toward any business strategies are fraught with failure. So when I put together case studies for this book, I wanted to provide a wide range of industry categories, products, and services. You've seen so far, with companies like the U.S. Army, Kodak, and Southwest Airlines, that vastly different organizations can utilize some basic strategies, such as an open, genuine culture and trust in their frontline employees, who have been well trained and handpicked to fit their individual needs. In your company, you can take those basic concepts and customize them.

The goal of this book is really twofold: one, that you would find a case study within this book most relevant to your organization; and two, perhaps more important, I wanted to provide evidence to show that digital strategies work in every organization when applied properly.

I think all of us have a reasonably good idea of what it takes to develop digital, new media, public relations, and marketing strategies around, for example, product-based companies. But what if you have a business that requires a person be there to experience the magic of what you provide? IndyCar is just that. It is an experience. I have to admit my prejudice here; I love IndyCar. I love everything they have done. And the fact that they were able to take one-dimensional digital media and make it multi-dimensional and truly customer connected is amazing.

In this Chapter I tell the story of how IndyCar has been able to utilize all the tools of the digital domain to drive customer connectivity, to support their customer community, and to provide significant and meaningful value-added resources by longer play video and interactive experiences. This is what it's all about: the ability to add more value, draw closer connections to customers and, in their case, it is a matter of industrial equilibrium since they provide a tremendous value to their customers, an amazing resource to their advertisers and customers, and a way to build upon their brand and business.

## Developing an Online Persona: How the IZOD IndyCar Series Has Added Value for Their Fans through Social and Digital Media

### About the IZOD IndyCar Series

The IZOD IndyCar Series is the premier open-wheel series in the United States, competing on a challenging combination of super speedways, short ovals, scenic road courses, and temporary street circuits. In 2011 the IndyCar Series will conduct 13 races in the United States, one in Canada, and one in both Japan and Brazil, all available worldwide through comprehensive, long-term agreements with ABC and VERSUS in high-definition. The IZOD IndyCar Series has a diverse lineup of drivers including Marco Andretti, Ryan Briscoe, Helio Castroneves, Scott Dixon, Dario Franchitti, Ryan Hunter-Reay, Tony Kanaan, Danica Patrick, Graham Rahal, and Dan Wheldon. A leader in motorsports technology, the IZOD IndyCar Series is the first racing series to power its Honda engines on 100 percent fuel-grade ethanol, a renewable and environmentally friendly fuel.

The IndyCar digital strategy gives fans what they want: a pass to the track and all that goes on behind the scenes, in preparation and on the day of the race. By giving an inside view of the unique experiences of the drivers, teams, and their stories throughout the season, the organization has created a variety of community-focused online platforms. This is the IndyCar digital story.

## Starting at .com

Like most companies, IndyCar maintains a main company website, IndyCar.com, that houses the majority of the information for the organization and provides a jumping off point for the company's digital strategy.

IndyCar's online team works closely with all members of the staff to create an online experience. To do this, there can't be walls inside the company. So the online team works closely with the editorial director, public relations, marketing, and sales teams. The .com experience provides IndyCar fans with direct access to hundreds of news stories published each year, as well as team and driver spotlight features. RSS feeds allow fans to get real time information that includes individualized stories about the drivers, tracks, sponsors, and more.

> IndyCar's online team works closely with all members of the staff to create an online experience. To do this, there can't be walls inside the company. So the online team works closely with the editorial director, public relations, marketing, and sales teams.

As any race fan will tell you, you've got to have the photo driven stories. So IndyCar also posts photo galleries that are categorized by event, tagged and integrated into the team and driver sections. This corporate jumping off point then feeds into IndyCar's Twitter account, YouTube videos, podcasts, and blogs that fall in the social realm of communications.

And then there are the super fans. Like me.

Linked from IndyCar.com is IndyCar Nation, an exclusive fan section, which has a global fan base that registers online to dive deeper into a more exclusive IndyCar experience by engaging with a number of interactive mediums. These include competing against each other and creating leagues through Fantasy Racing, access to Race Control (which provides live video, commentary, timing, and scoring from race events), as well as original IndyCar content, unique opportunities, and special offers from our sponsors. Visitors to the site are served with the ultimate IndyCar experience where they can see exclusive news and information related to the drivers, teams, racetracks, and sponsors.

In Chapter 4 we talked about the customer drive to get behind the velvet ropes, see what's going on behind the scenes. This need has driven the social networking evolution and will continue moving it forward. We like to peep. We want to see how things really work, maybe catch some scandal. This is what will continue filling spaces like IndyCar Nation.

During the 2010 race season (mid-March to early October), IndyCar.com received close to 20 million page views, with almost 3 million unique visitors. Everything IndyCar does for the fans, sponsors, drivers, teams, and members of the media begins at IndyCar.com, which keeps things simple and easy to navigate. Remember the keep-it-simple mantra from Chapter 2, The Digital Sandbox? Make the technology disappear for the best customer experience.

All efforts—online push brand awareness and content sharing outside of IndyCar.com—ultimately point back to the homepage. All of these options serve fans with a variety of media consumption options, and the easy-to-navigate layout provides a direct route back to access additional content at IndyCar.com. IndyCar subscribes to the same policy as mentioned in the mobile technology section of Chapter 2—keep things simple.

### Beyond.com

Outside of the IndyCar.com experience, the race series has purposely reached out to other online outlets to cultivate their fan base, discover new online communities, further expand its distribution of digital content, and experiment with new online platforms. Facebook, Flickr, Twitter, and YouTube have been important social platforms for fans to discover the stories behind the IZOD IndyCar Series. Most importantly, these platforms provide a unique online environment for IndyCar to learn from, experiment with, and respond to the requests of the online community. This is a strategy that will continue as the fan base grows and the IZOD IndyCar Series evolves. Agility and the ability to respond to changing needs and behaviors of fans are important to their vision for maintaining the optimal online experience.

Platforms like Facebook, Flickr, Twitter, and YouTube provide a unique online environment for IndyCar to learn from, experiment with, and respond to the requests of the online community.

The IZOD IndyCar Series utilizes new media platforms to support the needs of four targets: the fans, teams and drivers, corporate partners, and the sport.

For fans, the series utilizes online outlets to create and foster a community that shares the track experience, generates both anecdotal and actionable feedback, and provides exclusive opportunities for participants. The online arena is an opportunity for IndyCar to share content, but more important, it is a place to connect with and listen to its fan base.

When working with corporate partners, it is essential to generate additional ROI on their IndyCar sponsorship. This is generally accomplished by sharing content such as videos and photos, providing new ways for partners to engage consumers with their brand, and fostering long-term, mutually beneficial partnerships in the dynamic, ever-growing web.

Teams and drivers depend on IndyCar's new media team to share news stories, increase exposure, create sponsorship value on a team-level, and foster two-way support through sharing content, videos, and photos. The relationship between the sporting body (the new media, public relations, and marketing team) and the teams and drivers is incredibly strong. This allows for the seamless exchange of content and for new opportunities.

Finally, for the sport, new media works to communicate the brand, generate new awareness, and build the IndyCar name as a global entity, through digital media and social platforms, driving ticket and merchandise sales through e-commerce tools and developments, the promotion of open-wheel racing, and leveraging the web to reach new fans through the innovative and creative use of online tools.

## Behind the Scenes: The IndyCar Blog

The IndyCar blog is the vital mechanism that points visiting traffic from all social platforms to IndyCar.com. The blog includes content generated by internal writers from the IZOD IndyCar Series as well as guest authors, which can include anyone from drivers and team representatives, to helmet designers and IndyCar fans. Blog posts are conveyed in the original author's voice and meant to create further transparency to the series. IndyCar's internal authors are encouraged to write in their own voices in areas where they are most comfortable—emphasizing their professional expertise. It is vital that the blog represent real people, real personalities, and real stories from the world of racing. The approach is the same with guests—they're told, "Write in your own voice."

Posting through the WordPress platform aids the IZOD IndyCar Series' search engine optimization efforts by supplementing posts and media content with keyword tagging. Links within the blog point visitors to IndyCar.com and media content is first posted to YouTube and Flickr before being embedded into posts. This encourages everyone involved in the blog to think of digital content in a synergistic manner. The majority of all posts utilize links back to IndyCar.com, images from Flickr, video from YouTube, or external links to recommended partner sites.

Feedback from fans, via comments on the IndyCar.com blog and other social platforms, help direct the content for posts. At times, these comments can even serve as the catalyst for a more regular and in depth, blog series and allow IndyCar staff to hear instantly from fans.

Blog posts occur three to five times a week and feature a variety of voices and subjects. The success of individual posts has resulted in continued series. Through the blog, IndyCar has highlighted successes on Flickr by sharing images and analytics of our experiences on the site. User-generated content has been embraced by fans, so fans were invited to design their own IndyCars, which has been very popular. All designs become their own individual blog post. Technology, an important aspect of the IZOD IndyCar Series, has become a relevant category through the blog. Posts on technology have included IndyCar racing simulators and even a video series of how their drivers utilize technology in everyday life.

The IndyCar blog has created an ideal, informal environment where a diverse collection of stories are shared and fans can provide feedback. And like all other facets of the racing corporation, the blog directs visitors back to the main IndyCar.com site, which increases the already sizable web traffic numbers on the site.

> The IndyCar blog has created an ideal, informal environment where a diverse collection of stories are shared and fans can provide feedback.

## Making Friends: Facebook and IndyCar

Facebook supports the IndyCar new media strategy by serving multiple functions. To start, Facebook provides the opportunity to communicate information, connect with fans, and garner feedback on announcements and events—instantly. Real-time communications are a necessity in this day and age.

This deep level of fan engagement addresses both positive and negative feedback from fans in a manner that aids the overall transparency of the series, something that has been proven important again and again in each example of digital innovation leadership throughout this book. A dedicated IndyCar social media team posts content, monitors dialogue, and interacts with fans on a daily basis through Facebook. This fan engagement goes a long way in helping to shape the current online experience but will also influence future online objectives and develop better content for IndyCar.com.

The ability to embed audio, video, and photo files into Facebook posts provides the ideal platform to share content from all of IndyCar's new media and social platforms. Facebook has become a primary resource for distributing news stories, blog posts, Flickr sets, YouTube videos, livestream content, contests, and general status updates or questions for fans. IndyCar's team gets immediate feedback on that content and works diligently to capitalize on that information.

The evolving developmental API of Facebook has also allowed the IndyCar new media team to build seamless transitions between Facebook applications and, for example, promotional microsites. This solution benefits fans and IndyCar because the more tedious data capture processes inherent in such projects are no longer necessary. The result is a better experience for users and increased engagement to the benefit of IndyCar.

In the upcoming season, social gaming through partnerships with interactive media developers will play a more important role in engaging fans. The basis for this concept stems from successful fantasy racing enterprises offered for fans through IndyCar.com.

Social gaming provides the opportunity for fans to interact directly with IndyCar and immerses them in the technology, speed, and innovation synonymous with the IZOD IndyCar Series.

Facebook, arguably the most trafficked social media platform, truly supports multiple needs for the IZOD IndyCar Series while the developing platform continues to unveil even greater reasons to further engrain the platform into IndyCar's new media strategy.

## A New Community: Flickr and IndyCar

The IZOD IndyCar Series utilizes Flickr to organize and provide access to images for its fan base. Images are reduced in quality to a point that still allows fans to enjoy them, but avoids risk and concerns related to copyright or distribution licenses.

As images are uploaded to the IndyCar Flickr page, they are described, tagged, geo-tagged, and titled appropriately before being allocated into logical sets or groups based on content type. Images on Flickr are distributed via IndyCar.com, Facebook, and Twitter, and are embedded into the majority of all blog posts.

In addition to appealing to the IndyCar fan, Flickr also provides access to new online audiences that are passionate about imagery and photography. In the past year, they have reached an entirely new audience, entering the photography community by showcasing their digital assets—super-fast cars on track, the work in pit lane, driver appearances, and technological innovation.

Images are further shared through a variety of avenues, whether by embedding html codes generated automatically by Flickr or by distributing image-specific Flickr URLs. This practice focuses on creating a two-way stream of conversation between the IndyCar.com website and the IZOD IndyCar Series social platforms, including the blog.

Flickr benefits IndyCar in a variety of ways. Not only is it an outlet to share media, but it also serves as a tool to manage large amounts of content available for public consumption. Keyword tagging makes the bank of images searchable, providing easy access to the IndyCar image assets. The large volume of content also creates many opportunities for fans to help generate search-engine friendly data by uploading their own photos, creating sets, adding tags, and writing comments that become metadata for IndyCar search engine optimization.

In addition to supporting search engine optimization, user-generated content in the form of comments and tags also provides yet another touch-point to engage consumers with the IndyCar brand.

IndyCar utilizes various content themes via Flickr including racing action, major press announcements, parties, autograph appearances, and user-generated content. This approach has worked well in providing frequent updates to the feed and illustrating the diversity of the sport—there is always content and IndyCar is ready to share it with the fans.

IndyCar's approach on Flickr is similar to its blog. The racing company wants to provide behind-the-scenes access to its sport and wants to speak in an informal, familiar tone with its fans. Utilizing a variety of image content that includes race action but also shows user-generated content such as helmet designs by fans, different photographic approaches, and pre-race parties provides an authentic, personal experience with the sport in a manner that is not contrived.

Because the series has found Flickr practices to be so popular, a number of new Flickr practices are underway for the 2011 season, including leveraging the platform for contests and encouraging more user-generated content. Part of this practice will likely include the integration of a corporate partner to brand a set of unique image files that IndyCar fans upload to Flickr, tag as the IndyCar Series or sponsor with the possibility of winning exclusive Flickr prizes. The IndyCar new media team has been very happy with the Flickr experience in 2010 and wants to engage with more of the Flickr community in developing and showcasing its content.

Flickr provides a perfect stage for the IZOD IndyCar Series to share imagery that speaks directly to the race experience and accomplishes a major objective of the company's new media team: to provide a sensory experience online that will motivate a fan to attend racing events, thus generating revenue for IndyCar.

Flickr is a perfect stage for the IZOD IndyCar Series. It's probably one of the most popular fan platforms and is a great revenue generator for IndyCar.

## More Streaming: Livestream and IndyCar

When fans cannot attend racing events, IndyCar works to take the events to the fans. In Chapter 4, The Digital Video Revolution, you read a lot about the evolution of digital video. I can't stress how huge the video movement has become.

IndyCar is making the most of this massively popular medium with an agreement signed with livestream.com in 2010 to provide live video of major announcements and events. Livestream provided an additional video source that complemented IndyCar efforts on YouTube, as well as live coverage of race events on Race Control through IndyCar.com. Video delivery is an integral part of the Indy-Car digital strategy. The company will continue to utilize a traveling video production team to provide content for media, YouTube, Race Control, livestream, and archival purposes. Delivering high definition video content is another way of bringing the stories of racing alive, revealing the personalities of the drivers and showcasing the technology and innovation behind the sport.

Delivering high definition video content is another way of bringing the stories of racing alive, revealing the personalities of drivers and showcasing the technology and innovation behind the sport.

IndyCar is on the right track (no pun intended) with its live streaming video initiatives. Not only does that allow the brand to reach the audience that can't attend the event; it assures that the audience makes the appointment to attend that live web event, ensuring even greater audience participation.

In 2010, IndyCar utilized livestream.com to announce new race venues, the 2012 Chassis Announcement, new engine manufacturers, and driver signings. It was a new way for the racing company to transform the traditional press release into a live experience fans all over the world could access for free. Again this approach utilized many of the company's other online efforts—IndyCar.com, Facebook, and Twitter to promote the video stream—inviting fans to read IndyCar news at the same time as traditional media. The media team utilized livestream strategically towards the end of the year with plans to expand its video distribution and coverage significantly in the future. In 2011, IndyCar fans can expect more programming via livestream and more opportunities to view the stories and announcements coming out of the sport.

## Speed Tweeting: Twitter and IndyCar

The IZOD IndyCar Series' use of Twitter focuses on two core accounts, @INDYCARPR and @INDYCAR. Each of these accounts serves three specific audiences: IndyCar's media partners, teams, and drivers, and the general fan base.

The @INDYCARPR account has a steady flow of news items and exposure opportunities and is maintained by IndyCar public relations staff. The voice of this account focuses on the news occurring within the sport and issuing immediate news.

The @INDYCAR account provides a channel for race fans to interact with IZOD IndyCar Series digital content, events, and news stories. The primary focus of this Twitter account is sharing content from IndyCar.com. This content typically originates from the IndyCar blog, Flickr, YouTube, or Facebook accounts and is then tweeted through a social enterprise system to provide tracking and Web analytics. This approach allows IndyCar to measure analytics and report its online reach, while also monitoring fan engagement.

The release of this content is supported through retweets by a solid base of followers as well as teams, drivers, and racetracks that also participate on Twitter. Part of this support originates from the consistent participation in the Follow Friday or FF hashtag on Twitter. Follow Friday allows IndyCar to acknowledge new followers and recommend relevant Twitter accounts to current followers, building the network of engaged fans and partners. Follow Friday also provides for a subtle segue to another primary focus of the IZOD IndyCar Series' use of Twitter—corporate partner integration.

More and more, corporate partners are approaching the IZOD IndyCar Series with an interest in leveraging its Web presence. Through Twitter, this is accomplished in two ways. The first is a general awareness of a corporate partner's Twitter activity. The corporate partner is mentioned on 'Follow Friday,' in tweets regarding applicable promotional and track events, and, at the discretion of the company's new media team, promotional tweets of interest to race fans are retweeted. Secondly, IndyCar's official partners participate in various contests. These contests vary in scope and can be as simple as a trivia question where the nth-person to respond with the correct answer receives a prize package of items from the corporate partner. These contests are tweeted at specific corporate partner accounts and assist the company's corporate partners by driving follower numbers and allowing for further consumer brand engagement with a focused audience.

Twitter serves a further, pivotal opportunity for grassroots consumer survey efforts by allowing IndyCar's new media team to collect feedback directly from fans and act quickly to mitigate any potential concerns from upset fans. The IZOD IndyCar series is proactive and responsive to Twitter followers, rather than focusing on solely pushing out stories or videos, push content, the series works to engage fans and encourage pull feedback. And like many of their online efforts, it gives IndyCar an opportunity to truly connect with fans in ways they find meaningful and relevant.

Throughout *The Digital Innovation Playbook* you've seen again and again that developing meaningful connections with customers and fans is a goal anyone playing in the digital media space must attain. Genuine conversations provide the most meaningful results—information you wouldn't get any other way, loyalty, honesty, a community that will stand up for you and your brand, and more. The last thing you want to do is push a steady stream of marketing materials at your customer base. They're smart, they're savvy, and they know when the connection is a genuine one.

## Eyes on Content: YouTube and IndyCar

The IndyCar page on YouTube meets all of IndyCar.com's video hosting needs and is the single platform through which IZOD IndyCar

Series shares video content. Unique URLs generated by YouTube are shared through IndyCar's social media platforms and embedded directly into IndyCar.com to expand the reach of video as a complement to more traditional website content.

Videos typically include race highlights, exclusive driver interviews, and special announcements—all of which are available in high definition. Most of this video content is created in response to fan requests for specific footage or interest in seeing more of a certain type of video, such as driver profiles. Video content also follows editorial pieces throughout the season and reveals emerging stories throughout the season. Video also conveys the excitement and competitiveness a fan can experience by attending an IZOD Indy-Car Series event, utilizing the Web to encourage attendance at their race events.

The IndyCar page on YouTube reached the 7 million views mark in 2010 and will continue as IZOD IndyCar Series' primary video delivery focus. Video content delivered via SMS-Mobile, the Verizon Mobile application, and other outlets will play a big role in the company's new media plan.

## Verizon and the IndyCar Mobile App

In 2010, Verizon joined the IZOD IndyCar Series as a sponsor and with that came a host of new opportunities for technological innovation. Towards the end of the race season, Verizon and IndyCar launched a free mobile application for fans that included the majority of IndyCar's online digital content efforts. Built on the Android platform, Verizon users can access news, images, social media content, and videos, all related to the IndyCar experience. This opportunity will continue in 2011 with additional options with the application and an increased emphasis on bringing the race experience alive through fan technology.

## Talking Back to IndyCar.com

The strategy of the IZOD IndyCar Series will continue to utilize external online opportunities to develop engaging experiences for fans and encourage them to maintain a dialogue. The content used to feed these sites originates from IndyCar.com, but the digital assets need to reach out to other areas of the Web. Images posted to

Flickr, stories shared on Facebook, or videos uploaded to YouTube ultimately encourage fans to discover even more at IndyCar.com. It also creates new opportunities to convert a casual web user into an IndyCar fan (and repeat visitor).

The goal of hosting content at IndyCar.com and releasing content through other online outlets, such as Flickr, is to create an element of two-way communication between traditional Web traffic and online communities. In some cases, these new online communities may not consider themselves race fans. But, in the example of Flickr, IndyCar can showcase its imagery and photographic content to new users, revealing the new world and culture of IndyCar racing.

IndyCar's digital strategy will continue to leverage this back and forth approach because it allows flexibility as new online platforms emerge and the online behavior of fans continues to evolve. The company will continue to create engaging and innovative digital content to support the IndyCar experience. With that comes the responsibility of listening and responding to its online communities.

## The Ultimate Fan Experience

In anticipation of a major 2012 chassis announcement by the IZOD IndyCar Series this past summer, the online team developed a comprehensive digital strategy to engage IndyCar fans.

The date of the 2012 chassis announcement was highly anticipated by fans, the media, drivers, teams, and more. In preparation for this, the IZOD IndyCar Series reserved a 600-seat venue for the announcement. With most seats reserved for members of the media, series officials, drivers, and team officials, the online team from IndyCar turned to the blog to create a unique fan opportunity.

The blog became an invitation for fans to attend. A specific post was written asking fans why they should attend this historic announcement. Fans were competing for an opportunity to attend by revealing their favorite IndyCar stories, or why they deserved to attend as a fan. In reality, anyone that left a comment received an invitation, but it made for some compelling interaction with fans and some really powerful stories. In fact, the company received more than 100 comments on this post.

The night before the top secret announcement the online team leaked some sneak peak images through Flickr. None of the images gave away the final announcement, but they were selected to build excitement and capture fans' imaginations. These instantly became some of IndyCar's most popular images of the year.

Behind the scenes, the entire online department was working to build a new section of the IZOD IndyCar Series website focused on the 2012 chassis. In anticipation of the formal announcement, this new Web section was being constructed to go live at the flip of a switch, equipped with full descriptions of the announcement, images, video, and more.

Supporting content really came together on the day of the announcement. Video production teams grabbed interviews with team owners, drivers, and fans. IndyCar provided up-to-date information through Facebook and Twitter. Images from the day were gradually uploaded to IndyCar.com and Flickr to build on the anticipation of the event.

In addition to all these digital approaches, IndyCar also streamed video of the announcement via livestream.com, working with Livestream to publicize the event and produce the video broadcast. In addition to the 600 people in attendance, fans from all over the world were able to tune in and watch the historic moment. As people watched the live video stream, fans could also follow live tweets along with updates from a live IndyCar blog. Once the announcement was official, the online group activated the new site section and added in official imagery. It was a large-scale effort, leveraging all of the company's online outlets. Through one announcement, the IZOD IndyCar Series had utilized IndyCar.com, IndyCar blog, Facebook, Flickr, Livestream, and Twitter.

To keep content fresh between the announcement and 2012, IndyCar reached out to fans asking them for their design interpretations of the 2012 chassis. Part of the new 2012 section on IndyCar.com included downloadable graphics that could be used as design templates for any fan, anywhere. Fans could either submit hand drawn designs or more elaborate models utilizing advanced software. Again, this 2012 theme utilized many of the company's online outlets, including the design elements on IndyCar.com, the interaction and request to fans via the blog, and promotion via Facebook and Twitter.

IndyCar received designs from all over the world—North America, Asia, and Europe. Each fan that submitted a design received an individual blog post with their design and an explanation of their inspiration. Again, this was advertised through IndyCar.com and social media. In addition to this promotion, the designs were also uploaded to Flickr as a specific set.

This was an ideal project to connect with IndyCar's online audience and continue the momentum of the announcement via the web. Fans responded in a resounding way by sharing their racing memories as a way of gaining invitation to the announcement and responding to the release by submitting personal chassis designs.

## The Conclusion to the IndyCar Story: Keeping Up with IndyCar Communities

The 2011 season for IndyCar.com will consist of major web development projects, including a revamped IndyCar Nation section of IndyCar.com focused entirely on creating value and exclusive opportunities for IZOD IndyCar Series fans. In preparation for the launch of the new IndyCar Nation website, the IZOD IndyCar Series new media team has leveraged the blogging community to generate interest, embarked on a mobile site redesign, initiated improvements to the Race Control experience, and returned to its core focus of providing the content that fans ask for in addition to exclusive opportunities.

The single driving point behind the IZOD IndyCar Series web presence is to engage fans in a way that strengthens the brand and grows the series. This starts with a renewed focus on driving social media numbers in order to fully maximize the company's reach with open-wheel racing, sports and entertainment fans. While the company's current social media following is reflective of a highly engaged audience, the IZOD IndyCar Series is exploring how to integrate web development projects with social media content in order to achieve growth in both areas. Such short-term tactics will enable the Series to garner long-term interest in co-development projects and additional opportunities for corporate partnerships to deliver exclusive content and event opportunities to fans.

The single driving point behind the IZOD IndyCar Series web presence is to engage fans in a way that strengthens the brand and grows the series.

In many ways, 2011 will focus on the themes of speed, technology, diversity, greening initiatives, and innovation, propelling the Series into 2012. This follows on the heels of the 2012 chassis announcement, the integration of several new corporate partners to the series, and efforts in the 2010 off-season to distinguish the series from a spec series, including the welcoming of Chevrolet and Lotus as new engine suppliers and the continued involvement of IndyCar's current engine supplier, Honda.

Location-based initiatives, though not developed enough for the IZOD IndyCar Series to include at the date of this publication, will play an increasingly important role in connecting both corporate and supporting partners and the IZOD IndyCar Series with consumers. The Series is committed to evolving its web platforms along with changes in consumer preferences in order to maximize value for IndyCar's sponsors, teams, drivers, the Series, and fans.

The integration of corporate partners into the overall web media strategy will continue to focus on adding value for fans, rather than detracting from the IndyCar experience. Leveraging corporate partnerships enables the IZOD IndyCar Series to provide premium content, including mobile and social gaming applications, as well as exclusive opportunities and giveaways.

IndyCar.com and social platforms allow the IZOD IndyCar Series to participate in the discussion and serve as a reliable, go-to content provider for open-wheel racing fans. As the series evolves and Web media advance, the IZOD IndyCar Series will continue to respond to input from teams, drivers, tracks, and most importantly, the fans.

The opportunity for users themselves to generate content has been extremely popular and provides IndyCar fans with a creative outlet as well as an opportunity for discussion. Each user-generated design receives comments and discussion from other fans. This has kept the 2012 announcement a constant piece of news for the company and afforded its fan base an opportunity to be a part of this process. Importantly, it has also provided IndyCar.com with quality, authentic, fan-based digital content.

As IndyCar carves out its identity online, the Series will continue to experiment with new web applications, focus on the quality of content being provided to the web audience, and continue driving the online dialogue with the online community. The IndyCar brand is fast, exciting, thrilling, and ever-changing, attributes that need to be replicated online.

## Maximizing Innovation Potential

We've looked at several Innovation Superstars who have transitioned into the digital and new media world, combining their already innovative cultures with the new technology and platforms that are still growing and evolving as we speak.

Now we'll take the knowledge gained from these case studies and delve into several innovation concepts and programs that can further maximize your company's potential. Let's talk direct digital marketing and the RealOpen innovation strategy.

---

### Chapter Takeaways

- Focus on the story, not the technology. Allow the stories from your company or brand to determine the technology platform.
- Your .com site should integrate all of your other online efforts, including any blogs, Facebook or Twitter accounts. In turn, these outlets should point back to your website.
- Use emerging online platforms to showcase content to new audiences. New audiences are potential new fans or customers.
- Be open, be transparent, and listen to what your online community is saying.

---

*The Digital Innovation Playbook* is a living book. We are constantly updating the book online so you can watch uploaded videos, read the latest best practice on digital media, and even participate in free ongoing webinars.

To access this chapter's updated web page, please go to www.digitalinnovationplaybook.com/Chapter8.html or scan the QR code with your mobile device

# 9

# Digital Direct

## INNOVATION COMMERCIALIZATION THROUGH DIGITAL DIRECT MARKETING

As I have mentioned throughout *The Digital Innovation Playbook*, innovation has gone digital. I believe the term "digital innovation" will soon become as common as the term "open innovation" has been over the past decade. You can probably describe innovation in its totality of having three phases:

1. Listening to your customers, the market, and technology trends.
2. Creating or developing.
3. Commercializing with layered customer value (this is where digital direct marketing comes into play).

Innovation, product, and service marketing are now a digital phenomenon. One of the world's experts in the area of direct marketing is Ken Robbins, CEO of Response Mine (www.responsemine.com). In this chapter, through Ken's expertise, we look at how conventional direct marketing has now become digital direct.

## Direct Response Marketing: Advertising's Measurable Cousin

Over the last 40 years a scientific form of marketing, direct response marketing or DR, has grown to consume more than half of all U.S. advertising dollars. This alternative to more traditional brand advertising uses rational arguments to elicit real-time responses from the consumer. DR's objective is simple: increase sales and profits by maximizing marketing return on investment, rather than by maximizing general audience awareness.

How does DR maximize ROI? It tests different ads and media placements against one another, measures the results, then funds the winners and cuts the losers, thereby eliminating inefficiencies and only spending on the ads that have been proven to sell the most.

It started with a guy named Lester Wunderman. As an advertising copywriter in the 1960s, Lester would write ads with different headlines and benefits, and then measure which one sold the most. He developed some basic techniques we use today, techniques like benefit-oriented headlines, calls to action, and offers. By measuring which combinations of copy and creativity sold more, he could tell when he had a winner and then increase the advertising department's profits over time.

Wunderman's simple idea quickly took root in the marketing industry. By the late 1970s and early 1980s, product pitchmen like Ron Popeil and marketers like Peter Bieler had begun to apply the direct response-marketing concept to TV—and the infomercial was born. Using DR advertising, Popeil sold millions of Chop-o-Matics and Pocket Fishermen, and Peter Bieler introduced the world to the ThighMaster.

The dawn of the Internet ushered in a new era of direct marketing. By combining the time-tested techniques of DR marketing with the speed and measurability of the Web, innovative companies can drastically increase their returns on marketing investment. In this chapter I show you how to use digital DR techniques to improve your own marketing ROI, get more customers, and increase profits.

## DR to Branding: "We've Got Creative Differences"

Unlike branding, DR has certain fixed components. Before we get to digital direct response marketing and how it's applied on the Internet, the first step is understanding the four elements that form the basis of any good direct response marketing ad, regardless of its medium. These elements are *Benefits*, *Offers*, *Risk Reduction*, and *Call to Action*. They are the foundation of DR marketing—get to know them! Once you familiarize yourself with them, you'll begin to spot DR ads everywhere you look—in your inbox, on TV, on billboards, on the radio, on Google, in magazines—the list goes on.

**G**et to know the four elements that form the basis of any good direct response marketing ad: *Benefits, Offers, Risk Reduction,* and *Call to Action.*

## Benefits

In a Lexus ad for the new two-seater LFA, a hushed voice speaks about "the pursuit of perfection," and "the pursuit of the impossible," while the viewer watches a champagne glass being shattered by the reverberations generated from the car's engine revving. The voice doesn't ask you to buy the car, nor does it give you any specific reason to. The main purpose of the ad is to generate strong unaided recall. Lexus wants to create a connection between the product and the concept of luxury, deep within the subconscious. If someone off the street is asked to name a luxury car brand at random and they automatically think of Lexus, then Lexus has accomplished its goal to generate strong, unaided recall. They have successfully designed an ad to bolster the Lexus brand.

A good direct response ad, on the other hand, is much more straightforward. It lists the benefits of the item or service for sale and asks the consumer to respond. If my company is using a DRM ad to sell a wheelchair, rather than saying you're going to look sexy in this wheelchair, and surrounding it with strobe lights and glitter, a DRM ad is going to talk about specific features. It might say, for example, that the large wheel size means that less upper body strength is required for smooth movement, and the seat is made of memory foam, increasing comfortable seating for long periods. DRM is about making a hard-hitting, rational argument for the purchase of a product or service.

## Offers

In DRM, an offer is a form of bribe. There are many different ways to bribe a customer, but the most common and the most effective is a bribe to act within a certain deadline. You've seen them: "If you act before the end of the month, we'll give you 20 percent off any purchase over 100 dollars."

## Risk Reduction

Customers who buy from a DRM ad typically don't have the luxury of trying out the product before they get it, as they might in a retail store. DRM ads make up for this by offering some form of risk reduction. Free shipping, free return shipping of unwanted products, and a complimentary gift upon purchase are all common forms of risk reduction.

## Call to Action

A call to action is a request that the consumer respond to the ad immediately. The request can appear anywhere in the ad, and it is usually just a few words: "call now," "click here," "visit our store," "redeem your coupon," and so on. This request is really the core of any DRM ad. If the customer immediately acts in some form—whether by picking up the phone, clicking on the link, or running to the store—then the ad is a success.

# The Internet and Digital DRM: Your Media Roadmap

Companies ask themselves the question: Should we be using the Internet for marketing? Here's the problem with that question: The Internet isn't just one form of media. Marketing on the Internet is fractionalized into dozens of different categories, and each category has its own set of vendors. Buying a search engine ad from Google or Yahoo! or Bing is different from buying a banner ad on ESPN Zone or an ad on Facebook. To top it all off, the Internet is constantly changing. Social media didn't even exist 10 years ago, and now there are more than 3.5 billion pieces of content shared on Facebook alone each week.

To understand how digital DRM can be useful to your company, you'll need a basic understanding of some of the more common types of media currently being used and when to use then.

## E-Mail

Direct marketing e-mail is the more efficient, easier to measure, digital cousin of direct marketing mail. You might know direct marketing e-mail as spam, but it's also one of the most powerful DR tools if used properly.

There are really two kinds of e-mail used in DRM: database marketing and prospecting. E-mail database marketing is when companies send out an e-mail to a list of names it has generated on its own. Say a company offers white paper downloads off its website. Every time someone downloads a white paper, the company adds that person's e-mail to a list. The company develops a database of everyone who has requested a download. Next month, the company sends an e-mail out to that list telling them about the most recent white paper available for download.

Then there is what's called out-bound e-mail prospecting. That's when a company uses e-mail lists generated by third-party organizations. For example, a retail store might want to send out an e-mail to a list generated by the National Federation of Retailers.

### Paid and Organic Search Engine Marketing

Paid search ads are ads that pop up when you type certain keywords into a search engine. They're called sponsored listings, and Google charges on a cost-per-click basis. Every time a customer clicks on the ad, Google charges a fixed fee.

Organic search engine marketing isn't a type of media per se; it's a way of making your company's website show up at the top of a search. How high up a website appears on a list of website results from a web engine search is determined by how each site matches the criteria of the particular search engine's algorithm. Each search engine looks for certain syntax and HTML formatting and certain amounts of links going back to the page. My company runs a website, lawncare.net, designed to generate leads for a client in the lawn care industry. Right now, if you type in "lawn care" on Google, it's the first site that pops up. We didn't have that kind of visibility until we had a horticulturist rewrite the copy to include more industry specific terminology.

### Auction Marketing

Really, auction marketing boils down to companies using eBay. That's right—eBay. It's more than just an Internet yard sale where teens sell old Beanie Babies. Companies often use auction marketing to introduce new products to the market and liquidate excess products from old lines or models. Lots of companies that sell various parts, such as kitchen product companies, sell on eBay. In classic DRM style, in order to maximize price, companies often use one-day, three-day, and buy-it-now auctions.

## Banner Ads, Behavioral Targeting, and Cookies

Banner ads are one of the original, most varied forms of digital DRM. They range from a tiny $60 \times 60$ pixel ad—which might look like a button to click in the corner of a webpage—to quarter-page, half-page and full-page takeovers. The most common type of banner ad is the $240 \times 60$ rectangular one, usually displayed at the top of a webpage. Banner ads can be bought on a cost-per-impression basis (CPM), where the buyer pays every time the webpage with the ad is viewed, or a cost-per-click basis (CPC) where the buyer pays every time the ad is clicked on.

In the 1990s, banner ads were basically useless. Broadband connection was not accessible to the general public, so companies couldn't deliver anything more than a couple of images in rotation. A banner ad might get millions and millions of impressions, but people would pretty much tune it out.

By the early 2000s, the addition of broadband connections allowed Web surfers to view more complex and attention-grabbing banner ads. Thus, a new way of applying banner advertising that emphasized behavior targeting was invented.

There are two types of behavioral targeting: individual and groups. First, let's talk retargeting. Say you're surfing Delta Airlines' website—not looking to make a purchase, just clicking through. The website will upload a tiny file of code, called a *cookie*, onto your computer's browser, which essentially tracks your surfing activity. While you are surfing its site, Delta records that you visit its page for round-trip flights to Aruba. Three days later you are on the Internet again, this time on American Express's website, which is a close affiliate of Delta. While you continue to surf this site, it just so happens that you see a banner ad for "Aruba Getaways." That's no coincidence. Delta placed that banner ad for you to see on purpose.

American Express is retargeting you based upon your previous Web activity. The banner ad may even include an offer: "We've got a new Aruba getaway special: $199 airfare. But it won't last forever. . . ." And on top of that, it may offer you free upgrades if you fly on Delta because Delta is trying to fill seats.

Behavioral targeting can also work by targeting websites that have some relation to the product you are selling. For example, if a company is selling Adidas Shoes, it might place a banner ad on *Runner's World* magazine's website. Instead of targeting individuals, this method targets groups.

## Affiliate Marketing

Affiliate marketing is an affordable way to get ads on thousands of websites. There are two main affiliate networks: Linkshare and Commission Junction. These networks have about 10,000 and 300,000 partner sites, respectively. Companies can buy a placement with one of the networks, which will place their banner ad on every partner site. These ads are paid for on a commission basis, meaning the company only pays the networks if their product sells as a result of the ad. Depending on the conversion rate, it can be much more cost-effective than CPC, which requires companies to pay every time a link is clicked, regardless of whether the consumer makes a purchase.

## Directories

Most directories have gone online, and there are a host of new directories found exclusively on the web. They tend to be much more comprehensive than the yellow pages. For a price, companies can purchase more prominent listings, which often resemble classified ads.

## Mobile

From a marketing perspective, it makes sense to treat the iPhone and other smart phones as a pocket computer. Ads designed for mobile phones have to be smaller to account for smaller screen size, and they are often rapid fire. People tend to be moving fast when they are on their phones. They're not as likely to click through a series of ads to get to your product. There are also advertising opportunities through the thousands of applications available to users. But what makes mobile marketing really unique is the ability to incorporate GPS. There's a magical world of targeting related to local business that's created around the built-in GPS devices that are included on many mobile phones. For example, a marketing company can tell if the user is dining at a fancy restaurant in Atlanta and target him or her accordingly. It can offer a coupon for Screaming Eagle Cabernet, which might be on the wine list of that restaurant. It goes to show that with every advance in technology lies a new opportunity to improve the efficiency of DRM.

### Social Media

I was speaking at a marketing event in February 2009, and somebody asked me if I thought Twitter was going to become a competitor to Google. I thought, no way. Now I tweet 140 times a week and I have 4,000 followers.

Social media is the intersection of public relations, customer service, and branding. But what makes it great for DRM is how easy it is to measure an audience's response. If I put out tweets that are expertise-oriented, do I get more sales, followers, and re-tweets than if I put out tweets that are offer oriented? Dell sold a million dollars of product in one month using Twitter alone by putting offers out on the social site. Travelzoo is another company that releases offers on all kinds of airline fares using Twitter, and it's seen great results.

All these networks—Facebook, MySpace, LinkedIn, Twitter—are growing exponentially. The more people who join, the more useful the tool becomes, and the more popular it gets. Social media seems to be the next new thing, but I'm sure it won't be the last.

> All these networks—Facebook, MySpace, LinkedIn, Twitter—are growing exponentially. The more people who join, the more useful the tool becomes, and the more popular it gets. Social media seems to be the next new thing, but I'm sure it won't be the last.

## Using the Internet to Improve Allocation of Marketing Dollars

Direct marketing always starts with a financial goal, which is calculated as return on investment. The beauty of direct response marketing on the Internet is it becomes so much easier to predict the return on investment, and in turn decide how to better allocate marketing dollars.

Just like in the world of continuity sales, companies using direct response marketing decide upon customer acquisition price goals—the amount of money allocated to an individual customer—based on the calculated lifetime value of that customer. If a company expects a customer to generate $1,000 a year at a 5 percent discount each subsequent year, that customer is worth $3,700. The bottom line is, some customers are more valuable than others, and as such warrant more advertising dollars.

The Home Shopping Network can give a good estimate of the expected lifetime value of a midwestern male who purchased a piece of exercise equipment at 4 A.M. versus a northeastern female who purchased her first piece of makeup during the middle of the day. Even though the price of the makeup was only $50 and the exercise equipment cost several hundred dollars, the female has a higher expected lifetime value. The calculation to determine that comparison is complex, but essentially it resides in the fact that the female, given the time of day and the type of purchase, was more likely to make repeat purchases, whereas the Shopping Network found that 40 percent of the time, the man would return the exercise equipment, and was overall less likely to make a repeat purchase. Based on calculations of how much revenue it can expect from a certain customer demographic, the company decides how much to spend on ads for that target demographic.

### The Process

The Internet has made the DRM processes of hypothesizing, testing, measuring, and reacting more efficient. In particular, it has increased the amount of variables it's possible to measure and made it easier for companies to see how they need to modify the content of their ads.

What really separates DRM from more traditional forms of advertising, and what makes it that much more powerful, is its process, which it borrows from the scientific method. DRM starts with a hypothesis, which is then tested and measured. Based on the outcome of those results, you can choose to modify the hypothesis. If so, the creative content of the ads being tested is modified to match the new hypothesis, and testing begins again. The idea is to constantly improve marketing ROI by responding to consumer behavior, rather than, for example, just making an ad for TV, airing it, and hoping it works. Because of the process, it's okay if the first series of ads isn't as effective as hoped, because, as we discovered earlier, they can be changed or reformatted at very little cost.

### Hypothesizing

Coming up with a hypothesis boils down to deciding what is going to be tested. In DRM, almost anything can be tested—text, colors, images, videos, font, sound. Unlike general advertising, where companies conduct customer surveys prior to launching an ad campaign, the preliminary stages of launching a direct response marketing campaign are driven primarily by imagination, curiosity, and intuition. In the hypothesis phase of DRM we ask ourselves, "I wonder, if I run this ad at lunchtime will my outcome be better? I wonder, if I run 10 ads in this online newspaper. . . . I wonder, if I make the background of this banner blue instead of green or yellow. . . ." Anything is game.

In my experience, good hypotheses usually come from a thorough knowledge of the customer base. Once the results from the first series of hypotheses start coming back, a new hypothesis can then be created based on those results, and the process becomes more scientific and mathematical. However, it's often in the first stage of brainstorming where the most creative thinking happens.

> **G**ood hypotheses usually come from a thorough knowledge of the customer base.

## Online Testing the Quick and Easy Way

Offline, testing is cumbersome and time consuming. Online, it's quick and easy, so you can do a lot more of it. The more tests a company conducts, the better its chances of identifying weaknesses and strengths in its campaign, addressing them, and thus increasing its ROI.

If a company decides during the hypothesizing phase that it wants to test two different headings on the envelope of a direct mail piece—snail mail, that is—it's got to pay to print multiple copies of two different envelopes. If it wants to test four different headlines, printing costs double; six, they triple—you get the picture. The more the company wants to test, the more expensive the testing becomes.

Once the mail goes out, it takes at least a few weeks for the results to come back in. For any envelope that wasn't opened there's a host of possible explanations: It got put in a big pile and thrown out accidentally; it was dropped on the way to the house; or it was intentionally thrown away. It's also impossible to tell who actually opened the envelope, if they read it, or what parts they read. The only way to know for sure is if they make a purchase. With each one of these situations the company sending the mail is left guessing. The process is slow at best, and at worst, useless and costly.

On the web it's totally different. A company can send an e-mail to 10,000 recipients in an instant. Then the company can easily measure how many people clicked on subject line A versus subject line B to open it, whether they called the 800 number listed in the e-mail or filled out the online form or anything else that might help to refine the format of the e-mail.

Speed combined with low production costs means companies can test more variables at once: images, videos, text, colors, and any combination of these. Companies don't have to set up different screens and pantones in order to make changes and try out different variables; they can just have their Web designer click a button and switch the background from red to green. It's testing made easy.

### A/B Testing

There are two main types of testing. The first is called A/B testing. An A/B test is as simple as it gets. It's when a company tests two variations of the same ad or content against one another. For example, a company might set up two different landing pages to its website. The pages would be identical except for one variable. Let's say one landing page has a blue background and the other has a red background. The company is trying to figure out which color background delivers more responses from the consumer. The company puts the blue landing page up for one week to test what kind of response the website gets. The next week, the company puts up the red background and measures its traffic, clicks, call-ins—whatever factors are being measured—to determine if there's an increase or decrease from the measurement of the original blue background. The goal is to isolate one variable and test only that. If there is more than one variation between the two landing pages and one gets better results than the other, it's impossible to tell which variables account for the variation in results. If the blue background wins, then it can go up against green next.

### Multivariate Testing

The only problem with A/B testing is that sometimes variables work together. When companies test multiple variables working in different combinations it's called multivariate testing. Let's stick with the landing page example for now.

The truth is the background of a landing page is seen in relation to the color of the text and vice versa. White on black looks much different from green on black, and so it can be assumed that it will have a different impact on consumers. In fact, certain combinations are more than the sum of their parts—just because people like red print and green background doesn't mean they'll like red on green. In fact, that particular combination creates a shimmering effect called a duotone that makes it almost impossible to read, especially for seniors.

In multivariate testing a company will test 10 different headlines, in 10 different colors, against 10 different backgrounds. That's 1,000 variations. Add a few more variables and the number skyrockets. The catch is, companies need a lot of traffic in order to get a big enough sample size to get reliable measurements for each of the variations. If only 1,000 people visit the website, that means the company will only get one reaction to each variation, and you need a lot more than that to come to any kind of conclusion. Multivariate testing often needs hundreds of thousands or even millions of visitors each week before it delivers conclusive results. Smaller companies are better off sticking to A/B testing.

## Ad Measurement: How You Know You're Winning

Measuring is the heart and soul of DRM. If you can't measure and react to your test results, your marketing ROI will never improve, or worse, it may even decrease.

The Internet has made measuring a much deeper and more complex process than just recording when a consumer opens an envelope and makes a purchase. When used properly, the Internet has also made measuring more powerful and useful than ever before.

In digital DRM, there is a whole chain of events that precedes a purchase and each step prior can be recorded and measured. For example, the consumer opens an e-mail, which is measured as an open rate; views your ad, which is measured as an impression; clicks on it, which is recorded by the website as a click; surfs the webpage, which is monitored with cookies; fills out a form; and makes a purchase. The point of collecting all this data is to determine what the response rate is each step along the way; how many marketing dollars are spent on each customer at each step; and how that cost can be decreased by spreading them over more customers.

In order to measure all this data at my company, I allocate tasks to teams of employees. One team is responsible for measuring e-mail response rates, another for landing pages, and another for media. We all assemble our data and reconvene with the objective of trying to figure out which responses from the customer translate into the most sales. So, let's break down the different ways of measuring.

### Response Rates

Response rate is the general term used to describe the variety of different types of responses DRM tries to measure. In the real world, measuring response rates means measuring how many people called the number in the infomercial or how many people mailed in the order form from the catalog. We already know that, on the Internet, it means measuring all of the steps a consumer takes before making the purchase—mostly which links and ads he or she clicks on.

Here's an example of how to calculate a response rate: If 100 people view a banner ad and five people click on it, then that is a 5 percent response rate. The idea is to constantly increase response rates. Response rates can be broken down into different categories, which are described below.

### Open Rates, Click-Through Rates

Open rates are used for measuring consumers' responses to direct e-mails. Open rates measure the percentage of people who opened an e-mail they were sent. Click-through rates (CTRs) measure the percentage of people who clicked on a link contained in a DRM ad. The link could be in an e-mail, it could be a banner ad, a paid search ad, or anything that led to more DRM content.

CTRs are very easy to measure and the results are fairly easy to read. They're anonymous, so you're not learning any information about the person beyond the fact that he or she clicked. Often A/B tests measure CTRs. Say there are two paid search ads for similar services that use different text. One says, "Click here for freelance copywriting," and another says, "Click here if you're looking for a ghostwriter." And say there were 1,000 searches for each ad and the former got a 10 percent CTR and the latter got a 15 percent CTR. It's pretty obvious that the latter is a more efficient marketing expenditure. In DRM we often look at efficiency in terms of cost-per-click [CPC].

## CPC

Cost-per-click boils down to some simple arithmetic: It's the amount of money spent on an ad divided by the amount of clicks the ad gets. More specifically, if a company pays X for one ad and Y for another ad, and ad X gets 100 click throughs and ad Y gets 50, then X's CPC is $X/100$ and Y's is $50/Y$, so X has half the CPC as Y. In other words, X gives you more bang for your buck, so you cut Y and buy more of X.

You can make the same calculation for e-mail open rates or any other response rate. CPC is the bread and butter of applied testing in digital DRM.

As a side note, branding makes a similar measurement, but uses the metric of cost-per-impression (CPM) instead of CPC, which entails dividing the price of the ad by the number of views (more specifically, impressions). It makes sense with a TV commercial, but not so much with a banner ad. Just because a person views the webpage that contains a banner ad, doesn't means he or she notices the ad. It could be at the bottom of the page so the person had to scroll down; or it might be hidden in a corner. DRM is all about measuring responses, and there's no way to tell if a person responded in any real way to an ad unless they interact by clicking on a link, dialing a number, or watching a video.

The main difference in measuring between branding and DRM is that DRM can react immediately to new information in a variety of ways—increasing funding for certain ads, cutting funding for others, changing the content of ads, creating more variations of ads. In fact, one of the main problems that CEOs and CMOs run into with DRM is that they get so caught up with measuring and organizing data, they forget to react to it. It's important to always stay *focused* on reaching a real financial goal. Ask yourself, what can I do right now to improve my ROI?

## The Internet Makes Creative Fast and Easy

What's great about creativity in the digital realm is that companies aren't dealing with physical pieces of marketing material. Everything is cheaper, faster, and less work intensive to make, modify, and send. These qualities are particularly valuable when a company is testing thousands of different ads against one another.

In the world of branding, companies produce one set of creative assets, which replicate and play off each other. In the world of direct marketing, companies often produce radically different types of creative assets, which compete against one another rather than working in concert. The goal is to find a winner and cut the rest.

Often, finding the winner requires producing tons of creative content. Fortunately, on the Internet the cost of production is so low that there is virtually no limit to the amount of content a company can produce. You can get a video online for a few thousand dollars, whereas it costs hundreds of thousands to produce a video for TV. Alternatively, a company can just take some of the B role from an existing commercial shoot, splice it up, and put it on the web.

The cost of creating a banner ad with a few images is dust, and so is the cost of creating 90 characters of text for paid search ads, which make up two-thirds of all digital DRM advertising budgets.

The key to being creative is choosing the right format for the job. There are so many different formats and any of those formats can be combined. You need to figure out what combinations work in what contexts.

### Creative Isn't Flat

This brings us to the next point. Creativity in digital DRM isn't flat. There is an interactive, three-dimensional element to it. If someone is browsing their mobile phone, you don't want to shove a 30-second video down their throat or they'll click away. Instead, you want to give them the *option* to click on a banner ad, which leads them to video content, which in turn may lead to a page where they can purchase a product. The Internet allows you to not only target audiences based on their basic interests, but also to deliver certain content to them depending on their moment-to-moment interest level. It allows consumers to decide how much information they want or don't want, while simultaneously reinforcing their interest level at each step along the way until they finally click "Buy now."

Because it moves so quickly and has so many options, digital DRM can get overwhelming. That's why it requires more interdepartmental communication. Marketing, creative, and IT departments have to work together so that when that Mentos ad video goes viral, the servers can handle all the influx of traffic.

A more complicated example would be if a marketing company was going to issue a coupon to consumers offering 25 percent off a certain product. Then the company must tell the merchants to expect increased demand, and warn IT to expect more traffic to certain pages of the company's website, and then tell creative to make sure the landing page is ready to sell the product at the discount.

There are also issues of privacy on the web. If a company is doing health care marketing online, any health forms that people fill out are subject to the Health Insurance Portability and Accountability Act (HIPAA), and it requires a lot of work from IT to make sure that private information is visible only to certain people. The same issues apply to using information obtained from children online. If a firm is marketing for Toys "R" Us or Pottery Barn Kids, it has to be careful not to solicit or make visible certain types of information. Of all the pitfalls of digital DRM, this is the one to really watch out for.

## Media Optimization: More Bang for Your Buck

Good media optimization means getting the most out of your media marketing dollars. On the Internet, media placement is infinitely easier to regulate. Say a clothing store wants to run a Black Friday promotion for a line of dresses selling at a 70 percent discount, which they want to show to the public at 5 A.M. Friday morning. The company loads the ad content into its Google account, and coordinates with its vendors to turn the ad on at 5 A.M. Until 5 A.M., at any time, the buyer can postpone the ad, change the content, or even pull the ad completely.

Say that same company runs the same ad in the classified section of a newspaper. Usually the ad has to go out a few weeks in advance of the printing day. During that time, it's highly possible that the dresses will all be sold, and the newspaper ad will drop after there is none left. Then all the store will have bought is a bunch of customers who feel lied to and disappointed.

The ability to regulate when an ad runs, when it stops, and to change its content at a moment's notice is crucial to successful DRM, because so much of it depends on adapting content based on consumer responses. With offline DRM, it can take a week or more to change the content of an ad. With digital DRM, it can take minutes.

Another way the Internet helps companies optimize their media spending is by making it easier to scale up advertising. At any moment a company can go from sending 1,000 e-mails to sending 10,000 with barely any increase in overhead, because duplicating and even revising digital content is free. At its most expensive, digital DRM is much, much cheaper than offline advertising. With digital DRM, companies don't need to take time and money to print more materials and they don't need to drastically increase the size of their staff, even if they want to drastically increase the amount of material they are distributing. It's often simply a matter of using a larger list serve, or paying a vendor for more paid search exposure.

## Engagement Optimization: Keeping Up with Your Customers

Engagement optimization is actually a term I use to describe the art—or science, if you prefer—of interacting with customers. If a company has an e-mail list of 300,000 people who made a purchase off its website, should the company e-mail them all once a month or every two weeks? Should the company wait for the person to make a repeat purchase before it e-mails them? Should it send different e-mails to repeat customers?

Ideally, the company should send individualized e-mails to each of those customers based on their individual levels of interest. Let's say a customer named John buys a riding lawn mower off the website of a lawn care company. That company should send an e-mail saying something like, "Hello John, we see that you purchased a riding lawn mower last week from our store. We wondered if you were interested in purchasing some garden bulbs." Alternatively, the company could send John a coupon for a free set of replacement blades for the exact model number of his mower. It's easy to find software that will automate these individualized responses so a person doesn't have to type 300,000 e-mails.

Let's say a customer makes a large purchase from a company's website, but then shows no more interest in the company for three months. Because of this the company makes a follow-up call. This gives them a chance to find out if there were customer service issues, or issues with the product that the call could address to prevent more customers from experiencing the same problem. Making the follow-up call also gives the company a chance to win back that customer.

Here's another example of engagement optimization. Say a customer is buying camping gear for his family. He fills his shopping cart and is about to make the purchase when his phone rings, and he forgets to click "Buy." The next day when he goes back to the site, he finds that the page recognizes him and his shopping cart is still full of the items he planned on purchasing.

Think of it like this—engagement optimization is a form of digital customer service. It helps customers feel comfortable and familiar in a context that can easily feel disconnected and cold.

## Five Advanced Digital Media Tactics to Get Even More Customers

By now you should have a pretty comprehensive understanding of how DR works and the ways in which it can impact any marketing campaign. However, there is even more to it than that. There are cutting edge techniques that companies are using right now to win more customers, make more sales, and increase profits. These techniques are the shape of things to come in digital DRM.

### Click to Call

This is when someone clicks on a link, which automatically dials a phone number, either by syncing up with a mobile phone device or a software telephone service like Skype. It's a way of skipping all of the intermediary steps and going right to the action. The customer doesn't have to write a number down on the napkin or remember it, all he or she has to do is click to be connected directly with the vendor. It's great for selling items that require contact in order to complete a purchase, like certain airline tickets or hotel room purchases. It gets customers in touch with live customer service representatives.

### Modeled Chat

This is another great way to boost customer service. Some websites have the option to open up a chat box at any time and chat with an online representative. The problem is that if a site gets 50,000 hits a day, chatting with customers takes up all of the call center's resources. Modeled chat allows companies to offer customers the ability to chat only after they have demonstrated a high level of interest by spending a certain amount of time on the website or going to certain sections of the website. That ability to use resources only on customers who are likely to buy is what helps modeled chat dramatically increase ROI. It's a great way to convert customers on the brink of making a purchase before they leave the website. Often it's enough to push them over the edge and commit to the purchase. At the same time, it means not wasting valuable human and financial resources on customers who don't display a promising level of interest.

### Exit Pop-Ups

Pop-ups are another great way to grab customers before they leave a site. As they click out, a pop-up widow is displayed with a customized offer, based on what the customer was looking at while on the site. My firm used this technique with a florist and it ended up increasing his revenues by $1 million, about a 30 percent increase in profits.

### Co-Registration

Co-registration is when different companies, usually with similar services or products, share customers and information. After a customer fills out an online form for one company's product or service, the page will ask whether the user is interested in the other company's product or service. It's a great way for new companies to build lists and customer bases.

## *Klout*

Klout is a company with an extremely powerful and somewhat frightening idea. It assigns individuals a rating from one to 100 based on their social media following. It adds up an individual's Facebook and MySpace Friends, Twitter Followers, Blog Subscribers, and so on, and then plugs the figures into a formula. The higher a person's "clout," the more valuable he or she is from a marketing point of view. If an individual with a Klout score of 90 comes into your hotel, do whatever it takes—free room service or complimentary breakfast—to make sure he or she has a remarkable time. The hope, and likelihood, being that the person will in return post, tweet, or blog about his or her excellent experience and you'll win more customers and make more sales.

## What Now?

Now that you've glimpsed the vast array of possibilities in digital DRM, you might be asking yourself, what's next? How do I begin to apply this knowledge to my own company?

It's a good question, and the answer is you probably need a collaborator—a company or a consultant—who can help your company implement the science of digital DRM. You want your collaborator to be a digital DRM expert, but also to be curious and engaged in trying to understand *your* industry, *your* company, and *your* business philosophy. The relationship should be mutually educational, which is why it's important to arm yourself with as much information as possible going in.

For more information about the power of digital direct marketing, contact Ken Robbins at www.responsemine.com. Also check out www.webbnewmedia.com.

## Turning to Innovation Strategy

Now that you have an excellent handle on direct marketing, it's time to look at a great program that will maximize your innovation strategies. RealOpen is a system I created that allows companies to take their digital initiatives, their direct marketing programs, and using a customized system, automate some of the processes in order to make the most of the resources you have. Let's take the next step.

## Chapter Takeaways

- There are four elements of Direct Response Marketing (DRM) that can help you recognize it when you see it; these are Benefits, Offers, Risk Reduction, and Call to Action.
- DRM lists the benefits of the item or service for sale and asks the consumer to respond. DRM is about making a hard-hitting, rational argument for the purchase of a product or service.
- In DRM, an offer is a form of bribe. There are many different ways to bribe a customer, but the most common and the most effective is a bribe to act within a certain deadline.
- DRM ads make up for the fact that customers can't touch and feel the product when buying online or over the phone by offering some form of risk reduction. Free shipping, free return shipping of unwanted products, and a complimentary gift upon purchase are all common forms of risk reduction.
- There are really two kinds of e-mail used in DRM: database marketing and prospecting. E-mail database marketing is when companies send out an e-mail to a list of names it has generated on its own. Then there is what's called out-bound e-mail prospecting. That's when a company uses e-mail lists generated by third-party organizations.
- Affiliate marketing is an affordable way to get ads on thousands of websites. There are two main affiliate networks: Linkshare and Commission Junction, with each network having about 10,000 and 300,000 partner sites respectively.
- Five advanced digital media tactics that will get you more customers include click to call, modeled chat, exit pop-ups, co-registration, and clout.

 *The Digital Innovation Playbook* is a living book. We are constantly updating the book online so you can watch uploaded videos, read the latest best practice on digital media, and even participate in free ongoing webinars.

To access this chapter's updated web page, please go to www.digitalinnovationplaybook.com/Chapter9.html or scan the QR code with your mobile device.

# 10

# RealOpen Innovation

## DEVELOPING A FRAMEWORK TO MANAGE THE FLOW OF IDEAS AND TECHNOLOGIES

In *The Innovation Playbook* I devoted a chapter to the RealOpen system, a framework used to manage a company's flow of ideas and technologies. The same rules apply for *The Digital Innovation Playbook* and the need for a system able to manage innovative ideas arriving through digital channels might just be even greater. The key word in both books is *innovation* and as you read on, please keep in mind that whether you're already a highly functional, digitally connected company or you're a beginner in the new media world, you must first have the innovative, customer-centric foundation to be successful in anything you do. This is one system that optimizes the abilities of that foundation. So you'll find a mix of new media-specific information in this chapter along with the RealOpen system details that focus on a broader innovation theme. (You can see our logo in Figure 2.2.)

There are more than 170 different so-called innovation management systems—at least that I've found. The reality is, of course, most of these systems have two very basic problems. First, they're actually risk management, rather than innovation management systems, and as mentioned repeatedly so far, focusing on risk leads to failure. Next, most of these so-called systems use a cookie-cutter approach that almost always results in more failure.

Now it's time to examine just what I believe—and what I use—as a process in the real world to make innovation work. I must warn you now: If you were expecting a detailed step-by-step, fill-in-the-blank recipe, you'll be disappointed. Why? Because different processes work for different organizations, industries, and technologies. There is no grapefruit diet panacea solution that manages innovation. One size does not fit all.

And this should come as no surprise. As you could see in each of the case studies listed in this book so far—Southwest Airlines, NewTek, the U.S. Army, Spigit, Kodak, and IndyCar—despite some similar cultural values, customer needs and expectations can vary greatly depending on the products and services an organization generates.

Because of these differing needs, I developed a framework called RealOpen, which contains conceptual steps within which your organization can develop the specific processes and measures to succeed. I call it a "prescription" framework because it's like a doctor prescribing specific prescriptions to individual patients. The framework provides the diagnostic chart; the doctor applies it to the particular patient. I'll come back to this in a moment.

As the name implies, RealOpen is a holistic innovation framework and toolbox with a strong "open innovation" component. Why? Because in today's digital world, it is essential to utilize all sources of ideas and technologies, inside and outside, to meet the fast changing needs of the marketplace. We've discussed repeatedly the ways in which the Internet and social media have jump started communication methods to hyperspeed. Opinions, suggestions, comments, and everything in between are out there in droves, but to manage those ideas and innovations waiting to happen, companies *must* have some sort of system. So RealOpen starts with and manages open, external, and internal ideas, all with similar effect.

> In today's digital world, it is essential to utilize all sources of ideas and technologies, inside and outside, to meet the fast changing needs of the marketplace.

RealOpen is the perfect example of how you can computerize innovation. As discussed in Chapter 2, The Digital Sandbox, with the Spigit examples, a system like RealOpen allows both outside and inside innovators to easily submit innovations. The digital toggle approach allows innovations to be filtered in real time. This takes a major burden off both your fuzzy front end (FFE) and your new product development functions (NPD). Digital media provide a tremendous opportunity for us to gain large quantities of new innovations and directly filter them in real time against our innovation platform.

The digital world is evolving rapidly. The only way businesses can compete is to be *fast*. We need to play, listen, invent, and deploy. And I repeat: Focusing on risk is a recipe for failure. Remember the lessons from the IndyCar drivers. You end up where you focus, and keep your eyes where you want to go in order to get there. RealOpen combines all of these concepts in a system that is fast, efficient, and allows for rapid deployment on innovations that have already been filtered for a company's individual needs.

Remember: *Innovation is the process of delivering exceptional value through active listening*. RealOpen allows organizations to automate the process of listening. Moreover, it allows you to directly connect your listening to your innovation platform in order to deliver meaningful net customer value.

## A Prescription, Not a Diet

One of the things I believe in deeply is what I call a prescribed, or customized, approach to innovation management. No two organizations are alike; there are too many complex variables including technology, market environment, and organizational culture, not to mention the overall goals of the company itself. In fact, several organizations I work with have the goal of developing a range of technologies that would quickly position the company for increased likelihood of a strategic acquisition. Other companies are publicly traded companies that have a completely different goal in terms of their long-range planning.

So the first problem with most so-called innovation management systems is that they are designed with a one-size-fits-all mentality. And, as mentioned, they are almost all risk management systems disguised as innovation management systems. But what makes them even worse is that most of these systems create additional layers or barriers between you and your valued customers.

## Open Innovation

Open innovation is a catchy and oft-used phrase we've previously discussed in this book. In most cases it's a complete failure. Not because it isn't a fantastic idea; it's all about deployment. Remember: Culture is the collective focus of every member of your organizational team. When you have an organization that has a closed culture that's compartmentalized, it's virtually impossible to deploy internal or external open innovation initiatives.

But for those who do it correctly, open innovation is brilliant. The movement towards open innovation has helped a lot of companies.

A while back I posted some information about open innovation on several social networking sites and was surprised to see the wide variations of opinion on its benefits and usefulness. The people who sell open innovation solutions and services are, not surprisingly, widely in favor of it, whereas some organizations that have grown weary of the latest grapefruit, liquid, or cookie diet seem to yawn when you mention the name.

As I said, I think there is a real benefit to open innovation. But if your organization doesn't truly have the infrastructure to manage it—think Southwest Airlines—it's going to fail. The good news is digital innovation can allow some of the most bureaucratic companies to finally connect to their customer communities.

## What Is the RealOpen Innovation Framework?

Let's get down to the nitty-gritty of the RealOpen system. RealOpen is designed to do three things: Speed the process, provide results, and build profit. The system accomplishes these things by creating an external innovation sourcing function that is manageable, which includes a filtration process to quickly decide which innovations should be acted upon.

According to recent studies, the overwhelming majority of innovation gatekeepers are not open to external innovation. This is slowly changing, but one of the main reasons for this lack of openness is the fact that most organizations have 30 percent more technologies in their portfolio than they have resources to act upon. Companies just don't have the manpower for the huge influx of innovations they could experience in the right conditions. This is where systems like RealOpen are so huge.

Open innovation can be distracting and can bring with it a high resource "burn rate." Burn rate in innovation consumes fuel. It consumes people, time, and organizational bandwidth. But in this day and age, speed rules the day. So how do you reconcile the lack of resources with the need for speed? If you can speed products forward, speed them through what I call the Forget and the Forging stages in RealOpen, you'll have the ability to build bandwidth without increasing cost.

The system that we developed and have recommended to our clients is really not a system at all, at least not in the traditional sense. It's a toolbox—a toolbox full of tools that can be configured for any corporation or any industry of any size. It can also be configured to accommodate your current stage of corporate evolution. If you were to look at RealOpen, and compare it to the PC disc operating system (DOS) of the early 1980s or to the Windows or Macintosh graphic user interface, it's obvious that straightforward, clear, easy-to-understand systems, although more complicated in background, are far simpler to the user and have a higher adoption rate and, ultimately, a higher success rate.

The RealOpen system is like a graphic user interface. It is a fluid, nonlinear, and nonlegalistic system that makes it easy for companies to configure systems to help them find, filter, evaluate, and ultimately commercialize world-class innovations.

Everyone operates their system, and their web technology, differently, and they use different tools based on the specific needs of their business and their organization. I wouldn't expect a computer, iPad, cell phone, or other tablet user to be bound by a specific sequence of actions, such as being allowed to first check only e-mail before turning on the browser, and finally being allowed access to apps or other software items. RealOpen is no different.

In the process of researching Innovation Superstars, I was surprised to see many of them used systems similar to our RealOpen system. Without exception all of our Innovation Superstars used innovation management in a fluid and flexible manner, often with systems varying from department to department. Systems had one purpose and one purpose only—to speed great products to market.

The core concept of RealOpen is simple. First, with RealOpen, you pre-filter your innovations, the idea being to get highly vetted technologies that exactly meet your developmental platform (I'll explain this term later). Second, it is designed to move projects quickly, without spending too much time or resources on evaluating the innovations.

The term RealOpen really defines three different deliverables. First, as already described, it is a framework within which a specific process can be designed. Second, it is also a framework for innovation management training. More recently, it has also become a software tool used to manage the innovation process.

RealOpen includes fast-track methodologies to quickly move innovations forward, or to forget them if they don't belong in your building. It allows you to develop the discipline needed to create comprehensive product innovation platforms that assure you're developing technologies that make sense for your business and for the target customers of your business.

At this point, a picture may be worth a thousand words. See Figure 10.1.

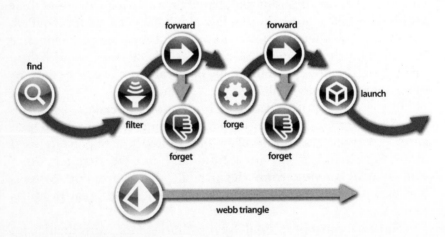

Figure 10.1    RealOpen Flow Image

The term RealOpen defines three different deliverables:

- A framework within which a specific process can be designed.
- A framework for innovation management training.
- A software tool used to manage the innovation process.

As you can see from Figure 10.1, RealOpen is a multi-step framework that moves you from idea stage (whether generated internally or externally) through to the launch phase for a product. As we will learn below, the Find and Filter stages—the gateways into the rest of the RealOpen process—are really the keys to making RealOpen work, and there are many tools in the RealOpen toolbox to help these two stages along. Find is a carefully orchestrated step that enables you to create the right ideas internally and source them externally, while the Filter step makes sure only the right ideas advance to the more expensive and in-depth Forge stage, and eventually to launch. Along the way, the transitional Forward and Forget steps help move the right innovations forward while getting rid of the failed ones with minimal pain and risk.

## What Is an Innovation Platform?

An innovation platform defines your product and customer vision precisely enough to use as a filtration model and focal point for incoming ideas and technologies. I've often said, if innovation is the answer, then what is the question? In this case, it's the innovation platform.

An innovation platform is like a conventional marketer's product platform, except it has current and future products in mind. The following Peter Drucker-styled questions help frame an innovation platform.

- What is our business?
- Who are our customers?
- What does our customer value?

When we're looking at these questions from the digital and new media standpoint, they still apply, but the social web presence adds new dimensions. Finding these answers, clearly defining your company's purpose must be done before any digital outreach takes place. As mentioned throughout the book, a bad culture is simply multiplied through the web—not fixed. The question "who are our customers" becomes a bit trickier when you look at new media. In the old days, this might have been a narrower profile, but the social web broadens your customer base simply because you now reach a much larger audience. You still need to know who you're aiming for, but remember, your customer communications are now influenced by digital multipliers that can seem almost limitless. And value? As mentioned over and over in this book, you must add value at every layer of the business, from pre-touch to in-touch.

It's surprising to see so many organizations that are failing to do innovation simply because they have not defined what success looks like for their business. This may sound simplistic, but the overwhelming majority of organizations that are using innovation management systems are evaluating technologies and ideas only against risk. This is simply a matter of playing the game not to lose rather than playing the game to win. At the risk of sounding overly philosophical, most organizations failure reference rather than opportunity reference. In other words, they evaluate technologies based on their likelihood of failing. That's a really bad idea; and it's used by most companies. My prescription for innovation success is to first identify what success looks like by creating a comprehensive innovation platform. Then filter innovations against your success platform based on the opportunity to deliver exceptional levels of customer value. Clearly that is a very different philosophy from the bureaucratic and legalistic approaches toward innovation today, but one that I can assure you will work every time.

> **M**y prescription for innovation success is to first identify what success looks like by creating a comprehensive innovation platform. Then filter innovations against your success platform based on the opportunity to deliver exceptional levels of customer value.

### *How Do We Create Value for Those Customers?*

With a proper innovation platform you can create filters to apply to ideas and technologies. Those filters use what we call toggles. As the name implies, toggles are a go/no-go switch that determines whether a technology should move forward. The toggles can be applied not only to internal innovations but also to external ideas. I explain further with an example shortly.

Innovation platforms not only keep your innovation efforts focused on the right products, they are also designed to simultaneously promote speed—a fast, fluid, smart system that is driven by time. They also take a lot of risk and wasted effort out of the initial stages of the innovation process. Innovation platforms help RealOpen move an idea from Find to Filter. If the filtering indicates a product meets your platform, the product or idea moves Forward. Then it gets Forged to the point of validation, then it goes Forward again. This process may repeat itself many, many times before it gets to Launch. Now, finally, it's time to examine RealOpen step by step.

## The Seven Ways to Find New Technologies and Ideas for Your Business

The first item out of the toolbox is *Find*. The idea of Find, or Fast Find, is easy to understand, easy to use, and implements tools that can be deployed in different ways by different companies. The main point is, in order for you to succeed, you must access technologies. You access technologies from two sources: the outside world, and inside your corporate walls, and both can be accessed digitally through a variety of mediums mentioned throughout the book—from Facebook to online communities to blogging sites. There are, all told, seven ways to find new technologies and ideas for your business.

1. External innovation portals. External innovation portals are tools that allow outside contributors—innovators or customers—to submit or push their ideas to your organization. Typically they contain some filtering mechanisms to capture only the most valuable ideas.
2. Internal innovation portals. Internal portals are like external portals except that they are for employees and others inside the walls of your organization.

3. **Captive R&D.** This is the traditional source for ideas and technologies—your own internal R&D or product development department.
4. **"Project Xs"** are simulations in the form of ersatz competitors. By creating competitive companies and observing what they would do to compete with your business, you can learn more about what you should do yourself.
5. **Frontline innovation** initiatives are campaigns that allow frontline employees—those with the most direct customer touch—to submit their ideas, from their experiences or customer knowledge, into the innovation process.
6. **Innovation Safaris.** As introduced in Chapters 6 and 7, these are team voyages into the customer world usually done by product development and higher level management personnel, in order to observe customer behavior, learn needs, and eventually develop ways to address those needs through ideation sessions.
7. **Micro-crowdsourcing** campaigns are usually done in conjunction with external innovation portals, but they are specific idea-generating campaigns done with carefully selected micro-crowds, or segments, of the external idea and technology-providing world.

All of the tools within our Find suite are designed to help you find products, both internally and externally. Figure 10.2 illustrates the components of the Find stage.

### External Innovation Portals

Closed organizations have become extremely averse to external innovation, and have developed a variety of ways to punish anyone who would like to submit an innovation to them. Great companies like Procter & Gamble have developed online submission portals that include explanatory videos that make it easy for anyone to submit an idea or technology to them. Online submission portals are a great way not only to get ideas, but also they are a great way to open up your organization to the outside world and do some "carpet time" with your customers—to learn what they're thinking and what they want.

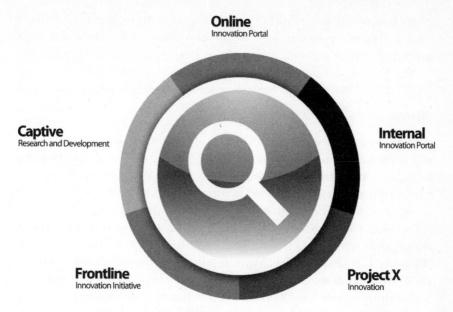

**Figure 10.2    Components of the *Find* Stage**

These are portals created specifically for submissions, but don't forget, as highlighted by Kodak and several other Innovation Superstars, conversations about your brand, including innovative new ideas for products or services, are constantly going on throughout the Web. Listening tools are out there that can help you track that information and join in the discussion.

To keep up with the available ideas and technologies of the outside world, you need to be marketing the planet looking for new innovations, but in order to manage the input of those ideas, you have to automate the process of submission. Online innovation portals are a great way to identify ideas and innovations, from within and from outside the organization, using tools like those mentioned in the Spigit chapter.

If you set up an online portal that allows an outside innovator, or entrepreneur, or customer, or field representative, or anybody to submit an idea, you can filter that idea by having the person answer the 10 to 30 toggle questions that are part of the Filter process step I describe further below. Ninety percent of those innovations will not qualify. But your product development and innovation folks have never had to talk to anybody, thus wasting resources, and you've never had to expose yourself to a third-party disclosure for intellectual property. That's powerful, because it builds speed and significantly increases your access in real time to external innovation.

### Internal Innovation Portals

You can use the same format internally, allowing anybody from service technicians to customer service representatives to engineering or marketing personnel to submit an idea. Any person in your organization can easily submit an innovation. And by the way, if the innovation isn't accepted, you're still giving the potential innovators something to do. Externally, you're giving them a shopping list of things that need to be done, and sometimes the resources to help do them. It is also helpful to give feedback to the outsiders, even in a standard form letter, advising them of status and why or why not their technology was or wasn't accepted. The principles of good customer relationship management apply here, too.

### Captive R&D on the Fast Track

There isn't much to say here about your R&D group, which probably already has its idea generation processes. The key is to make them observant, that is, in tune and in touch with customer and organizational needs, and fast—able to interact and respond to the outside and customer world quickly and effectively. R&D needs to be hooked into the other resources in the Find wheel. The new product development or R&D function should be able to fast-track methodologies with the right facilitation. Bureaucracy must be replaced with speed and results. We recommend a wide variety of fast-track methodologies to put speed in the driver's seat. Often established corporations will tend to roll to a stop in terms of managing speed in the innovation management process. Fast-tracking does not adversely affect quality, safety or market success; it simply collapses timelines in order to actually increase the likelihood of market success.

### Project Xs

I also like Project Xs. Project Xs involve taking an external team and creating a competitive technology to the technologies already in your product offering. We've been involved in five or six of these, and I don't believe I've been involved in one that didn't provide substantial new revenue with minimal investment.

You have two options when using the Project X tool. First, you can use it as an internal tool where you formulate a team inside your organization that has been put together with the express purpose of competing with your company.

The idea of being your own competitor may sound unusual. But because you know your technologies and your capabilities, your strengths and your weaknesses, you get a unique perspective that allows you to develop competitive products and solutions for your own business. As a result of this new vantage point, you see your weaknesses, or threats, more clearly. This then leads to the creation of new products, services, and technologies.

The second Project X option is to hire companies like ours, and we become the competitor. We design and develop a range of technologies and solutions to specifically compete against you. You can look at those solutions to see where potential threats come from—or you may, as has often been the case, adopt one of the competing technologies or solutions developed to compete against you.

In many ways, this is nothing but a change in vantage point, but it's one that works very well. I have watched amazing things happen both with internal and external Project Xs. In fact, a final footnote is in order. Probably the hardest part of the process for most organizations to deal with is the fact that you'll be exposing your own weaknesses. It is a true form of self-assessment and self-analysis, sort of an equivalent of an individual's self-help book, for a company. But I believe such self-assessment is not only necessary but can produce very positive unintended consequences.

### Frontline Innovation Initiatives

Another tool is what I call the Frontline Innovation Initiative. This means training your sales reps and marketing and customer service people to become active observers. Remember that active observation is the genesis of all innovation. I always say the greatest innovators of all time were not trained in innovation, nor were they particularly good at innovating—they were good at observing the opportunity to innovate. Then, they got help with the innovation (including even Edison)—and that's how it got done. Frontline innovation initiatives are critical in today's fast-moving markets and shortened product life cycles.

This translates well to your online communications teams, those listening to the ongoing conversations out there, such as at Kodak and Southwest Airlines. And, as we talked about in Chapter 2, not only do we need to listen or observe, there needs to be an action plan in place to take those observations to the action step.

### "I'm an Observer"—Innovation Safaris

In my last book and this one, I've repeatedly mentioned one of my favorite observation tools, the Innovation Safari. Innovation Safaris are an amazing way to connect to—or get reconnected to—your customers. It's really simple; the safaris are just a matter of venturing out from behind the desk and into the world where you can see who is using your product or service and how it's being used. You then take that information and layer on the value. Too many companies make the mistake of staying indoors. Now this still applies to the digital world, even if that means sitting at a desk. The safaris are simply on the digital highway rather than the physical one. As we've discussed throughout the book, those conversations are out there whether you hear them or not. Innovation Safaris will get you out there among the customers, the competition, and the ideas and solutions that could move you up to the next level.

Use Innovation Safaris as a way to identify what is important to your customers through active observation.

Active observation is an important point, and I'd like to examine it further. I have found that active observation is one of the true secrets to innovation superstardom. Haven't you noticed that people who pay attention to how they impact the lives of others tend to have a more peaceful, successful existence? The same is true for companies. Companies simply need to have the ability to pay attention to how their policies, procedures, methods, packaging, pricing, delivery, and everything else affect their customer. Because there are so many dimensions of interaction between a company, its products, and the customer, active observation is required. When people ask me how I've become such a successful inventor, my answer is, "Very simple. I'm not an inventor. I'm an observer."

The same is true for all great inventors. The ability to live consciously is a fundamentally important characteristic of the life of every individual. But it should be—and it needs to be—a matter of systematic deployment within corporations. It must become not only a habit, but part of the organizational culture.

And the open nature of the evolving social web makes huge amounts of information more accessible than ever before.

**Active Observation with the Innovation Safari Tool**    How do you become an active observer? Again, it gets back to the Innovation Safari tool. Great organizations like John Deere will go out into the field and spend months living with their customers. They observe the impact of fuel costs and the efficiency of being able to plant, manage, and harvest crops. They will look at every single ergonomic issue. Literally, everything that affects that customer is observed, not through some focus group member with a clipboard, but by living with the customer and plowing the fields together and observing—first hand—how to add meaningful net customer value through their observations.

Now in a more controlled way, we have had clients do one-day Innovation Safaris. Really, they work quite well. We had the privilege of working with a great medical company, but we were discouraged to find their engineering department had spent virtually no time in the operating room. So we set up three different Innovation Safaris in two hospitals and one ambulatory surgical center. Immediately after the safari, we facilitated an ideation session. That session resulted in a multimillion-dollar technology that wouldn't have been on the R&D radar screen had we not spent time in the field discovering where the problems, needs, and opportunities were within their market space.

Every company in every business in every space is different, so we begin each Innovation Safari with a meeting prior to the safari to make sure we've identified the best range of customers and to make sure about what kinds of systems and measurement tools we need to take into the field with us to gather as much information in as short a period of time as possible.

Innovation Safaris work with mathematical certainty. They're inexpensive to do, and they score points with customers, who typically like to be listened to and brought into the development process. Yet, most companies haven't made them part of a regular business practice, especially for the people who have the greatest decision making authority. I believe every organization should use the Innovation

Safari throughout the enterprise, even to discover the needs of internal customers.

We have also used Innovation Safaris in customer service to help companies learn opportunities to provide exceptional value in service.

### Micro-Crowdsourcing

One of the biggest problems with crowdsourcing is that the crowd is very, very big. As a result of that, the crowd typically isn't "vertical" enough to solve a problem; it is hard to get to the depth necessary with any part of the crowd at any one time. Yet, you're exposing your question to a very large audience.

We recommend the use of what we call micro-crowds. Using techniques that only attract relevant crowds will give the greatest likelihood of providing great solutions.

In our program we put a lot of work into developing innovation platforms. Maybe not in the old product platform sense—real platforms are highly customer connected, so that we know what our wish list looks like. By developing those platforms and comparing them to our business value and our net customer value, we're able to filter those innovations quickly, so they don't sit in the building for long periods of time and consume fuel.

This is critical: With innovations, you must learn to dump them quickly if they don't fit—"bail, don't fail" or "fail early," as I always say. That's critical to building speed and the bandwidth to focus on the right innovations.

## Creating a Filter with Customers in Mind

Innovation platforms are one of the key components of what I call the *Filter* step. Most organizations have filtration systems that identify whether an idea or project is likely to provide a profitable return on investment. Most of the filtering systems are really centered on the business-case analysis of an emerging technology. In fact, 90 percent or more of new product development systems are designed to build business cases around innovations.

For most people, that makes perfect sense. I, however, humbly disagree. When you develop filtration systems just to define the business

**Figure 10.3   The *Filter***

case around an innovation, somehow—in most cases, anyway—
you've left out the customer as the principal driver. Several amazing technologies would have never made it to market if you had used
the standard business-case analysis.

I believe an organization can get on the right track by having
the discipline to create a comprehensive innovation platform, and
that the innovation platform is what drives their product or technology platform. Many companies feel they actually have that through
their planning process. But do they really? Usually they have comprehensive business planning instruments or new product planning
instruments that are so complex and/or large that very few people
even know what's contained in the documents.

We believe it is important to develop a platform that says: "We're
in the X business, and we provide Y value to Z customers." That is
the basis of your filtration system (see Figure 10.3).

### Filter, Don't Evaluate

It's important to realize that, in our system, we separate filtration
from evaluation. We believe strong, well-thought-out filtration significantly reduces the burden on R&D organizations to evaluate or even
develop products or technologies that never should have entered the
new product development process in the first place.

This is important enough to restate: We believe that your focus
should be 80 percent on filtration and 20 percent on evaluation. Most
organizations have it backwards: They spend 80 percent of their time
evaluating and 20 percent filtering, which, at the very least, leads

to a lot of wasted time, and at most, to poor decisions and bad products, especially if the filtering process I just described doesn't happen at all.

The reason so many organizations focus on evaluation over filtration is that it requires a great deal of discipline—the discipline of customer focus, the discipline of innovating to customer needs, the discipline to say "no" in a way that removes risk from the idea creators. The result is a haphazard approach of dealing with what comes in the door. The wrong things get early focus and attention, and many of these things ultimately get tossed out later in the development process, if not by the marketplace.

I believe that an idea or technology should be thoroughly vetted—at a high level—before any team or resources are used in its evaluation. Filtration is best developed through the creation of what I call toggles. Toggles are the questions that go into the 20 or 30 key components of success, or at least the relevancy of an idea of technology submitted to, or within, your organization.

### Toggles

Toggles are gate-keeping questions designed to vet the external source and filter out innovations (or innovators) that don't fit. To create toggles, you first need to come up with a broad and deep understanding of what you want from your outside contributors; then you want a sequence of questions and filters that get you and the inventor to that want list. The thought process might look something like this.

Suppose we have a small medical start-up company looking to build its ophthalmic surgical adjunct business. They want to create an automated innovation portal to go out and aggressively look for new technologies. But because they're small, they have limited resources to evaluate those technologies. So, in this kind of case, you would sit and ask yourself, "What regulatory class am I looking for? Is it an FDA Class I? A Class II? Or a Class III?" Since it's a surgical adjunct company, they may be looking at innovations that are only Class I or a Class II. What about stage of development? Again, in this case, they may only want products that are in a mature stage of development. What about patents? Are they really looking for concepts? Products that are patent pending? Or products that have issued patents? The list goes on.

When we build an innovation portal for a client, we have anywhere between 15 and 30 simple questions a submitter can answer; the list does two very magical things. First, it provides a quick,
comfortable environment for the inventor to submit an innovation,
and—most important—without disclosing any intellectual property.
You don't have to worry about nondisclosure agreements, nor spending hours on the phone with someone who could be a crazy inventor
or a general malcontent. You simply send people to a site that honors
them and gives them an easy way to submit their idea.

Now suppose you're the ophthalmic company and someone
comes in and presses the "Class I" button. They're okay. Suppose they press the button for Stage of Development and they're
okay. Intellectual property status—they're okay, on and on down
the list.

If they hit the "go/no-go" buttons and they all say "go," then
the product or enhancement has already been pre-filtered for
you. So the innovations that come through this firewall are innovations that specifically connect or dovetail into your innovation
platform.

For the ones who do not go through, a mail-merge response
comes back: "Thank you for your submission. There were four areas
that don't meet our requirements; however, we appreciate your submission and would like to give you this gift of an educational CD, or
a Starbucks card, or something else as consideration." This message
is to give you the reputation of treating innovators well. When an
innovator honors you with a submission, you should give him or her
something in return.

Great companies develop a reputation for true and genuine
openness, and the beautiful part of automated innovation portals
is that they do not require you to spend time on the phone. Your
inventors are pre-building and pre-vetting the technology, and you
don't have to worry about the legal issues associated with intellectual
property disclosure.

A focus on filtration, rather than evaluation, significantly increases your access to world technologies. It significantly reduces,
if not eliminates, the cost of evaluating technologies that are fuzzy or
simply not relevant.

The best way to look at filtration over evaluation is automation. If
you've been hand-manufacturing a product for years, and suddenly
you get a large sales increase opportunity, you would have to look at

vertical integration and maybe even robotics. Unfortunately, it is a time-consuming process to go from a hand-operated factory to one that is highly automated, but that's what has to happen to modern organizations that want access to the next generation of technologies. You have to scale up in terms of volume.

What most organizations ultimately do, unfortunately, is push good innovations away because they don't have the time and bandwidth to evaluate them. What I'm saying is simply this—don't evaluate them, filter them—but look at more innovations, not fewer.

## Fast but Smart

Speed is an extremely important point. In fact it might be one of the most important in both *The Innovation Playbook* and *The Digital Innovation Playbook*. In order to keep up with your current market, with its short product life cycles and rapidly emerging technologies, you must look at a lot more.

The following paragraph and list of questions provides an example of a generic medical innovation portal submission questionnaire. These questions should be used to gather the type of information you need to pre-vet your submissions. The questionnaire should read something like this:

> Our goal is to connect with the world's best innovators to develop strategic partnerships to deliver world-class medical innovations. Therefore we have provided an online innovation submission portal that allows you to easily submit your innovation without disclosing the details of your idea. This process actually pre-screens innovations to verify that they comply with our innovation platform. Once you've submitted your innovation you will receive an instant response indicating that we either have no interest or would like additional information. This approach eliminates the runaround many companies put inventors through. In order to provide additional value to our external inventors, we also have a free e-book called "successfully commercializing your medical idea," which gives you valuable step-by-step information you can use to take your product to market in the event that it doesn't meet our current needs. You can also sign up for our monthly online newsletter that provides ongoing tips and market trends. On behalf of the entire XYZ medical team, we

sincerely appreciate that you are considering us as your marketing partner.

1. Type of Device. XYZ medical is currently looking for class I exempt, class I and class II medical devices. Is your product a class I, or class II device? Yes or No
2. Stage of development. XYZ medical is looking for products that have proven feasibility and functionality. We are currently not accepting concepts or unproven technologies. Have you verified the product's feasibility and functionality? Yes or No
3. Patent status. XYZ medical only accepts products that have a provisional or utility patent pending or issued that has been prepared by a licensed patent attorney or agent. Do you have a pending patent? Yes or No
4. Did you conduct a formal novelty search and/or market clearance search through a licensed patent attorney or patent agent? Yes or No
5. Are you a physician or health care practitioner? Yes or No
6. Have you conducted market and competitive research? Yes or No
7. Has the product been the subject of a white paper or other published article? Yes or No
8. What is the current stage of the technology?
   a. Concept validated
   b. Concept prototype ready for production
   c. Production currently in the market
9. Is the product a single use sterile disposable or is it reusable?
   a. Single use
   b. Reusable
10. Do you have revenue projections for the subject technology? Yes or No
11. Do you have a cost of goods sold of the subject technology? Yes or No
12. Does the product have a reimbursement (CPT) code? If so what is the number?

The list can and usually does go on, to perhaps 20 or 30 questions, with different technologies to make certain you're still in the game. But most organizations systematically push away inventors and entrepreneurs because they don't have the resources to evaluate the technology. Again, that's why we choose the Pareto principle of 80 percent filtration, 20 percent evaluation.

Build great filters, and you will have access to the best technologies on the planet. It's almost a self-fulfilling promise—if you're able to use and accept more ideas and technologies, you'll get more of them, and ultimately, more of them will make it through your filters and stick.

## Forward, Forge, Forget: Fast-Track Methodologies

Another set of tools we use that falls under the heading "fast-track methodologies" is a set of transitional tools we call *Forward* or *Forget*. Most people and most organizations allow ideas or technologies to stay in the building way too long. The bad and ironic thing is they allow both great ideas and bad ideas to stay in the building too long. As I said before, there's nothing wrong with failing, just fail early, or as I call it, bail early. So when you realize an innovation isn't working, bail and *Forget*, part three of my trio of F-words. (These are good F-words, not bad!)

You must decide—early on—does the idea match our product platform, or not? If it doesn't, get it the heck out of there, because the technologies and ideas waiting in your building for some sort of action are consuming fuel. So the point is—when they don't fit, *Forget* fast.

The flip side of the *Forget* tool is the *Forward* tool, and this ties back into the speed mantra I've been repeating. Once an idea or technology is vetted and accepted, and goes through the initial stages of development successfully, it must be put on into the *Forward* stage and given a detailed timeline. The reason for doing this is to keep it moving, and again, to avoid unnecessary consumption of organizational fuel—let alone, a delayed introduction into the market.

Filtration can be done almost completely automatically once you develop your business values, your customer net value, and your innovation platform. What happens after the filtration step? The answer is simple: move forward *fast*.

### Fast-Forward

Moving forward fast means taking a look at your risks and your rewards and assessing whether the innovation and its technology meet your business model and your business values. Make certain it delivers exceptional value to your customers—keep in mind ways to layer on that value at every contact point—and that you have all the requirements we've discussed earlier, including commitment, sponsorship, and support in the organization.

Once you do, get it to market as fast as possible and ahead of the competition (you should be in good position to do this if your boxes are checked). Speed rules the day. *Fast-Forward* should be part of every single thing you do in your business.

If you don't move forward fast, the resulting lethargy becomes a self-fulfilling ticket for failure. I was involved with a $400 million company that was an expert at going over and over an idea forever, and it seemed their strategy was to think about the technology until it finally became irrelevant. Why? Because at that point they had mitigated the risk that the technology would fail. In other words—try nothing; fail nothing. In this world of digital and new media, a slow pace means being left behind.

### Forge

Once you move your technology forward, it's time to *Forge*. *Forge* is the investigation and decision about product or technology feasibility—that is, "Can we make it?" or "Can we do it?" "Can we do it profitably?" *Forge* can happen in a variety of stages depending on the product, service, or type of technology.

We can go from *Forward* to *Forge* to *Forget* at any stage of the process. In fact, at all stages, there is an exit ramp for projects or ideas that don't make sense. As individuals and organizations, we need to be free to exit when necessary, and to cut the "fibers of emotional connection" to an idea. No matter who or what department is involved, we must feel comfortable forgetting technology that doesn't make sense. See Figure 10.4.

Don't spend years trying to develop elaborate spreadsheets based on data points that are wild guesses. As I discuss later, you should keep it to four testable scenarios maximum. At the *Forge* stage we set out not only to establish the manufacturability and deliverability of the product, but also the saleability and protect-ability of the product or idea. As the innovation enters the *Forge* stage, groups adjacent to the main development team should begin to forge the sales

**Figure 10.4    The *Forge* Stage**

conduit and the intellectual property protection necessary to bring it to market.

- Can the product be delivered to customers with the exceptional value we think it should have?
- Can we gain from protecting the innovation to create a monopoly and/or licensing revenue streams down the road?

### The Webb Triangle

As you enter into the *Forge* phase, now you actually start the process of evaluation. However, you do start that process with the idea that you're going to create this product or technology.

This brings us back to a tool called the Webb Triangle. The Webb Triangle is another one of those simple, yet powerful, tools that focuses and drives agile decision making about an idea, a technology, or an innovation in a nonlinear, not risk-centered way. I've invented dozens of products with a tremendously high success rate, and for the past 20 years, I've used this simple formula (see Figure 10.5).

**The Top of the Triangle: Need**    At the top of the triangle is the need, problem, or opportunity, and it asks a few important questions:

- Is there a need?
- Is the need widely recognized?
- Is the need large enough to constitute a viable market for a business?

**Figure 10.5   The Webb Triangle**
*Source:* © Lassen Scientific, Inc. 2010. All rights reserved.

Or . . .

- Is there a problem?
- Is the problem widely recognized?
- Is the problem fix large enough to constitute a viable market for a business?

And lastly . . .

- Is there an opportunity?
- Is the opportunity widely recognized?
- Is the opportunity large enough to constitute a viable market for a business?

In addition, lots of other questions can be addressed at this stage. For instance,

- Can we take an existing technology and possibly cross-pollinate it into another market segment?

- Can other existing technologies perhaps connect to some of our other products and services?

**The Left-Hand Corner: Build**    The build set of drivers can be found at the lower left-hand corner of the Webb Triangle. Perpetual-motion-fueled machines would be a tremendous breakthrough and energy saver; the problem is you can't make one. You can't make one because perpetual motion defies the laws of physics.

In the build section, you ask yourself if you can actually deliver on the need, problem, or opportunity.

- Can you create, obtain, or manufacture the subject product or technology?
- Can you do it in such a way as to be profitable and in line with the needs and value implied by the top tiers of the net customer value strata (see Chapter 2: The Digital Sandbox)?

**The Lower Right: Sell**    Now we move into the lower right-hand corner, the sell corner, which looks ahead to such questions as:

- Is there a market?
- What is the market?
- How do you define it?
- How do you position the product?
- How do you promote it?
- How do you sell it?
- What are all of the environmental factors that will determine the success of the innovation?

Now, for many, this model is oversimplistic. But since we know our product platform extremely well, and we've already prefiltered the idea or technology, we know that we can move it forward through more simple, nonlinear evaluation tools.

**The Center: Net Customer Value**    There's one final, important note. In the center of the Webb Triangle is the customer. This is where we ask ourselves the final and most important question: Can we provide net customer value? If the innovation meets the requirements, and can be manufactured and marketed with reasonable effort and cost, it forges ahead. You continue the process to get information with which to design and validate the product.

## Value Layerization

Also, during the *Forge* process, don't assume that the product is fixed in concrete at that point. You should always look for ways to improve the innovation, even at this stage. The new ideas and refinements that can come forward at this stage always amaze me. It also amazes me how many businesses fail because they develop a technology that was "not done cooking," that is, they locked into a specific delivery and failed to evolve it during or after the initial *Forge* stage.

I believe a final stage of *Value Layerization* should be hard-wired into your innovation process. Of course, you should make sure the innovation met the original design requirements, but you should also look for ways the innovation can deliver additional value prior to its launch—for instance, product or product line extensions, new channels, licensing to other companies, or altogether new uses.

One way many companies do this is to use Project X teams to look at internal innovations as a competitor to see what they would do better before a new product or technology is launched.

## Packaging for Launch

Another tool we talk about is what we call Packaging for Launch. So many—too many—technologies are launched prior to being finished. Once again, the Apple Newton—from a company proud of its innovations overall—is a great example. They identified a great need. They found some real problems to solve. Without question, they identified there was a market composed of people looking for a personal digital assistant. The problem was they weren't able to create a technology on the build side that met the needs of the hungry market at a reasonable cost. As a result, the technology failed.

So in this last packaging stage, you need to determine that the product has totally met its design requirement, not just in terms of functionality, but more important, in terms of its ability to deliver net customer value at a high level. Is the product exceptional or close to it?

Now at this point, the product may need additional layers of innovation. We may need to add additional functions in terms of value to really make it—and us—a superstar. That's what this phase of the developmental process allows us to do.

## RealOpen and the Four-in-One Garlic Press

I would like to tell you more about how I used the RealOpen innovation management system in my own business. In addition to being a management consultant working for some of the best corporations and universities in the world, I also own several businesses. A few years back I started a gourmet kitchen gadget company. I started it because I wanted to combine my expertise in handheld surgical ergonomics with my love for gourmet food.

The company I started is called Van Vacter. Van Vacter was named after my grandfather, a Dutch immigrant. The idea was to create unique and special tools that allowed for improved ergonomics and to provide better ways to achieve food preparation.

In the process of developing the company, the first thing we had to do was follow the RealOpen system and create an innovation platform. Before you can begin to innovate, you have to know what it is you want to invent. So we began by looking at the market and the competitive environment, and we settled on a platform in the general area we wanted to target. Once we did that, we set up an online innovation submission portal allowing people to submit their innovations.

We then marketed the innovation portal to the micro-crowds, getting access to the experts on kitchen gadgets. We connected to gourmet chefs and other experts in the food preparation environment. Once we had a well-defined platform and an online innovation submission portal, we began the process of working on our own internal methods, using, first and foremost, Innovation Safaris. We spent a great deal of time with gourmet chefs in Napa, California. We traveled around the country to look at regional foods to identify emerging food trends. Once we'd completed our Innovation Safaris, we went back to our office and conducted ideation sessions. As a result, we were able to create some amazing products. Meanwhile, our innovation submission portal, which was providing pre-filtered innovations, was filling up quickly—so fast, in fact, we had to take it offline because we were getting so many great ideas we simply didn't have the resources to develop them all.

Once we began to assimilate our external ideas coupled with our internal ideas, we used our fast-track methodology to move them forward or to forget them quickly. Once we passed the ideas through we were able to quickly develop the technologies. In fact, as a result of using Project Xs, in which we looked at competitive technologies, we actually created a company called "Hanz" for the purpose of being our phantom competitor. We developed competitive technologies, some of which, not surprisingly, ended up becoming part of our product portfolio.

As a result of using these various techniques—Project Xs, Front-line Innovation, Innovation Safaris, and all of the other tools within our Find program, we were able to access hundreds of ideas and technologies in unbelievably short periods of time. Because we committed to fast-track methodologies through our Forward or Forget program, we were able to move those with lightening speed. In fact, our largest competitor was a $500 million a year company with dozens of people in its R&D department. On our side, there were only two of us—myself and an industrial designer—and in that period of time we launched a new successful product every month for the first 12 months. During that same time, our large competitor had only launched two products. So the system was working and working with mathematical certainty. From the beginning of the process all the way to commercialization, we referenced the Webb Triangle to make sure there was a genuinely recognizable need, a problem or an opportunity we could take advantage of. We always looked at manufacturability in the context of price sensitivity. And of course we had the tools in place to keep us connected to the market environment and competitive scenarios, so as we were moving products forward we were getting real time information to help us make intelligent decisions. But even as we would move toward commercialization, we constantly tried to identify ways to layer new value. Often products were forgotten. We gave them a decent burial, grieved for a few hours, and then realized forgetting technologies at any stage of the process was fundamentally necessary in order to have the resources to develop market-leading technologies.

Even as we moved towards commercialization, we also looked at ways to layer the value for launch. Our most popular creation, for example—the four-in-one garlic press—was a tremendous product (see Figure 10.6). For years, people had been trying to create a multifunctional garlic press. We did it! Not for just two functions,

Figure 10.6    Van Vacter Four-in-One Garlic Press

but for four. However, as we began to test it with our customers before launching it, we identified that it was hard to clean. So we immediately designed a cap that also served as a cleaner. Again, this resulted in a product that has been so popular it is sold by more than 800 retailers worldwide and is constantly in demand.

So—the process works. We didn't use all the tools and, in the beginning, we used a different set of tools. As the company began to mature, we relied more on hard-wiring the systems to our front-line people and creating ongoing ideation sessions and pasteboard programs. You'll find when you use the RealOpen system that you'll customize it in a way where it becomes truly part of your organization. You'll also find you constantly rearrange it, just like the icons on your desktop, to optimize usage.

Over the past year, we've begun to use other tools in the RealOpen framework that we have used with our other clients over the years. We're finding now that we're looking to float innovations online, and we have set up an innovation digital command center—recall Chapter 2, with Dell recently embracing the digital command center idea—that allows us to manage our online reputation and access new ideas and float ideas to potential buyers before we put them to development.

As you can see, RealOpen is a system that is custom designed for your organization. Whether you are a financial services company, a medical device company, a software supplier, a university, or a research organization, the bottom line is companies and their organizations are so unique they must have a configurable system that allows for a prescribed approach towards accessing, filtering,

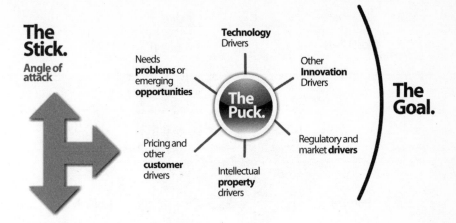

**Figure 10.7    Innovation Scenario Planning**

evaluating, developing, and commercializing ideas. I was excited to see that RealOpen worked as well on my kitchen gadget company as it has for micro-silicone implants and Class III medical devices.

## Innovation Scenario Tactics

Innovation scenario planning is one of the most useful tools in today's innovation management (see Figure 10.7). Not only is it exciting, but it is also fundamentally important that all organizations have an innovation scenario tactic. Innovation scenario tactics are especially important today because markets are moving more quickly than ever and product life cycles are shorter than ever before.

When things are moving very dynamically, you need to create multiple innovation scenarios so you're always moving toward the target or market goal, regardless of internal or external events.

In hockey, if a puck was always in the same place or on one trajectory towards the goal, the angle of your attacking hockey stick would always be the same. The problem is the puck is never still; today the puck is moving faster than ever before. There are technology drivers, that is, emerging technologies, and a lot of cross-pollinations of technologies between one market and another that can have dramatic effects on the movement of a market (like digital cameras and cell phones, for example). The changes in needs, problems,

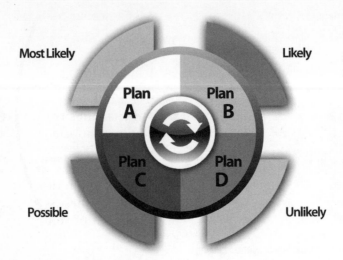

**Figure 10.8    Innovation Scenario Tactics**

technologies, and opportunities all drive the trajectory of innovation. Pricing and other customer drivers will also move the puck quickly. Also weighing in are intellectual property drivers, regulatory drivers, and other market drivers unique to a product or industry.

If the hockey puck is moving so rapidly, how then do organizations plan for the changes within their business? In the innovation scenario tactics, we recommend that you always create four possible scenarios. We break them down, simply, as Most Likely, Likely, Possible, and Unlikely. Those become Plan A, Plan B, Plan C, and Plan D respectively (see Figure 10.8).

The idea here is to examine two columns. One column would be known factors such as pricing trends, known technology changes, changes in consumer buying habits, competitive and emerging competitive factors, and so on. We look at all things known today and put them in a list in the first column. Then, next to that list, we add unknown factors, such as regulatory changes or other environmental changes.

Typically these lists contain from 30 to 50 items on both sides of the ledger. From these lists, and taking the listed items in combination, you build your four scenarios. Under "Most Likely" you list both your knowns and your most likely unknowns. This pattern is continued through Most and Least Likely scenarios, that is, Plan A through Plan D.

## A Medical Device Industry Example

Here I share some of the highlights of a rather elaborate scenario sketch developed for the medical products industry, and show how it might influence a company's innovation platform and ultimately drive its innovation.[1]

This is an industry-wide study, but it serves as an example of the kinds of externally driven scenarios you might develop for your own innovation and product platform. Each of these scenarios would in turn be used to create an adjusted version of your own product platform. There are four scenarios.

### Scenario A: Necessity Is Thy Mother

Driven by economic downturns and the ever-rising cost of health care, the federal government establishes universal data standards and open, medical device databases on patient outcomes (with appropriate privacy requirements). Health care data generally flows freely, with appropriate patient controls, from devices to doctors and across networks.

Highlights:

- New opportunities for informatics technology companies.
- Nascent efforts with disease prevention supported by new business models and data availability.
- Greater regulatory scrutiny of medical devices, with more emphasis on managing data and cost.
- Benefits of new products, combined with universal data standards across the system.
- CMS negotiates the rates for all drugs and medical devices (replacing private initiatives).

---

[1]This content is used with permission from a study titled "Future of Medical Devices: U.S. Trends and Scenarios Through 2015," co-authored by Jim Austin, Director of Life Sciences, Decision Strategies International; Terry Fadem, Managing Director, Corporate Alliances, University of Pennsylvania School of Medicine; and Paul J. H. Schoemaker, Research Director, Mack Center for Technological Innovation, The Wharton School of Business.

- Patients absorb more of the costs of health care and move towards self-care (education, online information, etc.).
- Driven by economic constraints, the general level of reimbursement for new medical devices and health care is reduced.

### Scenario B: Tough Love

In this scenario, the benefits of medical devices are well recognized and their long-term cost-effectiveness proven in a series of large population, well controlled studies. However, the federal government has imposed greater regulatory and data ownership/access constraints on private manufacturers in the effort to drive system efficiencies and business transparency.

Highlights:

- Positive reimbursement rates, especially for new approaches such as disease management, lead to a growth in procedures across all segments.
- Devices increasingly are neural networks—not only feeding back medical and ongoing performance data, but also linking to sophisticated patient and cost-benefit outcome databases.
- As the number of procedures performed increases, some question the cost/benefit of more aggressive cases (orthopedic implants for 90-year-olds, etc.) supporting increased patient/ provider emphasis on prevention rather than ever more sophisticated interventions.
- With heightened competition, many suppliers face declining margins in this world of resource plenty.
- Universities create multi-specialty disciplines combining informatics, biologics, material science, and engineering.

### Scenario C: Stagnation

Low reimbursement levels, technology snafus, and a lack of data standards slow the growth of the medical device sector.

Highlights:

- Health care cost containment, increasingly by rationing care and raising patient contributions, of primary concern to most stakeholders.

- Patient privacy a major issue for patients, effectively halting national database and registry initiatives.
- The potential of medical devices limited due to information sharing constraints and lengthening new product development cycles.
- Patients bear an increasing proportion of medical device costs, yet struggle to obtain information on the full range of options open to them.
- Investment in R&D declines from both private and public funding sources.
- Less skilled workers are more typical of those who must install, calibrate, and manage ex vivo medical devices (such as diagnostic equipment and IV pumps) in patient care settings.

### Scenario D: Isolated Islands

While reimbursement is readily available and innovation continues, medical devices have not fulfilled their potential in reducing health care system costs or improving life quality—in large part because of public data management and informatics limitations. Devices stand alone and do not benefit from being linked to broader networks.

Highlights:

- Reimbursement for medical devices is strong, supported by a growing economy and the aging of America.
- National or regional data management standards and protocols are lacking.
- Privacy concerns and increasing data security problems have further delayed the role of data sharing networks in medical device therapy or product selection decision.
- With lack of data sharing networks and increased privacy legislation, devices focus more on disease-specific treatments than on broader disease prevention.
- Medical device companies are growing, but within defined niches and established competencies.

The scenarios are summarized in Table 10.1.

From each scenario, an innovation, or product platform, is developed, with an assessment of the likelihood of the scenario. As an innovation organization, you would innovate to the most likely

**Table 10.1   Scenario Blueprint Summary–Key Uncertainties and How They Vary by Scenario**

|  | Scenario A | Scenario B | Scenario C | Scenario D |
|---|---|---|---|---|
| Level of Reimbursement | Tightened | Expanded | Tightened | Expanded |
| Legal Regulatory Environment | Restricted | Restricted | Unfettered | Unfettered |
| Role of Consumer in Selection | Large Role | Moderate Roll | Moderate Roll | Minimal |
| Level of Private Investment | Medium | High | Low | Medium |
| Availability and Utilization of Information | High | High | Low | Low |

*Source:* "A Look into the Future of the U.S. Medical Device Market," Austin, Fadem, and Schoemaker. 2009. Medical Device and Diagnostic Industry.

scenario, watching for external environment changes even daily that might change the likelihood of each scenario.

Companies that have not deployed the innovation scenario planning tactic in the past aren't usually familiar with the idea that the market is speeding up with shortening life cycles. Yet, one of the biggest problems we see is the time it takes most organizations to adopt innovation scenario tactics. I see innovation scenario planning as an idea that truly separates the mature, successful innovation organization from one with years of growth still left.

## Chapter Takeaways

- RealOpen is a framework for managing innovation with special emphasis on finding ideas and technologies from the inside and outside worlds, and filtering them quickly and effectively.
- The RealOpen process is not one-size-fits-all but rather a framework, which creates specific processes that should be developed for your organization.
- The Find step makes use of seven different processes to diversify and speed up your ideation processes.
- The Filter step makes use of a predefined innovation platform, a clearly stated vision of your business, customers, and products, both present and future.
- Innovation-platform-based filtration is preferable to case-by-case "business case" innovation evaluation.
- Forward or Forget stages help to move the process along quickly.

- The Forge process takes the product or idea into its first real stages of development, using the Webb Triangle to fine-tune the realism and viability of the project.
- Innovation scenario planning is a way to keep a few different irons in the innovation fire, and to be flexible according to the most recent "where the puck is going" market and technology changes.

 The *Digital Innovation Playbook* is a living book. We are constantly updating the book online so you can watch uploaded videos, read the latest best practice on digital media, and even participate in free ongoing webinars.

To access this chapter's updated web page, please go to www.digitalinnovationplaybook.com/Chapter10.html or scan the QR code with your mobile device.

# 11

# Creating a Digital Culture

## ORGANIZATIONAL CULTURE IS A SYMPTOM: THE UNDERLINING CAUSALITY IS COLLECTIVE TEAM FOCUS

Culture is an elusive thing. We know it's important and we know we need the right kind, but defining it and shaping it are two of the most difficult tasks companies face. We've already talked about culture quite a bit in this book, touching on it in each chapter. But because the right culture is so incredibly important, it is really the foundation of any initiative.

It's important to remember that organizational culture is a symptom; the underlining causality is collective team focus. In other words, your organizational culture is the net total of the pervasive thoughts of your internal stakeholders. As defined in Chapter 1, Mastering Digital Innovation, culture is the collective focus of every member of your organizational team. If your team members' focus is based in risk and fear management you will have an internal, slow, and ineffective culture. Conversely, if your team's focus is on delivering exceptional customer value, then you will have an innovative culture that is truly open.

We've talked a lot about *why* the right culture is so important and the types of culture that are important in order to become digitally successful. In this chapter we talk about *how* to build a successful cultural base to support innovation. It also examines how to best incorporate what we're now coming to call "digital innovation" as a tool to sustain not only the innovation process, but also the innovation culture.

In Chapter 5, The Anatomy of an Innovation Superstar, in my first book, *The Innovation Playbook*, I defined three essential parts of the anatomy of the body of innovation: Customer, Process, and Culture. The customer part was analogous to the head—containing the information and brains to decide what needs to be done in the interest of the customer. Process was compared to the torso, containing the vital parts necessary to keep the organization alive and functioning, while Culture was the legs, supporting the rest of the being and propelling it forward.

Culture is how the organization thinks, feels, and works as a whole to achieve excellence. It is about pride, passion, and environment. It's about whether the company provides a functional environment for employees to succeed, and thus, for innovation to succeed. It's about having the right empathy and focus on customers that allow their input and needs to get into the company brains in the first place; an organization that doesn't listen to customers won't make the right customer-focused decisions, and will thus be doomed to fail.

> **C**ulture is how the organization thinks, feels, and works as a whole to achieve excellence.

You may have recognized that love requires the same essential ingredients: a functional environment, a passion to think, feel, and work together, a consistent empathy, and, above all, the right focus. Consider this a chapter about love, only in this case, it is a love of customers that translates into a loving organizational culture that allows other great things to happen.

## External Focus versus Internal Focus

The starting place for both love and culture is focus. Without the right focus, all other efforts will be misdirected or misguided, and the best intentions will miss the mark or go unnoticed. As a result,

I believe the organization must start out focused in the right place, and that place is external.

External focus for an individual is simply focus on the other, not on oneself, and focus on listening with unfettered attention to the other person, with empathy, compassion, validation, and a top-to-bottom satisfaction of that other person's needs. In an organization, external focus is an unfettered focus on the customer, which also entails listening, empathy, and especially a top-to-bottom satisfaction of the customer's needs. A tangible example of this is contact point innovation, in which you focus on layering value at every customer contact point from pre-touch to in-touch.

Beyond satisfying these needs, in culture as in love, delivering beyond expectations brings delight and substantial reward to both parties involved. In the case of both individuals and organizations, love and culture bring about the right decisions—in the former case personal and in the latter business decisions—to bring mutual reward and beyond that, the visceral connections and loyalty that, if managed properly, can last forever.

We hear this question all the time: What is external focus and how do we, as an organization, get there? It's a great question. If you give a PowerPoint presentation in a conference room about external focus, or wander up and down the organizational halls whispering "external focus" in the ears of the occupant of each and every cube, will external focus happen? Maybe, for a while. But will it be sustained? Will there be a permanent commitment to external focus? Will it be ingrained and behavioral? Probably only until the next set of forms arrive that accomplish some mundane organizational task, or worse, that control the risk of the project or process you're working on. If you're this far into this book, you know how I feel about risk-centered processes.

Further, it turns out that almost everything we find wrong with innovation in an organization has, at its root, internal focus as a cause. Excessive risk management, delayed or slow launches (or no launches at all), inadequate resources, solutions that don't meet or exceed customer needs and thus fail in the marketplace—all can be attributed to internal focus.

The solution to creating external focus is simply to eliminate internal focus. Leadership that avoids internal focus creates external focus. Employees are more likely to become devotees and enthusiasts, which self-perpetuates into more external focus, and you have an oxygen-giving positive spiral of good feeling and external focus that satisfies customer and organizational needs alike.

Again, the solution is pretty simple but bears repeating: To achieve external focus, get rid of internal focus.

### Hewlett-Packard, Champions of Innovation

External focus may be the proper cultural foundation for doing innovation right, but it isn't the entire story. An organization that is externally focused, but still dysfunctional, still won't get there.

The best way I can expand on external focus is to summarize a lengthy interview I had with Art Beckman, Director of the Innovation Program Office for Hewlett-Packard's Software and Solutions operations. This interview session went into considerable detail about HP's innovation culture, methods, and processes. One of the simpler but more profound takeaways from the discussion was their definition of innovation culture. Innovation culture in HP's words is, "a combination of leadership and communication."

For HP, leadership is all about the fundamentals of leadership that I describe later in this chapter. But it's also about having a designated innovation champion within the organization to foster the right focus and climate for change, whether acting as an internal cheerleader, mentor, consultant, or "process engineer" for the various processes and tools an innovating organization might put into place.

HP has created the Innovation Program Office within the Software and Solutions organization, which has a largely unconstrained charter for making innovation happen throughout the organization. Some companies actually have a VP of Innovation. However it might be set up, the idea is that innovation gets the right kind of dedicated, flexible leadership; the position also validates the organization's commitment to innovation in the first place.

**The Garage**    The small Palo Alto garage where HP was born in 1939 has become an enduring symbol of grassroots innovation ever since. HP now not only uses the Garage metaphor as a historical reference to its innovative roots, but also as a name for the Software and Solutions business innovation portal bearing that name.

The Garage is set up as a source of internal information, collaboration, and feedback to guide innovation and its innovators. In

HP's words, the Garage ". . . was opened to systematically gather, organize and allow collaboration on ideas to improve our business. . . . It manages open idea submission, brainstorming, collaboration, and idea campaigns." The idea campaign is billed and designed as an intense two-week campaign to tease any and all ideas about a topic out of the organization. The Garage is part of a framework that has been established called the Elements of Innovation Success from HP Software and Solutions. These elements and the Garage tool can be applied by each organization in a manner best suited to match the individual business unit's innovation objectives.

The Garage serves not only as the daily news of what's going on with innovation in the organization, product launches, competitive products, and so forth. It's also a path for innovators, noninnovators, and management in the organization to share and communicate with each other in a way that doesn't consume much time, bandwidth, and organizational fuel. The Garage has worked wonders for keeping innovators and their innovations on track in the rather large and complex organization known as HP.

**You Cook It, You Eat It**   One of HP's strongest cultural strategies for success may have been somewhat inadvertent. Under CIO Randy Moss, the company embarked on a massive data center and software consolidation project in the mid-2000s. The goal was to save billions (yes, with a "b") by consolidating some 85 data centers at individual divisions in the United States into three data centers, and making similar cuts in the number of software programs that were run at these locations.

Quite clearly HP is a technology company that sells just this sort of enterprise IT solutions to its customers, so why shouldn't their customers benefit from the same tactics HP was employing internally? The Moss initiative required many of the same software and solution innovations as HP's customers needed. The fact that HP was using and benefiting from the same technologies it was selling to customers was a big plus for the organization's innovators—much as the opportunity to share the beer experience being created for customers is a motivator for the employees of Sierra Nevada brewery. The innovations are closer to home. The innovators, in many cases, become their own customers, one of the ultimate manifestations of customer connectivity.

## *Before and After*

You can almost tell a good innovation culture from the moment you walk in the door. There's a certain buzz in the building. There are examples of products in the lobby, often with pictures of customers using them. The products—or videos or facsimiles thereof—are displayed with such pride, as though the CEO of the company were giving a one-on-one presentation. There are written customer testimonials, industry awards for excellence on the walls. People look relaxed, content, even casual, but they're obviously working hard. They look, feel, act, and decorate their offices like entrepreneurs. The environment is conducive to work, but it is also relaxing—tastefully decorated with a warm atmosphere, plenty of open space, exercise facilities, and an attractive cafeteria. It is focused on employees, and more importantly, externally focused to the hilt.

But while good innovating companies start out this way, especially in the tech space, many more start with an old-school look and feel. Traditional offices have a certain chill and a lack of personality that includes off-white steel furniture, linoleum floors, pictures of assembly lines instead of products or customers, pictures of company leaders in the lobby instead of with products, awards, or customer testimonials. These are internally focused to the hilt.

In the words of Beckman at HP, many companies that "get it," like today's HP, made the switch from a "before" that could be described as pure innovation, not customer focused, risk adverse, top-down, internally focused. The "after," with the right culture, can be described as more organic, where risk is not punished, where as a result there are earlier starts, better starts, and earlier failures. The innovations are more grassroots, collaborative, open, co-created, and more customer focused.

## Success Referencing

Companies with strong innovation cultures also tend to success reference rather than failure reference. You can see it in the language the company uses in meetings. You can even see it in the body language.

Success referencing occurs when a company talks about its successes and measures new products or ideas against its successes. A new idea is assumed successful until proven otherwise, and there's an almost childishly excited hope that the new idea will have the same success as the old one. The idea gets a champion, gets sponsorship and resources almost right off the bat. People buzz about what the new product and its adjuncts could really become.

Failure referencing, on the other hand, occurs when a company always looks back on failures and uses those as a model for what might happen to a new idea. "We can't do this because . . . ." It's easy to play find-the-flaw with an idea, and often people think pointing out problems makes them look smart and avoid personal risk at the same time; it's also easier. It is easier to failure reference than to success reference.

So again, if a company holds up its own innovations with pride, and tries to fit new ideas into something resembling a success, the culture is right. If a company lives constantly in a world of fear, risk, and doubt about a new idea, especially based on some past experience, the innovation culture needs some work. To develop the innovation culture—think positive—and reference success.

There is one warning I'd like to include in this concept of success reference. Don't get caught up in the technology. It can be easy to get caught in the coolness factor and lose sight of what customers really want. If you think back to Chapter 2, The Digital Sandbox, you'll recall the section on the advancement of cell phone technology. The technology is advancing at such a rapid pace that it can outpace the customer. Developers must be careful not to become so technocentric that they lose sight of how customers use the product. Remember, they just want it to work. So when you reference the success, think positive but keep the customer at the forefront.

> **I**f a company holds up its own innovations with pride, and tries to fit new ideas into something resembling a success, the culture is right.

## The Four Characteristics That Define Cultural Excellence

There are four characteristics and checklists that define a company's cultural excellence: collective passion, craftsmanship, fear no more, and the right team. Each of these attributes flies a bit below the radar of the overall external focus mantra, but they're all part of the equation.

## Achieving Collective Passion

In assessing collective passion, the first question is whether or not a company really embraces or internalizes the importance of successful innovation as part of its long-term success. If it doesn't—that's big trouble. The answer, of course, is a long-term view of success, and a thorough understanding of the company's customers and what value they might want over the long term. To get to these places, a company must adopt—you guessed it—an external focus.

Aside from that, passion is really all about whether the company and its employees truly have passion for their customers and their products. Do they understand the customers? Empathize with them? Feel good when the customer feels good and feel bad when a customer feels bad? Really good, smart, people with balanced personalities and good training do these things. These concepts are hard to teach, but again, it's about putting oneself in other people's shoes. It's about external focus.

To get there, it's important to hire the right kind of people in the first place—positive, enthusiastic, energetic, and so forth. Remember the Southwest Airlines chapter? It is also important to stress the importance of the customer, and provide a reward and internal social system that fosters these feelings. Let people talk openly about customer successes and failures. Allow them the time to find out for themselves whether customers are having good or bad experiences. Send them on innovation safaris. Make each employee feel like every customer is both their friend and their responsibility. Reward them for doing so.

And finally, do away with the dry, dull, corporate-speak in visions, mission statements, and strategic and tactical plans. Make them fun and active. It's hard to instill passion in a person, but if you create the right environment for passion, whether with corporate culture or personal love, great things can happen.

## Achieving Craftsmanship

Craftsmanship is like passion, but it is more specifically directed at the product, not so much at the customer. The idea is to produce products that not only meet but exceed customer expectations or, more colloquially, to make the customer say Wow!

How you get there, of course, starts with external focus. A company or an individual within the company will craft the best products or customer experiences when he or she can feel that experience personally. When a customer says thank you or gives pleasant compliments about the product or service, you're there; when they come back (loyalty) or refer others (evangelism), it's even better.

A culture of craftsmanship comes about when management has a get-it-right mentality—and gives employees the time, resources, and recognition to do it. When employees are treated like entrepreneurs, and they feel that the company is their own personal small business, they will naturally deliver a higher standard of quality and take more responsibility for their products. So giving employees the time and empowering them to get things right goes a long way towards craftsmanship.

Further, in my opinion, one of the best ways to instill the idea of craftsmanship and entrepreneurship in an organization is to give employees an ownership share or a share of the profits. In large companies this can mean shares of stock or options or profit-sharing bonuses. In smaller companies it can also mean bonuses and shares of profits, and it may also be ownership depending on how the business is set up. Either way, when employees have skin in the game, better results almost always follow, especially in the area of craftsmanship but also in the area of passion just described.

### Achieving "Fear No More"

The fear factor has been addressed so many times in this book that to say much about it here would be repetitive. Simply, you must create a culture where employees can take smart risks. They can start—and finish—projects when it makes sense. In the fear culture, failure is rewarded and sometimes even celebrated as a necessary step to success.

Psychologists sometimes group people into two types: people who live in fear and dispense fear all their lives, and people who live in love and dispense love all their lives. We all know the types. And to get the right culture, management needs to do the latter (that love thing again). Positive reinforcement, and even delivering bad news with a soft touch and a "here's how things can work better next time" can help. Managing fear properly in an organization is a lot like providing a positive environment for children, where they can make mistakes, learn from them, and not feel like they have to lie or work around you to get what they want.

So give your employees a little empathy and love, reference success, and assume they're doing good instead of doing bad, and you'll build a culture based on success, not fear.

> Give your employees a little empathy and love, reference success, and assume they're doing good instead of doing bad, and you'll build a culture based on success, not fear.

Also realize a healthy organizational culture recognizes the fresh perspective that failure—tried, recognized, and learned from—can bring to an organization. Such an organization has a smart-risk culture. Remember that a tree, pruned of its dead branches, comes back healthier for the experience. Have a failure? Take the team out for drinks, talk about it, and celebrate it.

### Achieving the Right Team

Some businesses may be small enough to carry on as one-man bands, but it's not likely to be the case for long, especially if a business is destined for success. So I say that successful innovation is highly dependent on having a good team, and the right team, in place, with the right mindset. The right team has energy, collective enthusiasm, and diverse skills and personalities. They are interesting people, and they interest each other. And they can all put their own interests and rewards aside to honor one common bond: the interests of the customer. They are externally focused individuals, other-centric individuals who interact easily with others and realize that, in many situations, one-plus-one equals three.

Selecting such people isn't easy because these attributes are almost indiscernible on a resume. It's all about finding out what kinds of experiences these people have had with others, and with helping others—whether in a business or rock climbing on a 1,000-foot granite face. Signs of customer involvement and team involvement in the past should be observed. And of course, positive, forward verbal language (we, us instead of I, me, they, and them) and body language are all plusses.

A successful team culture shouldn't rely 100 percent on the individuals in the team. Of course, the environment created by management is extremely important. People need the chance to act and interact in positive team settings—at work and at play. Team oriented organizations have group functions, basketball courts, gyms, and organized after-work events. Teamwork is encouraged—and teams are built through team-building events. Team-oriented organizations consider these items as investments, not expenses, and they are all part of the investment an organization makes in keeping ahead of the game.

## The Critical Role of Leadership

It wouldn't be surprising if, by now, you've concluded that a lot of what we're talking about with respect to culture is really a matter of leadership. External focus, passion, craftsmanship, creating a safe environment in which to innovate, and building the right team are all outcomes of smart, properly focused, compassionate, and effective leadership. Specifically, I like to see the following characteristics of leaders and the leadership style they deploy in the innovation space.

### Keep—and Share—the Focus

We've made much of the external focus that gives oxygen and direction to innovations. Leaders must get focused, stay focused, and show that focus to their teams. Keep a long-term perspective. This one's easy: A leader focused exclusively on short-term results will get just that—and a company that runs out of ideas fails in the marketplace longer term. Keep your eyes on the prize—the prize is almost always long-term. Really understand the customer.

Sounds simple, but how many leaders really understand their customers—all of their customers, not just the biggest ones? How many have taken the inverted pyramid to heart? Remember, the inverted pyramid puts the decision makers of the company at the top of the pyramid, far from the customers. How many take the time to really get into the heads and into the experiences of their customers? How many of them innovate by walking around, taking innovation safaris? Do top management presentations, or company annual reports, reflect ideas taken straight from a customer's experience? Well, there are a few such leaders, like Howard Schultz of Starbucks, perhaps. But most rely on cumbersome market intelligence, or worse, try to dictate what the customer needs, as Microsoft does. These processes are seldom fast enough; they miss market opportunities—or tick customers off.

### Understand Innovation and Innovators

Leaders are simply more effective when they understand who and what they're leading. Do leaders in your organization really understand how innovation works? Or do they let their innovation program leads, where they exist at all, do that for them? Leaders who have "been there, done that," or leaders who take the time to work in the kitchen, so to speak, will gain a better understanding of what's eventually served up.

> Leaders are simply more effective when they understand who and what they're leading.

### Passion, Patience, and Perseverance

Here I combine an assortment of leadership qualities into a single bullet—for a reason. Passion without perseverance doesn't work, and without at least some patience, the organization will go into stop-start mode and overreact to every new input. Leadership is really about a combination of good elements and traits without too much emphasis on one trait; otherwise it looks false or contrived. Always think win-win.

Good leaders look for scenarios where everyone can win—the customer, the organization, the employees, the shareholders, the leaders themselves. Out the window go such examples as Merrill Lynch's John Thain, who had the gall to complain about not receiving a year-end bonus from his firm—which had lost billions. His argument that he prevented more severe losses rings hollow when you consider the win-win principle. And GM CEO Rick Wagoner—as justified as he might have felt in taking the corporate jet to

Washington, hat in hand, to ask for a bailout—clearly sent the wrong leadership message to everyone inside and out.

> **G**ood leaders look for scenarios where everyone can win—the customer, the organization, the employees, the shareholders, the leaders themselves.

### Be Quick and Patient

These seemingly opposing traits actually do work well when worked together in the right way. I just mentioned General Motors CEO Rick Wagoner as an example of poor win-win thinking; now I'll call his number as an example of an executive who failed via paralysis, by leaving a failed business model of too many brands and too many dealers unchanged as the Detroit-based corporation hemorrhaged shares and cash. Something needed to be done faster, and the organization would have responded well (I believe) to an executive who really had a clear vision and took charge. At the same time, I have a big problem with impatience overdone—leaders who don't appreciate that good strategy may take some time to implement and that initiatives need room to develop and mature. Such leaders will create frustration and stress in those beneath them. I need to also stress that good leaders don't have to be an expert in the field to lead well. Take Andrew Carnegie as an example. His management team knew more about steel than he did, and honest admission of that fact not only motivated his team but reflected his own culture of respect.

### Be Truthful

People—both customers and employees—are smarter than you think. They want honesty, and can generally see through the alternatives. Employees will respond better when a CEO admits a mistake or a hard truth about their organization or its innovations. Jeff Bezos, founder and CEO of Amazon.com, has often been quoted as saying that one of the key elements of being a good business leader is the capacity to tell hard truths, not run away from reality. And we all know what troubles can be caused when a company tries to hide its failures from its customers, as the recent Toyota debacle clearly illustrates.

### Have Fun

Too often I see way too much seriousness and dryness in corporate environments. I believe the best work is fun work; that is, when I'm having fun, I put more energy and thought into my work; I think frankly most people do. You may not have always observed it, for when the straight-laced, dark-suited bunch get together for an offsite all forms of productivity melt away into silliness—but I think it's because these people don't have much fun during normal work life, so they overcompensate. Fun leadership begets happy employees and expansive thinking.

### A Lesson: Even Mistakes Can Be Fun

The results at Southwest Airlines, which has led its industry in innovation and clearly in fun, speak for themselves. Even more specific examples arise, such as another in the airline industry. Recently, Eric Brinker, JetBlue Airways' director of brand management and customer experience, admitted to making a little mistake. His team decided to replace a popular, but hardly healthy, mix of Doritos chips called Munchie Mix. The junk food fans revolted.

It was soon clear; the customers wanted the junk food. Brinker realized they needed to reverse the action, but he didn't want his team to become dispirited. So he launched the "Save the Munchie Mix!" campaign that read: "Some pinhead in marketing decided to get rid of the Munchie Mix!" He invited employees to write poems and stories about why the snacks should return to JetBlue. He kept things fun, in hopes that the experience wouldn't cause employees to hesitate when making their own creative decisions. That such a leadership style stimulates passion, craftsmanship, teamwork, and a positive innovative spirit should by now be obvious.

## The Components of Digital Innovation

Not only has the world as a whole gone digital, but so has innovation. As in other aspects of business—marketing, operations, customer service—digital media will open the doors to effective innovation—and close doors to those who choose to lag or ignore it altogether.

My point is that today there is a tremendous opportunity to speed up customer input and innovation efficiency by using digital media as your platform. In fact, in our practice, we continue to recommend that clients set up what we call a digital command center. The idea of a digital command center is to be able to acquire great information quickly to aid in the innovation process, and to link innovation and other marketing and image activities in such a way as to improve your company's reputation and even to manage the brand.

We've developed a holistic digital innovation model that incorporates several digital platforms in and around innovation. Some of these activities, such as listening posts, have been discussed in earlier chapters, but I examine them again here just as parts of a whole. See Figure 11.1.

### Listening Posts

Listening posts were introduced in my last book as a carpet-time method to capture the buzz in the marketplace and media about your products and product concepts. Listening posts are easy to set up as keyword selectors for various media. For example, you can set up a listening post by entering a keyword—your product or your

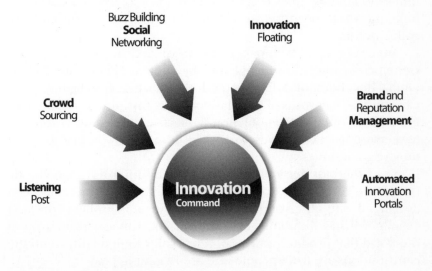

Figure 11.1    Digital Innovation Model

brand—on Yahoo! News or Google Alerts. It's a great way to quickly, and in real time, identify what people think about product concepts, service concepts, brands, and so on. You can also set up posts and questions on social networking sites and other new media to capture buzz and get more specific answers to questions you might pose. Listening posts are a great way to get real time feedback—for free. Probably the best example of a corporate listening post is Dell Computing's digital command center, which I talked about previously.

### Crowdsourcing: Getting the Best from the Madness of Crowds

I've said a fair amount about crowdsourcing already. Crowdsourcing is the process of sending out questions, or problems, to problem solvers, and providing rewards for people who deliver solutions to specific problems. Crowdsourcing can be done easily and cheaply on innovation portals like Spigit—www.spigit.com. I've also advocated (as described in Chapter 8 of *The Innovation Playbook*) managing the size of the crowd to get the kind of relevant feedback you want with micro-crowds.

Early triumphs like the Linux operating system and the Wikipedia Web encyclopedias brought the ideas of crowdsourcing and open innovation forward as emerging disciplines, but they aren't magic idea factories. A look at recent cases and research suggests open innovation models work best when carefully designed for a particular task and when incentives are tailored to attract the most effective collaborators.

In a February, 2009, paper, "Harnessing Crowds: Mapping the Genome of Collective Intelligence," by Thomas Malone and Robert Laubacher, both of MIT Center for Collective Intelligence, and Chysanthos Dellarocas of the Massachusetts Institute of Technology, the authors call this phenomenon "collective intelligence." You may have heard it called crowdsourcing, wisdom of crowds, peer production, or wikinomics.

Over the past decade, the rise of the Internet has shaped a variety of forms of collective intelligence. Wikipedia, which has been developed with almost no centralized control, is probably the best example. It has thousands of volunteer contributors from around the world that produce articles of remarkably high quality—and the contributions are from people who aren't getting paid.

Threadless—a T-shirt company—asks site visitors to submit to a weekly design contest and then vote for favorites. The entries receiving the most votes get sent into production and designers get royalties and prizes. In doing this, the company utilizes the collective intelligence of more than 500,000 people to design and then select its T-shirts.

In the 2009 paper, it is suggested that there's much more to this ideal of crowd intelligence that just a "fuzzy collection of cool ideas." To unlock the true potential, managers need a deeper understanding of how these systems work and what motivates contributors to contribute. The MIT Center for Collective Intelligence gathered almost 250 examples of Web-enabled collective intelligence. They looked at who participated in the organization and among the crowd, and the motivation behind the participation. Sometimes it's money, but it can also be love or enjoyment, glory, or a competitive drive. Money talks—for example, InnoCentive is a company that offers cash rewards, typically totaling in the five or even six figures, to researchers anywhere in the world who can solve challenging scientific problems such as how to synthesize a particular chemical compound.

They also looked at "what and how" behind the average project. This is the same as the project's mission or goal. It may be to create something new, it may be to decide or answer a question. Companies like Threadless both create and decide. The company found there is a difference between situations in which contributions are received or evaluated independently or in which there is a dependency between the contributions. Collaboration, which occurs when participants are working together to create something and must depend on one another to some extent, can be motivating. Wikipedia articles are a good example of independence but also collaboration—articles are created independently, but additions or editorial changes made within an article are strongly interdependent. It was found that the crowd mentality was most useful in situations where "the resources and skills needed to perform an activity are distributed widely or reside in places that are not known in advance." It was also found that, for this to work successfully, you must be able to divide an activity into pieces that can be performed by different members of the crowd. There should also be safety mechanisms in place that prevent people from sabotaging the system. In many cases the final decision is left to a specific internal group in charge of the crowd's task, even if some of the intermediate decisions are made by the crowd.

Not mentioned explicitly in this paper—but pertaining to culture—is the idea that to succeed, a company must have a culture open to outside ideas and a system for vetting and acting on them—as stated by Henry Chesbrough, one of the original champions of open innovation and the executive director of the Center for Open Innovation at the University of California, Berkeley, in a recent *New York Times* article. These thoughts will help guide you through the maze of crowdsourcing and the cultural characteristics important to pull it off.

## Buzz-Building

Digital innovation also includes what I call buzz-building. Historically, if you were a national company, building buzz could be an extremely expensive task. If you were a local company, it was slightly easier, because you had a local market and presence, and it was easier to "go viral" in such a market.

But now, with the Internet, you can build buzzes and get your products and services noticed by crafting intelligent blogs, posting on social networking sites, and the list goes on. In fact, most marketing departments and marketing agencies have created a digital media section, and in some companies, the marketing department has transitioned into a digital media department altogether. It's that important. So buzz-building through social networking and other digital marketing modalities is a powerful way to sell and to be successful in any market. That buzz, of course, can generate feedback useful to the innovation process, and more generally, to the development and strengthening of your innovation culture.

## Innovation Floating

Another concept that I call innovation floating is also very powerful. In fact, my company has created special and powerful websites and photo-realistic imagery on technologies that didn't even exist to send images out to the digital universe. Such images can also be presented as film clips for YouTube or other media. Floating can occur not just for the consumer space but also for the distribution and channel space. The purpose is to get feedback on the product, and learn whether people would buy it if it was in the marketplace.

We recently tested online a new product color for one of our clients that manufactures canes. We found that customers preferred black to chrome 90 percent of the time. This saved the company tens of thousands of dollars when compared to the nondigital approach.

One issue with innovation floating is intellectual property; it is important not to disclose your innovation before patent filings because, unless it is done right, it can negatively impact future patent rights.

**Online Brand Reputation Management**    Prior to engaging in innovation floating, particularly with people outside of your company, it is highly recommended that you consult with a registered patent attorney to ensure that your innovation floating program does not invite problems down the road. According to patent attorney Robert Siminski, one major risk of poorly structured innovation floating programs involves "public disclosure" of an invention which can serve as the basis for invalidating any patents that might be obtained. See the next chapter, Rules of Engagement, in which Siminski provides counsel regarding the potential legal pitfalls associated with using the available tools and opportunities to monetize your digital innovations through intellectual property protections. Another risk is that if not properly controlled, feedback can find its way into patent applications, thereby calling into question who should own any resulting patents. The bottom line is this: Properly structured innovation floating programs can provide significant value while poorly structured programs can have serious ramifications.

Another important area that can be addressed digitally with ultimate benefits to the innovation process is brand reputation management. Reputation management is the observance of online feedback from your customers about your products and services—and the corrective action you might take to turn the buzz positive. It's extremely important—whether you're a corner liquor store or a multinational company, your reputation online is your reputation. Naturally your brand reputation, in turn, serves to nourish your innovation culture.

In fact, many in the corporate world today keep track of online feedback just like a credit score; when there's a "ding" against it, you act. New firms have been set up to specialize in online reputation management. Sometimes the information is erroneous or laden with bad assumptions, but still it's important to keep track. Online brand reputation management provides a significant proactive opportunity to really build a brand, by creating your own Internet footprint that speaks favorably about your company and its products and services. But also, don't forget what people are saying, feeling, and experiencing becomes input to your innovation process.

### *Automated Innovation Portals*

Again, covered earlier, but really important, are the automated innovation portals that capture both external and internal ideas and feedback; they are the key to soliciting, acquiring, managing, and reviewing ideas on the open innovation front. The key is the automation, through the filtering and toggle questions I laid out in the RealOpen Innovation chapter. To reinforce the idea, remember that to make open innovation work through such portals, you need to clearly state your needs (remember the innovation platform?). Developing a platform not only gives the necessary structure to filter out unwanted ideas, but it also helps you as an organization to focus externally and to get your culture aligned to a set of products and product characteristics that really meet the needs of your customers. A well-defined wish list, to me, is a sign of a company with a well-developed innovation culture.

■ ■ ■

In summary, digital innovation is centric to almost all businesses today. You should be using listening posts, micro-crowd sources, buzz-building, innovation floating, brand reputation management, and most importantly, automated innovation portals. We're almost to the end, where we can tie all of these concepts together and you can run with them. But first, we go to a chapter devoted to protection.

---

### Chapter Takeaways

- Above all else, external focus is the cultural lifeblood that keeps innovation flowing in the right direction. Without external focus, the remaining cultural elements of good innovation will be difficult if not impossible to achieve.
- Almost all things that go wrong with innovation can be attributed to internal focus. Therefore, creating the right culture for innovation really starts with getting rid of the manifestations of internal focus—excessive risk aversion and process focus, bureaucracy, blaming, reactivity, failure referencing.
- Beyond external and customer focus, effective innovation cultures exude passion, craftsmanship, safety for risk takers, and good teamwork.

- Today's effective innovation culture must also be digital in order to keep up with the pace of change and to properly augment customer knowledge and ultimately the innovation process itself.

*The Digital Innovation Playbook* is a living book. We are constantly updating the book online so you can watch uploaded videos, read the latest best practice on digital media, and even participate in free ongoing webinars.

To access this chapter's updated web page, please go to www.digitalinnovationplaybook.com/Chapter11.html or scan the QR code with your mobile device.

# CHAPTER 12

# Rules of Engagement

## PROTECTING THE VALUE OF YOUR INTELLECTUAL PROPERTY

Throughout *The Digital Innovation Playbook*, I talk about the importance of creating digital resources or content that are valuable to the customer. These resources include everything from software applications to online, downloadable content in the forms of special reports, whitepapers, articles, e-books, podcasts, vodcasts, interactive training, instructional videos, and interviews.

And the list goes on. Whether your company is large or small, it is critical that you understand how to use the Internet and social networking to advance your innovation initiatives. That said, it is also important to understand the potential legal pitfalls associated with using these tools and the opportunities to monetize your digital innovations through intellectual property protections. For this, I turn to my Intellectual Property Counsel, Robert (Bob) Siminski, of the law firm Harness, Dickey & Pierce, PLC, to provide an overview.

Successful participation in the digital sandbox requires good, old-fashioned common sense and a genuine desire to connect to your customer community. But in today's litigious society it is also extremely important that you understand the rules of the digital road. To better understand these issues, I've asked my good friend and colleague Bob Siminski, a world-renowned Intellectual Property Attorney, to write this chapter.

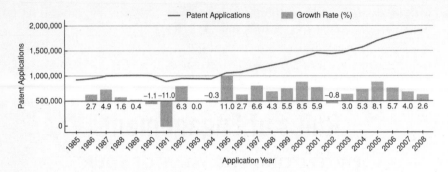

Figure 12.1    Trend in Total Patent Applications and Patent Grants

## One Giant Leap for Mankind

In my 20-plus years of practicing intellectual property law, I have seen a lot of cool technology developed and have witnessed the acceleration of technological growth first hand. While it is difficult to accurately quantify the rate of technological growth, the fact is that technology is rapidly expanding. For example, as shown in the Figures 12.1 and 12.2, the number of patent applications filed worldwide since 1985 has about doubled to nearly 2 million.

The rate of technological expansion took a quantum leap with the introduction of the information superhighway, the Internet. Since opening up to the general public in the late 1980s, the Internet has grown from a proverbial two-lane dirt road with a few million users (with an "M") to an eight-lane, multi-level mega highway

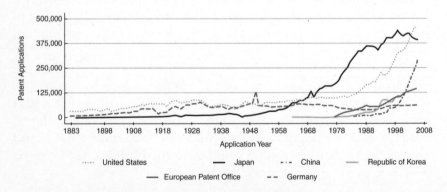

Figure 12.2    Trend in Patent Applications at Selected Patent Offices

with nearly two-and-a-half billion users (with a "B") worldwide. That's nearly one-third of the world's population!

New forms of information have been specifically developed for the Internet. One such form is digital media. Early examples of Internet-enabled digital media included basic software downloads, simple single-player games, primitive file-sharing, and (if you waited 30 minutes or more for the download and were lucky enough to not have your dial-up connection disconnected), a few seconds of video. How times have changed, indeed.

More recently, advances in wireless telecommunication technologies have provided digital media with an alternative communication pathway. Estimates are that roughly 72 percent of the world's populations uses cellular telephones. In fact, as of 2008, the number of cell-phone-only households surpassed the number of land-line-only households in the United States for the first time (about 60 percent of households have both). The funny thing is that most people don't even use their cell telephones primarily to talk—they use them to communicate visually via texting, instant messaging, and e-mail (in 2009, non-voice data surpassed voice data on cell networks for the first time).

As with the Internet, wireless-enabled digital media are being developed almost daily. Some examples include video calling (such as iPhone's FaceTime), Internet calling (such as Skype), location-based coupons, multi-player remote gaming, and stock trading.

Almost as quickly as the technology is developed and placed into use, legal questions arise regarding the digital media itself: Who owns the digital media being used on the Internet or in electronic wireless never-never land? If I didn't create it, can I still use it? What if I take someone else's concept and change it to be more useful, can I claim it as my own? How can I determine what intellectual property rights others have claimed for their technologies? These and other commonly asked questions will be addressed below in my *Rules of Engagement*—essentially a summary of the do's and don'ts of creating and using digital media on the Internet or via wireless networks.

The Rules of Engagement are intended to do two things:

1. Give you, the innovator, the guidance you need to use the intellectual property laws to protect your digital creations.
2. Keep you out of trouble in your digital endeavors.

The Rules of Engagement are general guidelines, and they are not intended as legal advice. You should always consult an experienced intellectual property attorney (preferably a registered patent attorney) prior to proceeding.

### Digital Media *per se*

While the Rules of Engagement are generally applicable to various types of digital media, I have chosen a wildly popular genre as a practical example—smartphone technology.

Smartphones, of course, are wireless telecommunication devices with multi-functionality. In essence, a smartphone is a hand held computer capable of being used as a cellular telephone, an Internet surfing tool, a word processor, and a texting device all wrapped up in one. The amount of digital media content that is accessible via a smartphone is nearly endless. You can use your smartphone to get the weather, breaking news, sports scores, stock quotes, YouTube videos, play interactive games with other gamers throughout the world, book airline tickets, check-in for a flight, track the location of your friends and family, and access any number of social media networks, such as Facebook, Twitter, and LinkedIn.

Perhaps the best known smartphone technology today is something called a smartphone application, or *app*. A smartphone app is essentially software written to operate on a smartphone operating system, such as the iPhone iOS. The software can be for something as simple as an offline game, such as checkers, to a program that communicates with the Internet to transmit and receive information, such as E-Trade's stock trading app. Some of my favorite apps include the Southwest Airlines Ding® app and major league baseball's "At Bat" app, which allows you to watch nearly every major league game live on your smartphone.

The popularity of apps is mind-boggling. According to recent reports, the one billionth (with a "B") iPhone app was downloaded in 2009 and over 300,000 different apps are currently available for download from Apple's App Store alone. I have received countless inquiries from people who have said, "How can I protect this killer app that I came up with?" Clearly, apps are a worthy subject for outlining the Rules of Engagement.

While some apps involve very little intellectual property, other more elaborate apps involve aspects relating to essentially all of the major categories of intellectual property: patents, trademarks, copyrights, and trade secrets. In the Rules of Engagement, I attempt to touch on all of these aspects while trying to keep the legal mumbo-jumbo to a minimum.

## Rules of Engagement

Rules No. 1 through 6 concern intellectual property protection considerations, Rule No. 7 concerns due diligence, and Rule No. 8 concerns fair use.

### Rule No. 1: Memorialize Your Concept and Document Your Development

When I first meet with a new client, before we talk about the *thing* itself—the innovation—I go through a fairly rigid set of questions. Basically, these questions are intended to provide me with a fundamental understanding of how the client got to this stage. With this fundamental understanding, the discussion then turns to the thing. As we delve into discussing this thing, I am often surprised at how little new clients can tell me about their innovation. Either the thing isn't past the concept stage or new clients don't realize how much detail intellectual property attorneys need to best protect their interest. With regard to apps, for example, we need to know at an absolute minimum: No. 1, what the inventor thinks the invention is; No. 2, how the invention is different from previously existing technology (so I can determine if the invention is really what the inventor thinks it is); No. 3, who else, if anyone, was involved in the development of the invention and what their contributions were; No. 4, whether the inventor is under any obligation to assign the invention to another, such as an employer; No. 5, whether the invention was disclosed to others and, if it was, what was disclosed to who and when; and No. 6, what work the inventor has done thus far on the invention, and what work he/she thinks remains to be done.

Without question, the best way to provide this information is by having a written record of it. It is imperative that you write all of your ideas down in as much detail as possible, and that you date your entries—keep a journal. Until you decide whether to pursue patent protection, this may be the only evidence of your "killer" app. I highly recommend having the entries attested to by someone you can trust to keep them confidential. Not only will your written record help you explain the invention to your intellectual property counsel, but it also can be important for proving your invention date. Proof of an invention date becomes important in the event that someone else comes up with a very similar invention and there is a dispute as to who has rights to it.

It is imperative that you write all of your ideas down in as much detail as possible, and that you date your entries—keep a journal.

### Rule No. 2: Don't Let the Cat Out of the Bag Too Early

When I meet with a new client, one of my questions is, "Who have you told your idea to?" Often the response is: to my friends, my co-workers, my family, and so on. Once in awhile I will even get an answer such as, "I didn't tell anyone, I just posted the idea on Facebook." Can you see me cringe?

Once you disclose your idea publicly, the U.S. Patent Office's clock starts. If after one year you haven't filed a patent application, your opportunity to obtain a valid patent has been lost.

In the United States, the one-year clock essentially starts upon: first, selling the invention or placing the invention on sale; second, publicly using the invention; or third, publicly disclosing the invention. The good news is that if the year hasn't run out, you still may be able to get a patent in the United States.

The rest of the world isn't so generous though. In most foreign countries, you lose your opportunity to obtain valid patent rights at the very moment of your first public disclosure.

Thus, prior to any disclosure it is vital to meet with your intellectual property attorney to consider whether to, first, file a patent application (provisional, utility or design); and/or obtain a *customized* nondisclosure agreement to protect against violating the one-year rule. I say "customized" because the form agreements that you find on the Internet will often do you more harm than good.

My suggestion: Don't talk to anyone about your idea, other than someone you can absolutely trust, until you have decided whether you want to protect it (especially if you want to try to obtain a patent).

A little paranoia about others stealing your innovation is a good thing.

### Rule No. 3: Forget the Handshake—Get It in Writing

Often a new client will want to talk about their killer app. The problem is that what they have is not an app, but rather a concept for an app. Typically, no software to execute the app has been developed and the client isn't able to write the software. Now what? Generally, the client needs a computer programmer to help reduce the invention to practice. This can open up Pandora's box. When you find a developer to write the software, make sure you have a written contract in place. Don't rely on a handshake. Without a written contract, questions almost always arise as to who owns the software.

But use extreme caution when presented with the software developer's standard contract because it may state that the developer owns the software—not you! Don't let your enthusiasm cloud your judgment. Before signing *anything*, make sure to get your attorney involved to read the contract and advise you on its content.

Instead of relying on the software developer's contract, I highly recommend that you have your attorney prepare the initial contract. This will give you control over the terms and conditions that are important to your situation. For example, make sure that your contract includes a formal assignment provision whereby the software developer assigns all rights, title, and interest to you, including rights to all future modifications and additions.

A noncompete provision is also important, such as to guard against the software developer offering a similar version of the software to the next guy that comes along. Still other provisions will be important depending upon your circumstances, so it is imperative that you consult with your intellectual property counsel for questions.

In my opinion, a handshake is appropriate only after a written contract is executed and a fully functional software package has been delivered.

### Rule No. 4: Protect Yourself—Secure Your Intellectual Property Rights

New clients invariably show up at my office thinking that they need to get a patent on their concept. Maybe—maybe not. But the general understanding that they need to do something, whatever that something is, to protect their interest is spot on.

The type(s) of protection that will best secure their interest frankly depends on the nature of their innovation, their business plan, and their budget. What they often do not realize is that they may already have certain rights once they memorialize the concept. At this stage, I usually discuss their innovation in view of their business plan to work up the appropriate strategy. Taking the app example, I explain that they can protect their rights to the software by obtaining patents and/or copyright registrations.

Utility patents generally protect "any new and useful process, machine, manufacture, or composition of matter, or any new and useful improvement thereof" (as opposed to design patents, which only protect nonfunctional design features). App software can qualify as a process, machine, or manufacture, depending on the nature of the invention and how the patent is written. A utility patent grants to the patentee the right to exclude others from making, using, or selling the patented invention throughout the United States and importing it into the United States for 20 years from the date the application for patent was filed. A U.S. utility patent does not protect the following: nonfunctional design features; the name of the product, its features, or your company; musical works; character personalities or images; photographic images; or protect against infringement in foreign countries (unless you file your patent abroad, of course).

Copyrights, on the other hand, protect original works of authorship fixed in any tangible medium of expression, now known or later developed, from which they can be perceived, reproduced, or otherwise communicated, either directly or with the aid of a machine or device. Computer software, which is the technical basis for an app, is a "work of authorship" under U.S. copyright statutes.

Copyright protection extends not only to computer programs written in conventional human language, known as source code, but also to programs written in machine-readable language, known as object code. Both qualify as "literary works" under the Copyright Act.

Screen views are automatically protected by copyright because they are "fixed in a tangible media." Computer programs can qualify as audiovisual works as well. While the Copyright Office allows a single registration of a computer program to cover all components therein, it may be beneficial to register the screen views separately. Your intellectual property attorney can explain when this is appropriate.

It should be noted that copyright registration is not a condition of copyright protection; however, there are a number of important incentives for registering copyrights, including the ability to sue for infringement and the option to recover statutory damages (in lieu of actual damages and infringer's profits) and attorney's fees, among other benefits.

By sitting down with your intellectual property counsel, a plan to protect your rights can be outlined and executed.

### Rule No. 5: Name That App

Most new clients have already thought of a name for their app by the time they arrive at my office. Like the title of the old movie starring Clint Eastwood, the names range from *The Good, The Bad, and The Ugly*! Naming your app is one of the most important decisions you can make because consumers will use the name to identify and reference your app. Ideally, the name you give your app should serve as a source identifier for consumers so they are not confused as to the origin of your app. The name of an app may also serve as a trademark.

Only certain types of trademarks are entitled to protection, however. Trademarks that are arbitrary/fanciful are generally considered to be the strongest. Such marks convey no information about the product itself. They are inherently strong because they have a substantial impact on the buyer's mind. Examples include Apple® for personal computers, Arm & Hammer® for baking soda, and Exxon® for gasoline. Southwest Airlines' DING® trademark likely also qualifies as an arbitrary/fanciful mark.

The next strongest category of trademarks is known as suggestive trademarks. They suggest, rather than describe, characteristics of the goods or services. A suggestive mark requires a consumer's imagination to make a connection between the mark and the product. Examples include The Money Store® for a mortgage lending company, and The Music Makers® for a radio show.

Descriptive marks are often the most desirable, but are not protectable unless they have secondary meaning; in other words, consumers must identify the name with a particular source. Such marks describe the product and/or its functions. Examples of descriptive marks include Computerland® for a computer store and Vision Center® for an optics store.

After selecting a name, it is often desirable to file a trademark application to register the trademark with the United States Trademark Office. Similar to registered copyrights, there are numerous benefits to registering trademarks. These benefits include: No. 1, public notice of your claim of ownership of the mark; No. 2, a legal presumption of your ownership of the mark and your exclusive right to use the mark nationwide on or in connection with the goods/services listed in the registration; No. 3, the ability to bring an action concerning the mark in federal court; No. 4, the use of the U.S. registration as a basis to obtain registration in foreign countries; No. 5, the ability to record the U.S. registration with the U.S. Customs and Border Protection Service to prevent importation of infringing foreign goods; No. 6, the right to use the federal registration symbol ®; and No. 7, listing in the U.S. Patent and Trademark Office's online databases.

There are two important caveats regarding trademarks. First, rights are based on use, thus you must continuously use your trademark in commerce or you will lose your rights. Second, trademarks are not self-policing, so you must be on constant lookout for infringers. Failure to enforce your rights can cause you to lose them, particularly if the third party use causes the mark to become generic. Trademark watching services are available to keep a lookout for potential infringes. Obviously, you should consult your intellectual property attorney immediately after becoming aware of a potential infringement.

### Rule No. 6: Brag about Your Rights

Once intellectual property rights are secured, or at least in the process of being secured, I remove the gag order and advise clients to begin touting their innovation. Letting others know about the innovation and that you have taken steps to protect it affords numerous benefits. From a pure business standpoint, touting the innovation can lead to increased sales and generate much needed revenue through a well thought out marketing initiative. It can also serve to attract investors if capital is needed. Virtually every financing deal I have been involved in has required a showing that intellectual property rights have been secured.

An important aspect of your marketing initiative should be highlighting the intellectual property rights you claim title to. Patents applied for or obtained, registered trademarks and trademark rights, copyrights, and exclusive rights held through licensing are all worthy of discussion. As a practical matter, putting competitors on notice of your rights can lower the chances that your rights will be misappropriated. Registering your rights and notifying others of your registrations allows you to seek enhanced damages and attorney's fees in many cases.

Registered trademarks should be designated with one of the following notice indicators: ®; Reg. U.S. Pat & Tm. Off.; or Registered in U.S. Patent and Trademark Office. To recover profits or money damages in a federal trademark infringement suit, the trademark registrant must give this notice of registration, unless the alleged infringer received actual notice in the form of a written or oral communication.

If the trademark is not registered, care should be taken to use a different type of notice indicator, such as TM. Falsely using the ® symbol when in fact the trademark has not been registered is not allowed and can serve as the basis for a misrepresentation of a rights claim against you. The TM symbol is sufficient to notify others that you are claiming trademark rights.

While the current Copyright Act does not require notice of the copyright on copies of the work, providing notice will generally defeat a claim of innocent infringement. There are three basic elements of notice: No. 1, the symbol ©, if registered (which is recommended because some countries and treaties do not accept alternative types of notice), or the word "Copyright" or the abbreviation "Copr."; No. 2, the year of first publication of the work; and No. 3, the name of the copyright owner, or an abbreviation by which the name can be recognized, or a generally known alternative designation.

As far as patents go, when a patent is obtained it is strongly recommended that you mark the product, packaging, or instructions with the patent number. Examples include U.S. Patent No. 5,842,941 for a utility patent and U.S. Pat. No. D295,716 for a design patent, both of which are products that I have obtained patents on personally. Marking products covered by your patent puts the world on notice of your rights and entitles you to recover damages from infringers (failure to mark may limit or entirely prevent recovery of damages). But be careful to mark only products that are covered by the patent because falsely marking an item as patented when it is not is an actionable offense.

If you have not yet been awarded a patent but you have filed your application, you are entitled to mark your product or packaging with the phrase "Patent Pending." This effectively notices that you are in the process of obtaining a patent, which should serve as a warning to others not to copy the product.

### Rule No. 7: Do the Due

Frankly, "doing the due" could be listed well ahead of some of the other Rules of Engagement. "The due" is short for due diligence, and in the intellectual property context it generally relates to accessing and evaluating the rights held by others for similar innovations. Believe me when I tell you that the last thing you want to happen after you introduce something like a new app into the marketplace is to be dragged into court and charged with infringing someone else's patents, trademarks, or copyrights. Some of the most expensive litigation today involves intellectual property rights disputes. Patent infringement litigation through trial can run into the many millions of dollars and I have seen many businesses fold as a result of prolonged patent litigation. So the question is "How can you avoid this?" The answer is by doing at least some level of due diligence prior to product launch.

The good news is that you can do some of the due diligence yourself, while saving the more complicated stuff for your intellectual property counsel. Start with some key word searching on the Internet. If you can concisely define what it is you have developed or wish to develop, chances are that you can find important reference information before you expend a lot of time and ever so important working capital. If you find something you consider relevant—don't throw in the towel! There still might be an opportunity. Talk the situation through with your intellectual property counsel so you don't make a huge mistake. Whatever you find, compile the information so that you can discuss it with your intellectual property counsel.

Another free resource is the U.S. Patent and Trademark Office's website. On their website (uspto.gov), you can access separate "patent search" and "trademark search" databases that generally work on a key word basis. At a minimum, you can get a general feel for what others have protected via the patent and trademark registration process. Unless you are extremely familiar with these databases, I do not recommend that you rely on your own search results. Rather, you should compile your results and share them with your intellectual property counsel for evaluation. It often takes many years to master these databases, and doing a mediocre patent or trademark search can, in some instances, do more harm than if no searching had been done at all.

If your business is sufficiently funded, you are better off leaving the due diligence up to your intellectual property professional. By understanding the inner workings of the U.S. Patent and Trademark Office and having access to various proprietary databases that are specifically designated for use by the patent and trademark professionals, a carefully crafted due diligence study can be outlined and executed on your behalf.

Taking the app example, depending on the nature of the app it is entirely possible that one or more patents have been applied for on a similar app. A quick review of the U.S. Patent Office patent searching database revealed the following patent applications for apps: cruise ship services app (publication no. 2010/0306075; Apple, Inc.); travel planning app (pub. no. 2010/0190510; Apple, Inc.); home electronics and appliance control app (pub. no. 2009/0239587; Universal Electronics, Inc.); and location specific content app (pub. no. 2010/0120450; Apple, Inc.).

A quick review of the trademark database tells me that trademark applications and registrations for apps are becoming commonplace. For example: AT BAT for Major League's Baseball's iPhone app (U.S. Serial No. 77/864,767; MLB Advanced Media); PATH for a social networking app (U.S. Serial No. 85/170.620; Path, Inc.); IBOOKS for a book reader app (U.S. Serial No. 85/008,412; Apple Inc.); and TOUCHSPORTS for a sports gaming app (U.S. Serial No. 77/564,657; Handheld Games, Corp.).

By knowing what others have done and are doing in your technology space and knowing what intellectual property rights they may hold, you can determine whether a new course needs to be taken or if you are free to proceed.

### Rule No. 8: It's Better to Ask for Forgiveness than Permission (NOT!)

Let's face it: There is a lot of cool stuff available over the Internet. Just type in a few key words on your favorite search engine and voila! Publications, photographs, music files, video content, social media,

media renderings, artistic content, and on and on—all for the taking. Or is it?

Maybe you want to use the content in something you are working on—an app, for example. In your app, you have a number of musical snippets by famous artists playing while a catalog of photographs of famous people flashes across the screen. I ask you, "What's wrong with this picture?" Well, that depends, of course, on where you obtained the material. Was it from a website authorized by the artist or recording industry to allow content to be downloaded and used in other "publications"? What about the photographs? Were they downloaded from a website authorized to distribute them? Even so, are there restrictions on further use?

With respect to copyrighted works, you may use them for a variety of noninfringing purposes such as criticism, comment, news reporting, teaching, scholarship, or research. But you don't have absolute freedom to use the work. Whether your use is a noninfringing "fair use" will be judged based on a number of factors, such as:

- *The purpose and character of the use.* A commercial use is unlikely to be judged a fair use; exceptions include parody and satire.
- *The nature of the copyrighted work.* Use of an informational or functional work is more likely to be a fair use than use of a highly creative work.
- *The amount of the work used.* To constitute fair use, the amount used must be reasonable in light of the purpose.
- *The effect of your use on the work's value.* If the use will result in a substantially adverse impact on the potential market for, or value of, the original work, the use is unlikely to be a fair use.

With respect to trademark fair use, you may use another's trademark to describe your own goods or services. For example, while Payless is a trademarked name of a shoe store, you may still use the term to describe you own app—"Buy my app and you will pay less!"

You may also use another's trademark to identify their goods or services. This is not an infringement as long as there is no likelihood of confusion. Such a fair use often occurs in comparative advertising. For example: "Buy my app because it has video, unlike the XYZ App from Acme Company."

Finally, if you absolutely must use the content or trademarks of another in your project and you aren't sure whether your use would be a fair use, consider obtaining a license to do so from the rights holder rather than risk a charge of infringement. In my opinion, artists are generally willing to work out a deal with you, many times without costing you an arm and a leg, if what you plan on doing with the material is tasteful.

## Chapter Takeaways

- Memorialize your concepts and document your developments.
- Keep the concept to yourself, except for a witness.
- If you work with others to develop the product, get contracts in place.
- Protect yourself by obtaining patent(s), trademark(s) and copyright(s).
- Put others on notice that you have obtained patent(s), trademark(s), and copyright(s).
- Know what rights others have obtained before you proceed with your innovation.
- Consult with an intellectual property attorney to help protect your innovation.

*The Digital Innovation Playbook* is a living book. We are constantly updating the book online so you can watch uploaded videos, read the latest best practice on digital media, and even participate in free ongoing webinars.

To access this chapter's updated web page, please go to www.digitalinnovationplaybook.com/Chapter12.html or scan the QR code with your mobile device.

# 13

# The Innovation Game Plan

## ARE YOU READY TO DEPLOY?

**H**ere we are. In the previous chapter we went over how to protect your properties in a digital world. Before that we talked about the elusive culture ideology and we talked about streamlining your innovation processes through the RealOpen platform.

One of the overarching concepts discussed throughout the book has been knowing your customers and understanding who you are as a company. Since every company is different, to be successful at digital innovation you must define the term in a way that directly connects to your organizational mission. One last time, here's my definition of innovation: *Innovation is the process of developing exceptional value through active listening*. I'm not suggesting there's one perfect definition, but I can tell you organizations that have not defined innovation in a way that is directly connected to their organizational mission fail with mathematical certainty.

Also, when defining innovation for your organization, make sure to use a vernacular that's clear and easy to understand for your entire team. Make it short, but most importantly make it deployable. As you begin to develop your innovation game plan, recognize that innovation success requires a willingness to openly communicate with both internal stakeholders and outside customer communities alike. Digital innovation requires organizations to develop digital connections in virtually every department and every job function.

**D**igital innovation requires organizations to develop digital connections in virtually every department and every job function.

## Learning from the Best and Brightest

Throughout this book, we have talked about the importance of creating a digital culture that gives employees the tools for success and, in turn, allowing innovation to succeed. By providing a number of company examples, we talked about the anatomy of an Innovation Superstar, which includes a functional environment, a passion to think, feel and work together, a consistent empathy, and above all, the right focus. Southwest Airlines shines with its love-driven culture and carefully crafted, fantastic employee base. NewTek and Kodak gave glimpses of the digital revolution we're currently experiencing and all of the amazing opportunities available to those brave enough and smart enough to embrace the possibilities.

IndyCar showed us how to create super fans on and off the track, and both Kodak and the U.S. Army showed us how large, entrenched corporations can still be open, developing avenues for honest, genuine conversations that benefit the communities and provide a path for incredible innovations in both products and services.

Spigit and Radian6 highlighted some great tools that are available for those focusing on one of the most important tasks in the digital world—listening. And then they provided some fantastic examples of how to turn that intelligence into actions that improve the customer experience and add layer after layer of value so companies can reach the exceptional level—and escape from baseline, a dangerous place to be.

## The Most Important Takeaways

Alongside the important company examples provided to you throughout this book, you should also keep the following three success drivers in mind as you move forward.

## Know Your Target

Before deploying any digital innovation strategy, you must first know your target. You need to know who your customers are, what they care about, how they use your product or service. And you need to know what influencers are out there in your industry.

I believe that organizations should employ the use of an innovation interventionist to review your organization's innovation game plan. The reason I'm suggesting this is that it's virtually impossible to have objectivity of any kind when you've created the innovation plan for your own organization. An outside innovation interventionist or innovation strategy consultant can really help you identify potential pitfalls. And it makes certain that you have a fresh, outside, nonpolitical view of your game plan.

Innovation requires clearly identifying who you serve. Most organizations define the people they serve as internal customers, or stakeholders, and external customers. We find that mapping those relationships to identify how best to serve them at all contact points is a useful tool and should be part of your innovation game plan.

Remember to identify stakeholders within your organization that you and your department deliver value to. This is the only way you can actually invent. You must understand who is in your value chain. Map out the value flow, looking for needs, problems, and opportunities within the internal stakeholder relationship. Develop listening connections to that relationship in order to identify new value propositions. Identify external digital communities and develop active listening resources to monitor the digital communities for innovation opportunities. Host regular ideation sessions to review digital opportunities to create improved value within your organization and your customer community. And make certain to use contact point innovation (which I describe in full shortly) so you can invent an improved experience throughout the innovation cycle.

Your success as a digital innovator will be highly dependent on your ability to prepare yourself for the digital universe. Remember that our working definition of innovation is: the process of delivering exceptional value through active listening. So the question then is: value to whom? You have two basic communities you should be delivering value to: first, your internal customer, or stakeholder; and second, your external customer community.

Value mapping, or innovation value mapping, is an extremely useful tool in identifying the participants of my value chain and helps us look at ways to identify problems, seize opportunities, and recognize needs. Value mapping is very much like mind mapping. The map explodes out to your internal and external communities and helps you identify the flow of value that you provide. When organizations collectively work together to identify value maps, they're able to provide specific innovation propositions throughout their internal and external value chain.

### Ready Your Team with Training and Rewards

Before you begin your digital innovation game plan, you should bring in your entire team—that is, everyone who will be involved in its deployment. We know programs that are co-created with our internal stakeholders have a much higher likelihood of success. You also need to provide the necessary training for your team. The digital media space is changing quickly and it's complicated. And your team frankly needs help.

First provide them with the training and the tools for success. Then acknowledge their success by developing recognition programs like the Innovation Superstar awards program, which provides incentives to your stakeholders.

First provide your team with the training and the tools for success. Then acknowledge their success by developing recognition programs like the Innovation Superstar awards program, which provides incentives to your stakeholders.

Don't forget to develop digital rules of engagement to eliminate most of the risk and drive initiative success. And also remember that teams must be open and flexible in reacting to the changes of the digital platforms.

I can't emphasize strongly enough that your organization needs to train its team. No team succeeds without training and preparation. And many organizations have failed at both innovation and digital innovation because their team simply did not know what to do. Your team needs to clearly define the term *innovation*. It should be very much like a mission statement; your team members all need to be playing from the same playbook.

They also need to know what's in it for them. I repeat, there should be recognition and other compensation programs that are directly tied to mission success. They also have to know—and this is very important—that everything is going to be okay; that your organization recognizes the fact that you cannot succeed without exposing yourself to failure.

The great motivational speaker Les Brown once said, "Anything worth doing great is worth doing poorly." And by that he meant, in order to be a good skier or in order to be a good anything, you need to be willing to be bad at it, at least for a while. If you expect perfection and a lack of failure on the part of your team, you will create an organizational atmosphere that will not move forward. Successful organizations have an entrepreneurial spirit. They don't take stupid risks; they take smart risks. They don't control risk through risk management; they control it through a high level—and I mean a really high level—of real rich, real time understanding of what their customer community cares about.

Your team also needs to have authorship, and by that I mean they need to participate in the development of the program that will ultimately be deployed by them. Statistics show clearly teams that help in the development of a plan will do a much better job in its deployment. You also have to make sure your team has identified both the internal and the external value of innovation. They need to see how innovation is providing economic value and customer value. That needs to be part of your organization's regular dialogue.

You also need to make sure your team is aware of how innovation plays a role in the development of improved experiences throughout the innovation cycle. Sometimes that's products and technologies, and other times it's improving the experience in other parts of the innovation cycle. And lastly, your team needs to learn the techniques of active listening and active observation.

Your team also needs to be recognized! This is a basic human reality. We need to connect customer and economic value to your compensation and rewards programs. For some teams and organizations, this can be complex because you have to find a way to install innovation incentives in a way that ties into your HR policies and other organizational factors. I said it was hard, but I didn't say you shouldn't do it. You must find ways to reward your team members for adding economic value and customer value alike.

I also strongly recommend that you host frequent Innovation Superstar awards programs that recognize the successful application of innovation within your organization. I believe you'll find that if you develop an Innovation Superstar program that the Innovation Superstars within your organization will ultimately become your organization's royalty.

Organizations rely heavily on their teams to identify new opportunities to add value to their customer community. Unfortunately, most organizations do not properly train their stakeholders to be innovators, and we all know there is a wide range of skills needed to do this right. You should have a comprehensive innovation training program to make sure all members of your team are contributing profitable innovations to your enterprise.

In addition, individuals need to be recognized and awarded. Different organizations have different philosophies about how awards connect into their human resource policies. In my career I have found the most effective form of motivating employees isn't through cash incentives but rather through recognition. In my practice, we use the Innovation Superstar award, a regular awards program, to identify and recognize employees who have provided contributions to the organization and the customer community alike. These programs work amazingly well. Any innovation game plan would be incomplete without them.

### Creating Avenues for Active Listening and Identifying Points of Experience

Organizations must create digital command centers to manage their online reputation, to listen to their customer communities, and to participate and innovate in the digital sandbox. Your innovation game plan should include the development and deployment of a digital command center.

This center should be staffed with employees that live and breathe your brand and can quickly respond, listen well, and are given the ability to use the gathered intelligence to promote exceptional innovations.

**Contact Point Innovation**  When you have a digital commence center, you should be able to identify who's using your product, how they're using it, and—most importantly—where things can be improved. Do you remember Contact Point Innovation, mentioned earlier in the book? Contact Point Innovation is extremely useful in the development of your innovation game plan. Look for ways to layer on the value at each point of contact—before a customer purchases, how a customer purchases, and how the product is used/updated/maintained. Identify each point of experience throughout the innovation cycle of your customers. Here's a reminder of each of the five phases or areas of engagement in Contact Point Innovation. See Figure 13.1.

The first is *pre-touch*. This is the reputation and is what is known by our customers prior to their contacting us in the first place. The best way to describe pre-touch is that it's essentially your brand's reputation. And by that I mean the holistic reputation. Many organizations have great products but bad service. Some have great service but bad products. Some have good technologies but bad customer service. So as you can see the brand reputation is comprised of how other people have experienced your brand throughout the innovation cycle.

Next is *first-touch*. First-touch is heavily weighted. Some suggest that 80 percent of what a customer will feel about you and your brand will be determined by the very first contact point. As the axiom suggests, first impressions do last a lifetime. As we're inventing, we should attempt to invent at each point of contact in the innovation cycle. What is that first experience like for your customer? How does

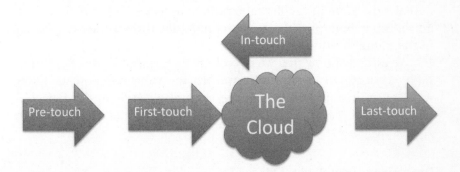

Figure 13.1    Contact Point Innovation Model
*Source:* © Lassen Scientific, Inc. 2011. All rights reserved.

it look? How does it smell? How does it feel? How does it make them feel? What is their perception of your quality? Your technology? Its functionality? Its reliability? And the list goes on and on. Remember that successful innovators invent throughout the experience cycle by using contact point innovation.

The next contact point is *the cloud*. The cloud is when you have them. They're in your sphere of influence. They're in your restaurant or they're using your product. They're experiencing you. What's that like? Is it fun? Is it interesting? Are they happy? Do they love it? Is it exceptional? Human beings are multi-sensory and they are emotive. As emotive beings, we feel. And our feeling is the net result of our sensory contacts. As we look to invent in the experience cloud, it is critical that we look at all aspects of how our customer experiences our products, technologies, and services.

The next phase of Contact Point Innovation is what I call *last-touch*. Last-touch is where you send them off. It's your last point of contact. This point of contact is also heavily weighted, as often customers will remember most the last thing you said or did. This is another important area where there are tremendous opportunities to add layered value throughout the innovation cycle.

The next phase of Contact Point Innovation is what I call *end-touch*. End touch is a way that we connect to customers in a way they want to connect. This is not about putting someone on a mailing list and sending them newsletters or e-mails. In fact, that's probably the opposite of what I'm suggesting. What I'm suggesting, in the end-touch phase of contact point innovation, is that you use this opportunity to identify the communities your customers live in and to play with them in the digital sandbox; to listen, to learn, to invent, and ultimately deploy the best technologies through active playing in the digital sandbox.

We already know that we need to map through innovation value maps in order to identify who we provide value to. Now we know we need to invent throughout the innovation cycle at the five contact points of *pre-touch*, *first-touch*, the *experience cloud*, *last-touch*, and *end-touch*.

## Becoming a True Digital Enterprise

It is critical that you become a digital enterprise so you can identify and connect to all of your communities in order to play, listen, invent, and deploy the best technologies on the planet. You also need to monitor, measure, and ultimately deploy and test all of your initiatives through your digital connections.

These processes can be highly automated through great resources like Spigit. As I have mentioned many times in this book, you are a digital enterprise. Your innovation processes are successful to the extent that you are digitally savvy.

### Avoiding the Digital Pitfalls

Remember that most digital initiatives fail because they are incomplete. They are a fractional solution applied to a holistic problem. Many organizations that believe creating a Facebook page, a blog, or participating in some online communities means they have become a digital enterprise. Nothing could be further from the truth. Make certain you develop a holistic, complete digital strategy that addresses all the fibers of connectivity to the digital world.

> **R**emember, most digital initiatives fail because they are a fractional solution applied to a holistic problem.

Also know that an analog approach to the digital world will never work. And again, when I use the term analog, I mean closed, an old-fashioned hierarchical view of the innovation world. Without a shift in cultural vantage point, you'll never be able to take advantage of the digital opportunities. As I have mentioned throughout the book a risk-centered view of digital innovation will always fail. The digital universe, and for that matter, the universe in general, is a dangerous place. But we also know, in order to explore and to identify great opportunities, we need to pull out of our driveway. Digital innovation is risky, but what is more risky is your unwillingness to take the risk. There is proportionality between risk and reward. This is, for all practical purposes, a cosmic law. Reward is always proportionate to risk. The key is to take smart risks and if you're going to fail, fail early. But don't focus on risk.

This will stall any innovation initiative. Another digital pitfall I commonly see is organizations not playing well with others. Most of us live in markets. And these markets, for all practical purposes, are like small towns. There's gossip and there's talk. In order to succeed in a small town, you need to become politically savvy. We don't use our digital connections as a way to talk poorly about our competition or to do anything that would damage our brand.

There are bullies in the digital sandbox. We need to recognize them, and to the extent we can, ignore them. But you must develop rules of engagement with all of your stakeholders to protect your brand and your digital innovation initiatives.

Another major problem with digital innovation is what I call passive listening. It's that Sunday morning listening you do while reading the newspaper that fades in and out, and that's not deep or analytical. In order to understand what our customer community cares about, we need to interact with them. We need to be lucid. We need to have our heads in the game. Passive listening creates bad innovations. Your team needs to learn how to be active observers and active listeners.

■ ■ ■

In researching and writing this book, I experienced an amazing journey. I got an inside view of the transformation of organizations that are taking advantage of the power of the digital universe to plug in to their customer community to provide exceptional levels of customer value. And without exception, these organizations are providing the highest level of top-end earnings, profit brand value, and organizational durability. I hope you can find the case study that best fits your company profile and use the fantastic examples given by these industry leaders to grow your own success. For more information on how to drive innovation in your organization, visit www.lasseninnovation.com.

*The Digital Innovation Playbook* is a living book. We are constantly updating the book online so you can watch uploaded videos, read the latest best practice on digital media, and even participate in free ongoing webinars.

To access this chapter's updated web page, please go to www.digitalinnovationplaybook.com/Chapter13.html or scan the QR code with your mobile device.

# About the Author

Nicholas J. Webb is a world-renowned innovation thought leader. He is the author of *The Innovation Playbook*, *The Digital Innovation Playbook*, and *The Innovation Superstar Workbook*. He is a successful inventor with a wide range of technologies, from one of the world's smallest medical implants to consumer and industrial products. He has been awarded more than 35 patents by the U.S. Patent and Trademark Office. He has launched hundreds of technologies in his 25-year career. He currently provides innovation strategy consulting to a wide range of clients, from small start-ups to Fortune 500 companies.

## Body of Research

In researching his books for one of the world's largest nonfiction publishers, John Wiley & Sons, Nicholas Webb has identified the key success drivers for innovation. Researching organizations from the vantage point of an innovator has given him a unique and special knowledge on what works in the real world. His research has included organizations such as the U.S. Army, Hewlett-Packard, Kodak, Indy-Car, Southwest Airlines, and NewTek, to name just a few.

## Keynote Topics

### Digital Innovation

Nicholas J. Webb has researched hundreds of companies while writing his book, *The Digital Innovation Playbook*. What he has discovered will astonish your audience. He learned how some of the best organizations in the world are using digital and social media to drive unprecedented levels of customer value. His case studies include how the U.S. Army has solved its image problems through its digital presence. He'll show how great innovators like Yamaha and Kodak are creating world-class innovations through digital connectivity. Digital innovation is literally the next generation of innovation and best practice. This information is extremely fresh and updated prior to every presentation. Your attendees will learn:

- How the digital universe is driving the most innovative companies
- How to increase access to breakthrough in incremental innovation
- The power of the digital sandbox
- How to digitize open innovation
- How to build sales while reducing costs

This program is available as a keynote and as a workshop.

### Innovation Leadership

The rules of successful innovation management have changed, and they have changed drastically. Our digitally connected world has mandated that leadership understands the role of social and digital media in innovation. Leaders today also need to understand new methods of driving speed to market while concurrently increasing efficiencies. In this keynote, Nicholas J. Webb literally creates a roadmap for innovation and leadership success. Attendees will learn:

- The best systems and practices for innovation management
- How to digitize your innovation function
- How to reward and motivate stakeholders
- How to connect to external customer communities

This program is available as a keynote and as a workshop.

### Innovation Superstars

Nicholas Webb has been involved in innovation for more than a quarter of a century. His success as both an inventor and an innovation strategist has taught him the key elements of innovation success. This real-world experience, in combination with his research on hundreds of companies, has given him the secret formula for innovation success. In this powerful keynote, Nicholas Webb identifies the anatomy of Innovation Superstars®. He provides real-world case studies and takeaways that allow you to apply this formula to your businesses immediately. In this program your attendees will learn:

- The anatomy of an Innovation Superstar
- The power of passion
- The will of innovation craftsmanship
- How to create an innovation culture
- How to avoid the five common innovation mistakes
- How to create your innovation game plan

This program is available as a keynote and as a workshop.

## Custom Keynote Topics

Nicholas Webb can provide custom keynotes that are surgically targeted to the specific needs of your organization and industry. Other topics include:

- The future of innovation in medical technology
- Innovation in the delivery of health care
- Managing change and the future
- The great news about the current economy
- The power of innovation in sales and marketing
- Contact point innovation and driving customer experiences
- How to achieve business excellence

## Retreats and Customized Events

We provide a wide range of customized training, coaching, and retreats. We also provide many workshop programs.

 *The Digital Innovation Playbook* is a living book. We are constantly updating the book online so you can watch uploaded videos, read the latest best practice on digital media, and even participate in free ongoing webinars.

To access this chapter's updated web page, please go to www.digitalinnovationplaybook.com/speaking.html or scan the QR code with your mobile device.

# Special Book Offer $149 Value

**W**ith the purchase of your Innovation Playbook, you are entitled to our introductory training program called The Innovation Superstar Level I. This program is an interactive innovation-management training program. It provides a series of audio and video lessons and allows you to test your innovation skills. The program includes the following features:

### Innovation Superstar Certified* (ISC) Level I

- Introduction to the state-of-the-art RealOpen innovation management system.
- How to automate innovation filtration.
- Developed world-class innovation platforms.
- Value layering your innovations with Project X.
- Fast-track innovation assessments with the Webb triangle.
- Hard-wire internal and external innovation to your corporate culture.
- Replace risk management with opportunity management.
- Build a systemic culture of innovation.
- Lead your market with customer and market-driven innovations.

**Certification is available at an additional cost.**

The free offer does not include the certification fee. Certification is issued to program participants who complete an online training program and have completed the test questions with an 85 percent or better score and paid the certification fee. The purpose of certification is to validate satisfactory course completion. No certification accreditation is expressed or implied. Innovation Superstar and RealOpen are pending trademarks of Lassen Scientific, Inc. a California corporation.

Visit the web site at: www.innovationsuperstar.com.

# Index